HAUNTS OF VIOLENCE IN THE CHURCH

A Look at the Answer
That Overcomes Violence

A Biblical Interpretation
Of
Peace and Violence

HOWARD GOERINGER

Copyright © 2005 by Howard Goeringer

ISBN 0-7414-2494-0

Published by:

INFINITY
PUBLISHING.COM

1094 New De Haven Street, Suite 100
West Conshohocken, PA 19428-2713
Info@buybooksontheweb.com
www.buybooksontheweb.com
Toll-free (877) BUY BOOK
Local Phone (610) 941-9999
Fax (610) 941-9959

Printed in the United States of America

Printed on Recycled Paper

Published May 2005

To my wife Marge,
and our five daughters,

Karen
Gwynne
Gretchen
Kristen
Kathy

Note:
Howard Goeringer, the author, died in 2001 before the publication of this book. His family and friends have had the manuscript published in accordance with his wishes. It is published in loving memory of his lifelong work.

I BELIEVE

God has created me to do Him some definite service; he has committed some work to me which he has not committed to another. I have my mission—I never may know it in this life, but I shall be told in the next . . . I have a part in a great work; I am a link in a chain, a bond of connection between persons. He has not created me for naught. I shall love as Christ loved; I shall do His work; I shall be an angel of peace, a preacher of truth in my own place, while not intending it, if I do but keep His commandments and serve Him in my calling.

Therefore I will trust Him. Whatever, wherever I am. I can never be thrown away. If I am in sickness, my sickness may serve Him; in perplexity, my perplexity may serve Him; if I am in sorrow, my sorrow may serve Him. My sickness, or perplexity, or sorrow may be necessary causes of some great end, which is quite beyond us. He does nothing in vain. He may prolong my life, He may shorten it; He knows what He is about. He may take away my friends. He may throw me among strangers. He may make me feel desolate, make my spirits sink, hide the future from me—still He knows what He is about.

-   John Henry Newman

Contents

Foreword

I never met Howard Goeringer. But every month, his little, self-published *Jesus Journal* would arrive at my door, and every month I would immediately devour it. It was the only journal of the myriad that I receive that got such preferential treatment. You have to understand that I generally read journals that are two to three years old. I just loved Howard Goeringer's polemic against churches that had sold out the gospel of nonviolence to the "just war" theory.

In high school I had embraced a Methodist version of nonviolence, but had most of it knocked out of my guts by my teacher Reinhold Niebuhr. When I found myself reconverting to nonviolence during the civil rights movement, the anti-Vietnam struggles, and the nuclear war crisis, I began looking for someone who could bring me more clarity about Jesus' teachings on nonviolence. I found immediate help in the New Testament itself. Jesus himself was my exegete. But Jesus never made nonviolence programmatic. It waited for Gandhi to perform the task, and then King and Chavez.

As I was widening my search for light on Jesus' teaching, synchronously I began receiving the *Jesus Journal*, free. (Later I caught on: I was supposed to make a donation, which I finally began to do.) It was an instant match. The Jesus as portrayed by Goeringer was one that I could take as my guide.

I used to fret that so few people had been exposed to Howard's writings. This little book, packed with some of his deepest insights, gives those who have not been introduced to them a chance not available during his lifetime. I hope you find him as helpful as I did. He had a message for all times and places, and it is time he be discovered.

Walter Wink
Professor of Biblical Interpretation
Auburn Theological Seminary
New York, NY

Introduction

Written for the approximately two billion Christians in the world, this book has a three-fold purpose:

One, to see clearly God's gospel of peace which is the good news that by Jesus' death-resurrection-ascension-rule-indwelling Spirit, the nonviolent kingdom of God has been restored on earth as it is in heaven, waiting to be consummated at the End of human history. God's saving Peace-Plan has been completed in Jesus Christ, the nonviolent Messiah. Nothing more will be added to bring peace to a fallen world. It is finished.

Two, to expose the centuries-old false "just war" teaching of mainline Catholic, Orthodox, Protestant, and Pentecostal churches which in the twentieth century has been responsible for more Christians killing Christians than in all centuries combined since the time of Jesus, making a mockery of His life and teaching.

Three, to make clear the eight things mainline "just war" churches must do to enflesh the peace of Jesus and be free from the heresy that "good wars" can be fought by Christians with the blessing of God.

The unique value of this book is that it brings these eight things together in a single volume as it:

1. Reexamines what the Gospel means by peace in the light of Jesus' life and teaching, including the life-style and writings of the Twelve Apostles and their pupils in the

early church, which rejected war for more than two centuries.

2. Confronts and exposes the violence of Rome's emperor, Constantine (312-337 A.D.), falsely hailed as the Lord's Anointed and lauded as the champion of the faith whose influence as "benefactor" of the church led to the involvement of Christianity in the world's systems of coercive and violent power Jesus rejected.

3. Examines in detail the "just war" teaching whose Graeco-Roman rational philosophy, not God's Self-Revelation in Christ, was the foundation of the heresy, which has destroyed the authentic peace-witness of Jesus' church.

4. Deals with the question, Why so much violence and war in the Old Testament? The terrible violence in these Scriptures must be understood in the light of Jesus, not followed as though they are on the same level of truth as the New Testament. They are not.

5. In the light of the life and teaching of Jesus, examines the New Testament passages used (misused) by mainline churches to support a fallen world's war system. If we cannot know from Jesus that His life and teaching is the Way of nonviolent love, there is nothing we can be sure about in the New Testament.

6. Acquaints the reader with the strand of Jesus' church that has for centuries rejected war in the face of persecution and death at the hands of mainstream Christianity. In every age, a strand of the church has been faithful to Jesus' gospel of peace. It is of crucial importance that Christians know about this church.

7. Presents the biblical truth that all humans are part of a fallen world of violence and war, and that only as humans repent and are created anew in Christ can we become citizens of God's peaceable kingdom that Jesus enfleshed and proclaimed. The culture of a fallen world

is violent and must be rejected in a radical act of repentance.

8. Rethinks the schooling of children of the church and the crucial need to provide children with the kind of education that exalts Jesus as the nonviolent Messiah of the world. Public schooling and violent nationalism go hand in hand.

At a time when the public is deluged with the media's entertaining voices and news-print which either fail to understand God's gospel, or politicize the gospel, or ignore Jesus completely, Christians are in dire need to make this eight-point journey and become members of the authentic Body of Christ in Whom is a fallen world's only peace that reconciles brothers and sisters to the Eternal One and to each other.

It is impossible to thank everyone who has helped give substance to these pages. Endnotes list some of the major works the author has used. The books and teachers who have molded his mind are countless, the master Teacher being Jesus, and the key book, the Bible.

I especially thank my wife, Marge, who has faithfully stood by my side through our sixty-six years of marriage, during which time I have tried to put first the kingdom of God in my stumbling human way. This requires a wife's patience and partnership. Our five daughters, Karen, Gwynne, Gretchen, Kristen and Kathy, have accepted our many moves with grace, largely because of the example of their mother. Our family remains intact and whole in a hostile world.

Chapter 1

How and Where Peace Is Found

> HE IS OUR PEACE, who has made us both
> one and broken down the dividing wall of
> hostility . . . that he might create in himself
> one new man in place of the two, so making
> peace, and might reconcile us both to God in
> one body through the cross, thereby bringing
> the hostility to an end.
> - Ephesians 2:14-17

What was it that transformed the author of these words from
a killer of Christians to the most powerful preacher of Jesus'
gospel of peace the church has ever had? It wasn't the ethic
of the Sermon on the Mount. Paul knew all about these
ethical principles and the Golden Rule long before his
Damascus Road conversion.

What was it, then, that transformed the life of Paul and the
other Apostles so powerfully that within a generation the
Roman world was being turned upside down by the gospel?
(See Acts 17:6)

It was the "new man" Paul became in Christ.

If we had been living around the eastern seaports of the
Mediterranean in those first generations after Pentecost, we
would have seen the answer to our question scratched on

1

walls or buildings, perhaps even on the ground, in the crude outline of a fish. We might have passed it off as doodling, especially where fishing was the common occupation. This was not doodling. The five Greek letters, which spelled "fish", were the first Greek letters in the words, "Jesus Christ, Son of God, and Savior".

Hard pressed by the ruling authorities of Rome who now saw the authority of the Head of the church as a threat to the authority of Caesar, Christians met secretly in the catacombs. The head of the fish would point in the direction of the place where they would meet to worship Jesus as the Christ, the Son of God, the long awaited Savior who had come as the blessing of peace God had promised to every family on earth (See Genesis 12:1-3).

This was not just another prophet, another wise man from the East. Jesus was the fulfillment of Old Testament prophecy, God's promised Messiah who had said,

> He who has seen me has seen the Father. I and the Father are one. In me you may have peace.
> - John 14:9; 10:30; 16:33

Why did these first Christians believe Jesus to be the Son of God, who had been sent by God to save them? Save them from what? For one thing, save them from fear, especially the fear of death in that each and every human dies is proof of our organic relation to the world of nature. This relationship would seem to prove that the fate of humankind and the fate of beasts are the same; as animals die, so die people. Man has no advantage over the beasts; for all is vanity (Ecclesiastes 3:19).

But the universal fear of death is also an expression of that in us which transcends nature. Our fear of death springs from our capacity not only to anticipate our death but to wonder about what lies beyond: "to die, to sleep" may mean "perchance to dream", as Shakespeare's Hamlet put it, an indication that humans are capable of something more than dust and death.

Jesus had been crucified and put to death. The three Marys and the Twelve saw the blood flow from Jesus' wounds. But three days later, the same Jesus showed Himself alive at different times and places. The accounts of Jesus' resurrection are meager, but the power of His Risen Presence so removed their fear of death that they faced their own death with songs of joy, remembering Jesus' words:

> Yet a little while, and the world will see me
> no more, but you will see me; because I live,
> you will live also.
> - John 14:19

Unlike other religions, Christianity is distinctive. It is marked by the joyous songs of victory, inspired by the indwelling Spirit of eternal life; the foundation of nonviolence; love of enemies; rejection of all war; and refusal to fight as the world fights to protect one's physical existence and material goods.

As a stanza of one Christian hymn puts it:

> I fear no foe, with Thee at hand to bless:
> Ills have no weight, and tears no bitterness.
> Where is death's sting? Where grave thy victory?
> I triumph still, if Thou abide in me.

If no enemy can destroy our life in Jesus and take away our most cherished wealth, then of whom, or what, need we fear? In Christ we have become part of an imperishable realm.

Christ-likeness is like Eternity. Present and Future have merged in Christ! Our real Homeland is not of the flesh in one of the planet's many nations and their inherent violence and death.

> It does not yet appear what we shall be, but we know that when he appears, we shall be like him.
> - 1 John 3:2

We were not made for death. Not made for the trash heap. Not made to slaughter one another. We were made for life. Endless life. Merciful life. Life infinitely valued in Christ, who said,

> The thief comes only to steal and to kill and destroy. I have come that they may have life, and have it abundantly. If any one keeps my word, he will never taste death.
> - John 10:10, 8:51

In addition to being saved from fear, the early church called Jesus Christ their savior because His cross lifted a second intolerable burden: the burden of sin's guilt in missing the mark the Eternal has set for us in the Christ-Example (1 Peter 2:21-25). Because we were created in the image of God, we all draw distinctions between what is better and worse. We ponder how it might have been, if . . .

We are told that more Vietnam veterans committed suicide than were killed in battle. Eighty thousand! Why? Part of it must have been the awful feeling of shame and guilt in killing elderly folks, mothers and little children, not from bombers in the sky a mile overhead, but face to face, close enough to hear their cries. This violence is contradictory to the teachings of the One, who said,

> Let the children come to me, and do not hinder them; for of such belongs the kingdom of God.
> - Luke 18:15

For a time, we can avoid feelings of guilt while escaping into some bit of pleasure, entertainment, or other addiction. But when the sun goes down and we are alone in the night with our thoughts, we remember what cannot be hidden. The Bible calls it sin and its consequences . . . and its shame.

Famous generals have commented on war and its characteristics. "War is HELL", said William T. Sherman, General of the Union forces that sacked Atlanta in 1864 during the "march to the sea". Douglas MacArthur, General of the U.S. Armies in WWII said, "Yes, I know war as few other men now living know it, and nothing to me is more revolting." Yes, war is hell. War is revolting. War is sin from which "Jesus Christ, Son of God, Savior" frees a fallen world (John 1:29).

Though killing is made legal by the state when it declares war and puts a soldier's uniform on a man or a woman, and a gun in their hands, there's something about that Man on the cross that fills us with shame. This shame arises from the image of running a bayonet through a so-called enemy also created in the same image of God (Colossians 3:9-11).

The crucified-risen-ascended-ruling-indwelling Christ teaches us that our fellow humans are not the enemy to slaughter in order to solve the "problem". The real enemy is sin's evil, which only the sword of God's Spirit can conquer. In fact, killing only makes us like the killer and fuels evil's fury.

This is not an easy truth for the finite mind of humans to grasp since we are prone to view life from a short-term, politically oriented stance. The ancient Israelites didn't grasp it. They knew God wanted them to enter the Promised Land, and the Canaanites stood in the way. The only solution was to kill those who stood in the way. It must be God's will to fight as the world fights because the whole world can't be wrong.

5

The logic was correct except for one thing. God promised to give Israel the Promised Land without killing (See Exodus 23:28, Deuteronomy 7:20). Significantly, Israel lacked the faith in God's capability to do it a different way, one that included the Canaanites in the Holy One's salvation plan.

It isn't God's intention to destroy the enemy. The good Lord's plan is to REDEEM the enemy—all people created in His image and destined for eternal life (John 3:16). The cross of Christ teaches that God so loves every soul on planet Earth that He came in the flesh and "was wounded for our transgressions" to assure us that His infinite love is greater than our sin and will never let us go (Romans 8:35-39).

This love is explored in the marvelous eighth chapter of Saint Paul's letter to the church in Rome, after asking the question, "Who shall separate us from the love of Christ? Shall tribulation, or distress, or persecution, or famine, or nakedness, or peril, or sword?" the Apostle shouts, "No! I am sure that neither death nor life . . . nor principalities nor powers. . . nor anything else in all creation, will be able to separate us from the love of God in Christ Jesus our Lord" (Romans 8:35-39). Explain the cross as you will, there is a purifying mystery about Jesus' love that is willing to suffer for you and me—God's kind of love the gospel calls "agape"- a self-giving love that makes us feel clean and peaceful again. As Paul put it:

> In him all the fullness of God was pleased to
> dwell, and through him to reconcile to himself
> all things, whether on earth or in heaven,
> making peace by the blood of his cross.
> - Colossians 1:20

It's the kind of agape-love that is seeking to reconcile the world, not blow the world to bits. It's the transforming love Christ shares with us when we abide in Him and share His

Spirit. Moreover, Jesus bids us go the second mile with others, even our enemies. The love that embraces enemies is God's agape-love abiding in us, not our own willpower to follow an abstract ethic. *God's peace in Christ is all about a personal relationship with the Infinite, not an attempt to obey an abstract moral law.*

The Homeland of Christians

The early Christians were not only saved from fear of death and a life burdened with sin's shame and guilt. Those guided by the "fish" to secret meetings in the catacombs experienced a third burden which "Jesus Christ, Son of God, Savior" lifted from their weary and heavy-laden hearts: their constant self-centeredness, their nagging ego always craving to be recognized, praised, and served in one way or another. We are all born with this sinful self-addiction.

All wrapped up in ourselves, we make a very small package, even when we tack on our family . . . our job . . . our race . . . even our nation. If we are to live nonviolently as conquerors, and not as victims of sin's violence, the circle has to be enlarged.

Those who scratched a fish on walls had discovered from their personal experience that this God-Person expanded their consciousness of self to infinity, breaking down the "dividing wall of hostility" (Ephesians 2:14). Because Jesus, their indwelling God and Savior was alive and well in them, the whole world became their Homeland. About the year 130 A.D., an unknown author described these "fish people" to the Romans in these words:

> They dwell in their own countries simply as sojourners. . . Every country is their Homeland. They pass their days on earth, but they are citizens of heaven. They obey the prescribed laws, and at the same time, they

7

surpass the laws by their lives. They love all men, but are persecuted by all.

Can you imagine such disciples of Jesus joining a band of soldiers called a Roman Legion and going forth with Caesar to kill barbarians on the other side of the mountains? It is unthinkable. Why? Because their self-protecting egos had been replaced by the indwelling Holy Spirit of "Jesus Christ, Son of God, Savior" in whom "there cannot be Jew or Greek, circumcised and uncircumcised, barbarian, Scythians, slave, free man, but Christ is all and in all" (Colossians 3:11).

This new oneness with the Father and with the Father's one Family, each one created in God's image, are one and the same reality. "How can we say we love God whom we have not seen, if we do not love our brothers and sisters whom we can see?" the Apostles asked (1 John 4:20). This oneness of Jesus' disciples with Abba and Abba's family is to be a sign that the Father sent Jesus as the Messiah whose gift is peace to a warring world (John 17:21). Understandably, a cynical world asks if Jesus has overcome sin's world of violence and death, why is there more violence and killing among Christians than any other identifiable group? Christianity as a religion has been taught and preached throughout the world for almost 2000 years. Where is the peace Jesus proclaimed? How many more churches do we need?

A good question. It needs to be asked over and over again.

Peace IN Christ

This answer: the peace of Jesus becomes a reality precisely where it was experienced 2000 years ago in Galilee, where it is found now, and where it always will be found: IN CHRIST. Not by "going to church" or establishing more churches. A church no more guarantees peace-people than a garage assures a car inside. A purchase has to be made. The purchase was made on a cross and to have His peace, the

Person on it must become a living, indwelling reality. We have the answer in Jesus' last conversation with the Twelve in the Upper Room the night of His arrest. In between the Teacher's words in John 14, "My peace I give to you", and His words in John 16, "I have said this to you that in me you may have peace", are His words in John 15 upon which the other two depend:

> ABIDE IN ME, and I in you, as the branch cannot bear fruit by itself, unless it abides in the vine, neither can you unless you abide in me. I am the vine, you are the branches. He who abides in me, and I in him, he it is that bears much fruit, for apart from me you can do nothing.
> - John 15:4-5

The peace of God is the fruit that comes from abiding in the Vine, the Spirit of the Holy One Jesus perfectly enfleshed and made accessible to a fallen world that we might be reconciled to the Eternal and to one another through His crucified-risen-indwelling Person. Apart from abiding in Christ-God and in the Holy One's Spirit, there is no peace. Peace is a living relationship between the Christ-person and every human who learns to be still in Abba's Presence, obeys the still small voice of Abba, and then trusts Abba to deliver from every enemy with a sword not of man, as He promised to do.

This is the good news: in Christ we are delivered from a fallen world's dominion of darkness and transferred into the kingdom of God's light and love:

> He has delivered us from the dominion of darkness and transferred us to the kingdom of his beloved Son, in whom we have redemption, the forgiveness of sins.
> - Colossians 1:13

Why does the gospel teach that God's peace is in Christ? The quintessence of life is Person and Spirit, not matter and molecules. Not a force like nuclear energy but Mind and Intelligence like that of the God-Person. This is why Paul told everyone in the church he would not be satisfied "until Christ be formed in you" (Galatians 4:19).

Why was Paul in travail until Christ be formed in each and every soul? Because the salvation he proclaimed in Christ is our only peace:

> peace in a warring world,
> life in a world of death,
> wholeness in a fragmented world,
> renewal in a tired world,
> purpose in a confused world,
> reconciliation in a racially divided world,
> security of Spirit amid our decaying life of flesh,
> a love that never lets us go, come what may.

The New Testament church testified that God has made known his plan to unite all things in heaven and on earth in Christ (Ephesians 1:9-10). Why in Jesus and not in Moses, Buddha, Mohammad, or in some great scientist like Einstein, or in the technology of science, or in a super-nation? Jesus has already overcome a world of discord and death. After saying to the Twelve, "in me you may have peace", Jesus gives us the answer: "I have overcome the world." (John 16:33)

What did Jesus mean when He said, "I have overcome the world"? To understand these words of Jesus, we must understand what the New Testament means by "world". In the New Testament it is the Greek word "kosmos" which, geographically, refers to the whole world, with its limited time of existence. (See Ephesians 2:2 and Matthew 4:8) This is the time-spatial "kosmos".

10

In the Gospel of John where "world" is used almost one hundred times, the word has a unique theological meaning. Here "kosmos" refers, not to the time-spatial world God created and adjudged to be good (Genesis 1:3), but to the world of humans estranged from God, bent on doing their own thing and playing God:

> I have given them thy word; and the world has hated them because they are not of the world, even as I am not of the world. I do not pray that thou shouldst take them out of the world, but that thou shouldst keep them from the evil one. They are not of the world, even as I am not of the world.
> -John 17:14-16

Like John, his fellow Apostle, Paul testified that the church has received "the Spirit which is from God, not the spirit of the world" (1 Corinthians 2:12). The Apostle James also made clear the same theological meaning of the "world":

> What causes wars and what causes fighting among you? Is it not your passions that are at war in your members? You desire and do not have, so you kill. And you covet, and you cannot obtain; so you fight and wage war. You do not have, because you do not ask. You ask and do not receive because you ask wrongly, to spend it on your passions. Unfaithful creatures! Do you not know that friendship with the world is enmity with God? Therefore, whoever wishes to be a friend with the world makes himself an enemy of God?
> - James 4:1-4

This is sin's fallen world estranged from God, spending time, energy, and money primarily on one's self-centered well-being, then resorting to violence to protect one's own little world from others who might interfere and take away from the stock-piled goodies. This is our unredeemed world, violent by nature.

Self-centeredness underlies the Genesis story of the Fall, something our secular age prefers to talk about in psychological and sociological language. The biblical narrative of the Fall and its explanation of real and radical evil in the world is not a temporal event that happened only once in the history of two people. The narrative of Adam and Eve is a myth in the sense that its truth is <u>always present</u> in the life of every human being and every human structure. That is, the story of Adam and Eve is the story of Every-Man and Every-Woman, the story of the world into which we were all born. The Powers and Principalities impact all of us, individually and collectively. It's the symbolic story of Man/Woman who become separated from God by freely choosing to pursue <u>self-elevating</u> happiness instead of happiness that comes from the Holy Spirit. The resulting expulsion of Adam and Eve from Paradise is the beginning of the deadly conflict of brother against brother, family against family, race against race, nation against nation, a debacle called the "Fall of the human race".

Throughout the Bible, estrangement from God is expressed in our distorted desires and ambitions the Bible calls "sin". Used in the singular, "sin" in the New Testament refers to a demonic quasi-personal power loose in the world, which Paul refers to five times in his letters as the "Powers and Principalities" (See Romans 8:38; Ephesians 3:10 and 6:12; Colossians 1:16 and 2:15). Their evil attacks both individuals and institutions, including the church. Used in the plural, "sins" refer to specific sinful acts such as killing, stealing, adultery, lying, greed, cursing, and the like. Such particular sins break the laws of God and have their inevitable consequences. But it is not disobedience to a law, which makes an act sinful. It is the fact that it is an expression of our separation from God symbolized in Adam and Eve's loss of at-one-ment with God and His peace.

All humans sin because we all belong to a human race corrupted by hubris; vain pride in the creature and the things he created rather than in the Creator. Our essential self of Truth has been lost in our sinful self-deception, which caused Paul to cry out,

> Wretched man that I am! Who shall deliver
> me from the body of this death?
> - Romans 7:24

And then to answer:

> Thanks be to God through Jesus Christ our
> Lord.
> - Romans 7:25

On the cross, Jesus conquered the sin of hubris by His completely unselfish giving of Himself, and then empowered us by His indwelling risen and deathless Self to follow Him into the kingdom of God and Eternity's peace on earth as it is in heaven. The night before His crucifixion, speaking of His return to His disciples on Pentecost in the gift of the Holy Spirit, Jesus said to the Twelve,

> In that day you will know that I am in my
> Father, and you in me, and I in you.
> - John 14:20

Jesus overcame the world of God-alienation (John 16:33). He did this not by mimicking the world and becoming its Super-Star, nor by trying to maneuver in the sphere of power politics and its systems as many mainstream Christians do today. He enfleshed the Eternal's Holy Spirit and witnessed to the new creation, thereby making reality when believers abide in the God-Vine. Whereas coercive power can only restrain, the mission of Jesus and His church is to redeem and reconcile, which leads to the rejection of all violent power.

What about justice? Justice always has to be enforced by coercive power, which elicits resistance, and the state deals with resistance by using police and military power. Given the self-addiction of the human race, the use of such coercive power always corrupts. The state's dominative power is never redemptive and must never be regarded by the church as the answer to evil. Agape is both the end and the means to the end. The end and the means to the end are one and the same.

To be sure, just laws are preferable to laws which are favorable to a particular class of people, but even equal justice under law, the ideal of state government at its best has to do only with human rights, not with the ultimate questions of life and death. At the graveside, the deceased's political affiliation does not matter.

The gospel is the good news that Jesus has overcome all evil. He did this by making accessible to the human race the fullness of God's Holy Spirit who is the quintessence of life! Peace is the indwelling God-Spirit who gives us what Jesus called a "new birth" and the Apostles called a "new creation", or a "new self", as we abide in the cosmic Person. In this way we become citizens of the peaceable Realm which Jesus called the "kingdom of God". Jesus' teachings clarify several things about the kingdom of God. The kingdom (or rule) of God is not peripheral to the gospel; it is central. Jesus began His public ministry, saying,

> The time is fulfilled, and the kingdom of God
> is at hand; repent, and believe in the gospel.
> - Mark 1:15

In Christ the time has been fulfilled and the kingdom of God has begun on earth as it is in heaven (See Matthew 6:9-10), to be consummated at the End of history as we know it.

What did Jesus mean by the kingdom of God? His many parables of the kingdom and His use of the term a hundred times make clear that He was proclaiming a new and unique quality of life in the present, not just a future realm called "heaven". The good news is about a God-restored life in the present, to be perfected in heaven. In the coming of Jesus, the time was fulfilled for God to act to reveal the mystery of his peaceful kingdom (See Ephesians 1:9-10). In other words, the all-encompassing peace of God in Jesus is not a continuing hope for peace when this world of time and space as we know it shall be transformed politically; it is realized in the present by abiding in His Person. (Revelation 21:1).

In Christ the peaceable kingdom of God has come into a fallen world (only to be received) to restore us to the first-fruits of Paradise. In this world we live in a time of disease and death, a perishing, troubling time of violence. The law of dying and death is at the heart of the world into which we were born. The gospel's good news is that in the Lord Jesus, the Spirit of life and love in God's kingdom has come. He is the living and resurrected One who has come to us from Eternity. Even in the midst of a fallen world's darkness, in Christ we walk in God's Light and Peace and rejoice in the victory Jesus has won for all of us.

Moreover, life in the kingdom of God Jesus inaugurated is not eclectic, composed of bits of truth gathered here and there from the great philosophers, based on a pluralistic life-view, which prides itself on being open to every idea trickling down from the human mind. The kingdom of God reflects the unique mind of Christ (Philippians 2:5), and the mind of Christ was not eclectic. His spirit was focused on the Spirit of the Holy One who sent Him, saying,

> I can do nothing on my own authority; as I
> hear, I judge; and my judgment is just,
> because I seek not my own will but the will of
> him who sent me. If I bear witness to myself,
> my testimony is not true.
> - John 5:30-32

In the same authoritative way, Jesus said, "I am the truth . . .
without me you can do nothing." (John 14:6, 15:5)

As we see in Jesus' trial before Pilate, the kingdom of God is
not a super-state like the United States of America. The
nonviolent Messiah said to one of Rome's top political
figures,

> My kingdom does not belong to this world; if
> my kingdom belonged to this world, my
> followers would fight to keep me from being
> handed over to the Jewish authorities. No, my
> kingdom does not belong here.
> - John 18:36 CEV

The capital of Jesus' kingdom is not Washington; its power
resides not in the Pentagon, the Congress, the Supreme
Court, in a man elected to be President. Jesus' kingdom has
no borders, no national anthem or flag.

In his *Story of Civilization*, historian Will Durant concluded:

> There is no greater drama in human record
> than the sight of a few Christians, scorned and
> oppressed by a succession of emperors,
> bearing all trials with a fierce tenacity,
> multiplying quietly, building order while their
> enemies generated chaos, fighting the sword
> with the word, brutality with hope, and at last
> defeating the strongest state that history has

known. Caesar and Christ had met in the arena, and Christ had won.

How could it be made any clearer that the church of Jesus does not fight like the world fights to save our life in this violent world of the flesh- the world He has overcome? Here the Ruler of the kingdom of God encounters the ruling authorities of this world. The difference between the two authorities could not be more obvious. One rules by the Eternal Spirit of holy self-giving agape, whereas the other rules by the temporal power of law enforced by self-protecting, coercive, and dominative power.

We are free to deny Jesus' Lordship. We are not free to use the name "Christian" and then eclectically pick and chose the parts of His life and teaching we happen to like. For Christians, it is required that the kingdom of God and the sovereign Holy One be FIRST:

> Do not be anxious, saying, "What shall we eat?" or "What shall we drink?" or "What shall we wear?" For the Gentiles seek all these things; and your heavenly Father knows you need them all. But seek first the kingdom of God and his righteousness and all these things shall be yours as well.
> - Matthew 5:31-33

In the eternal kingdom inaugurated by Jesus Christ, Son of God, Savior, the peace that He gives is more than *inner* peace that comforts and forgives the individual's sin. It is that, but it is more. Salvation in Christ includes reconciliation with all of planet-Earth's families whom God loves (Genesis 12:3; John 3:16).

In Christ, Abba not only offers peace of mind to the individual, but also peace in the realm of ALL human relationships – racial, ethnic, national. The Gospel of the

Eternal's reconciling agape speaks to the whole of life. Prejudiced and violent by inherited instinct, all humans have been reconciled in Christ and are one (See Galatians 3:27-28). Like the walls of Jericho, the walls separating races and nations come tumbling down when God's ministers sound the bugle of the Holy One's agape-love.

The Holy Spirit does not suffer from schizophrenia, one Spirit empowering God's people to love personal enemies, and a different Spirit inspiring us to butcher political enemies (See Ephesians 4:4-6). This is nonsense. There is ONE indwelling Spirit who speaks to ALL aspects of our life at ALL times.

When one of the scribes asked Jesus which commandments came first, He answered,

> Hear, O Israel, The Lord our God, is one, and you shall love the Lord your God with all your heart and with all your soul and with all your strength. The second is this; you shall love your neighbor as yourself.
> - Mark 12:28-30

When asked who His neighbor was, Jesus told them the parable of the Good Samaritan, the hated enemy of Jews (See Luke 10).

The unique ministry of the church is one of reconciliation (See 2 Corinthians 5:18-20), not incineration. No part of the New Testament makes this as clear as the First Letter of the Beloved Apostle John:

> He, who says he is in the light and hates his brother, is in the darkness still. He, who loves his brother, abides in the light, and in it there is no cause for stumbling. But he who hates his brother walks in the darkness and does not

know where he is going, because the darkness
has blinded his eyes.

We know that we have passed out of death
into life, because we love the brethren.

By this we know love that he laid down his
life for us; and we ought to lay down our lives
for the brethren. But if any one has the
world's goods and sees his brother in need,
yet closes his heart against him, how does
God's love abide in him? Little children, let
us not love in word or speech but in deed and
in truth.

By this we know that he abides in us, by the
Spirit, which he has given us.
- 1 John 2:9-11; 3:14, 16-18, 24

Citizens of the kingdom ruled by God's Spirit have
overcome every so-called enemy "by a sword not of man"
(Isaiah 31:8), the weapon of absolute trust in the God of love
made flesh by Jesus on the cross and set loose by His
resurrection and indwelling. Our new life in the kingdom of
God is our only real security where no enemy can harm us,
not the vilest of dictators, not cancer, not death. We are more
than conquerors in Christ who loves us.

In the most revealing book in the Bible, John recorded these
words to assure us of the victory which the King of kings
and the ascended ruling Lord of lords gives those who abide
in His Person and Word:

Now the salvation and the power and the
kingdom of our God and the authority of his
Christ have come, for the accuser of our
brethren has been thrown down, who accuses
them day and night before our God. And they

have conquered him by the blood of the Lamb
and by the word of their testimony, for they
loved not their lives, even unto death. Rejoice
then, O heaven, and you that dwell therein.
- Revelation 12: 10-12

The task of the church is not to reform the nations and
Christianize a fallen world; the result of this effort has been a
compromised church and a more secularized world. Rather it
is the task of the church to demonstrate an alternative
society, a counter-culture which, instead of reflecting the
brilliance and greatness of humans, loses its life in following
the Holy One, who made the most daring claim ever to come
from human lips:

He who has seen me has seen the Father.
Believe me that I am in the Father and the
Father in me.
- John 14: 9,11

Jesus invites us in our discord and death to participate in the
fullness of the Eternal Now in the kingdom of God. It is
there that we find our rest, our peace, and our reason for
living:

Come to me all who labor and are heavy
laden, and I will give you rest. Take my yoke
upon you, and learn from me; for I am gentle
and lowly in heart, and you will find rest for
your souls. For my yoke is easy, and my
burden is light.
- Matthew 11:28-30

As we receive the whole Jesus as Lord and Savior for our
whole life, we are restored to a new and eternal life. In place
of our old life of violence and turmoil, it is one of gentleness
and rest.

To be sure, the Powers and Principalities remain in sin's world and continue to confront us. They have not yet been destroyed, but in the crucified, risen, indwelling Christ they have been DEFEATED! This is our assurance,

> He who is in you is greater than he who is in the world.
> - 1 John 4:4

No matter what happens to our mortal flesh, our soul, our real self, abiding in the Eternal is indestructible. When we abide in the Risen Christ, our real self is <u>beyond tragedy</u>. No enemy can defeat us!

Christopher Reeve's book entitled, *Still Me*, is the amazing story of his response to an accident; instead of making a jump, the horse stopped suddenly, throwing Reeve to the ground. He was left completely paralyzed. Unconscious for five days, Reeve awakened with numerous tubes and steel supports in and around his body. After listening to what the doctors had to say about his condition, and realizing how seriously his body had been injured, Reeve concluded, "Why not die and save everyone a lot of pain and suffering?" When his wife, Dana, came into the room and heard him say, "Maybe we should let me go", he heard her say something that changed his life. Starting to cry, but looking into his eyes, she said, "This is your life and your decision, but I want you to know that I'll be with you for the long haul, no matter what." Then she added these words that transformed the patient's wish to die: "You're still you. And I love you."

In that moment, Christopher Reeve realized he could say, "no matter what the condition of my physical body may be, I AM STILL ME". Unable to breathe without a respirator or move a muscle, barely able to speak, he understood a fundamental biblical truth: his is an eternal soul who is loved, not a temporal body of flesh, not merely muscles, nerves, blood, organs of the flesh which soon perish and return to dust. This epiphany assured Reeve that to abide in "Jesus Christ, Son of God, Savior", is to abide in His Holy Spirit; therein we discover who we really are: each one a unique and precious soul loved by God as though there were only one of us to love.

There are those who will say, "I'm a pragmatist, a person who likes to take control and get things done. Talking about abiding in Christ and God's Holy Spirit is too vague and unreal for me. I can't get my teeth into anything like that." Such a sense of vagueness is the result of separating the Lord's indwelling from His teaching. His Person and teaching are inseparable. Said Jesus:

> If you keep my commandments, you will abide in my love.
> - John 15:1

The Apostles testified,

> All who keep his commandments abide in him, and he in them.
> - 1 John 3:24

There is nothing vague about Jesus' teaching. His words are disturbingly clear:

> Love your enemies and pray for those who persecute you.
> - Matthew 5:44-45

> A new commandment I give to you, that you love one another, even as I have loved you. By this all men will know you are my disciples, if you have love for one another.
> - John 13:34-35

In his last parable Jesus said that when we feed the hungry, clothe the naked, visit the sick and those in prison, and welcome the stranger, when you do it "unto one of the least of these, my brethren, you do it to me" (Matthew 25:31-40). This is not vague.

When we abide in Jesus, we hear His disturbing voice calling us to walk as He did with the least, the lowest, and the lost.

> In haunts of wretchedness and need, on shadowed thresholds dark with fears, from paths where hide the lures of greed, we catch the vision of Thy tears.

God's peace for which we were created is not merely an idea or a philosophical concept. There are all kinds of ideas and concepts of peace floating in the minds of brilliant people. Some are connected with "peace" in the Middle East, some with "peace" in Northern Ireland, or in countless trouble spots in a sinful, violent world. This is not peace, certainly not the "shalom" of God. This is only a politicized world's attempt to get groups to stop killing each other long enough to form a different kind of government based on a different arrangement of political and economic power. These solutions are very temporary. And when such "peace" is arranged, the parties still hate each other as much as ever, as we see with the so-called "peace process" between Israel and the Palestinians.

In the same way, there are "57 varieties" of so-called pacifism floating around in the world: some religious, some secular, some objecting to a particular war or kind of weapon, hardly any mentioning the "name which is above every name" (Philippians 2:9).

The peace of God proclaimed by the gospel is Person-centered-union with God's Person, who became flesh in Jesus that we in our person might possess the peace of God (Ephesians 2:14). It's God's plan,

his purpose which he set forth in Christ . . . to
unite all things in him, things in heaven and
things on earth.
-Ephesians 1:9-10

Not Man's plan, waiting for our brilliant strategies and
diplomacy to achieve. Peace is gift, the fruit of complete
trust in God. He is the process.

He is the Vine, the Spirit (See 2 Corinthians 3:17-18) and
when we abide in Christ as the branch abides in the vine, we
possess the fruit of the Spirit:

> . . . love, joy, peace, patience, kindness,
> goodness, faithfulness, gentleness, self-
> control, against such there is no law. Those
> who belong to Christ have crucified the flesh
> with its passions and desires.
> - Galatians 5:22-24

The Biblical Meaning of "Flesh"

More than fifty times in his letters, Saint Paul contrasts life
in the flesh with life in Christ and His Spirit. Life in the flesh
is beset by trouble and tragedy. Life in the risen Christ is
beyond tragedy. The mind-set of the flesh is death and its
Darkness. The mind of Jesus' Holy Spirit is life and its
Light. In this world of dark suffering and sadness, we are
saved from despair by abiding in Christ and sharing in His
resurrection-victory and indwelling Spirit whose fruit is
peace our peanut minds cannot grasp.

According to the gospel's foremost evangelist,

> To set the mind on the flesh is death, but to
> set the mind on the Spirit is life and peace.
> For the mind that is set on the flesh is hostile
> to God; it does not submit to God's law,

24

indeed it cannot; those who are in the flesh
cannot please God.
- Romans 8:6-8

Like some other passages from Paul, this is not easy to understand. From our birth in the flesh until the moment we die, we live in the flesh God created. We think about our flesh continually, taking a refreshing shower in the morning, satisfying our hunger, and so on until we go to bed at night. We ask, what is so evil about our flesh? "Sarx", the Greek word for "flesh" in the New Testament, can refer to the physical body, or to one's self, but as Paul's Letter to the Galatian church makes clear, "flesh" means the <u>carnal life that is alienated from God, fixated solely on the gratification of physical appetites and desires, even at the expense of the well-being of others.</u>

Let's look at Galatians 5:16 to 21 and see what Paul means by "flesh."

> But I say to you, walk by the Spirit, and do not gratify the desires of the flesh. For the desires of the flesh are against the Spirit, and the desires of the Spirit are against the flesh; for these are opposed to each other, to prevent you from doing what you would. But if you are led by the Spirit, you are not under the law. Now the works of the flesh are plain: fornication, impurity, licentiousness, idolatry, sorcery, enmity, strife, jealousy, anger, selfishness, dissension, party-spirit, envy, drunkenness, carousing, and the like. I warned you, as I warned you before, that those who do such things shall not inherit the kingdom of God.

In contrast to life in the "flesh" <u>alienated</u> from God, is the same life in the flesh <u>reconciled</u> to God and <u>abiding in the</u>

25

Holy Spirit whose fruit is peace. This is still life in the flesh, but it is life transformed in Christ, the abundant life of the Spirit Jesus enfleshed. Moreover, this life is to be enfleshed in every soul in order to restore the joyful, abundant, and eternal life of God's Paradise lost. This loss comes about when we attempt to play God managing our own life apart from the Creator. This is why the "flesh", estranged from God and dominated by the Powers and Principalities must be crucified with Jesus on the cross to be able to live in the Spirit and walk in God's peace. This is why Paul testified,

> Those who belong to Christ Jesus have crucified the flesh with its passions and desires.
> - Galatians 5:24

The Biblical Meaning of Baptism

What does baptism in the church signify? It signifies dying with Jesus to the world of the flesh alienated from God and controlled by the Principalities and Powers, then being raised with Jesus to a completely new life of the Spirit (Romans 6:1-8) in God's here and now kingdom, a kingdom liberated from the demonic spirit of discord and death. This is the essence of the gospel. The resurrection was not meant for Jesus alone. The new resurrection-life of the Spirit is for all who confess Christ as Lord and walk in His Way of nonviolent love; dying to a world of violence and death and being raised to the Savior's kingdom of peace. In other words, baptism signifies nonviolent people at peace, not violent people at war. This is not what baptism means to mainline Catholic, Protestant, Orthodox, and Pentecostal churches whose members are taught to kill in "good" wars. Nothing is more futile than the attempt to justify a "good war". There is no good war. In war the "good" guys act exactly like the "bad" guys -- same weapons, different uniforms.

According to a legendary tale, dying to the old violent self and being raised to the new man of God's agape Spirit is not what baptism meant to the Russian ruler, Ivan the Terrible. In their search for his ideal wife and companion, his aides chose Sophia, the daughter of the king of Greece.

Ivan was agreeable to the marriage, but there was one problem. Sophia's father agreed to the marriage only if Ivan submitted to baptism in the Greek Orthodox Church. Ivan agreed until he was told that baptism would mean giving up his profession as a soldier. The warrior-monarch of Russia refused to do this until he came up with his own style baptismal twist. When he and his army of five hundred walked into the water to be baptized by five hundred priests, Ivan and his soldiers raised their right arm, holding their sword above the water. The warriors were baptized, but not their weapons of slaughter.

This is what the tradition of infant baptism means in mainstream Christianity. Babies receive a name at baptism as parents and congregation are admonished to lead the child in such a way that he or she will join the church at confirmation and be faithful followers of Jesus all the days of their life. But the hand holding the gun put there by the state is held outside the waters of baptism. The hand of the soldier is not baptized in the Spirit and words of Jesus.

As we shall see later in detail, the Scripture, "Let every person be subject to the ruling authorities" (Romans 13:1), is interpreted by "just war" churches in a way that the one baptized is not only allowed to follow the soldier's profession; the soldier with special courage in battle is honored as a national hero with special qualifications to be elected to the highest political office in the nation and become Commander-in-chief of the Armed Forces.

Museums are dedicated to "The Greatest Generation"— soldiers who confront the enemy the same way the enemy

27

confronts them: with lethal weapons legal on the battle-field but illegal when the soldier returns home and puts off his military uniform for civilian dress. As an expert in killing on the battlefield, the soldier receives a medal of honor from the state, but when he uses the same weapon without the state's soldier uniform, he earns the state's death penalty. How confusing! Such is the confusion of mainstream Christianity.

In popular mainline churches, baptism no longer means dying to radical evil, living anew in the Holy Spirit, and loving enemies as Jesus loved and taught His Apostles and His church to love (See Romans 12). In war there is little difference between the baptized and the unbaptized. All are trained to kill. With the exception of the church we will examine later, all give their absolute obedience to the state, which is part of a fallen world (See 1 Samuel 8).

It is interesting to note that in the last two thousand years, the only churches that have totally rejected all violence and war have been churches that have rejected infant baptism and linked a believer's baptism with the rejection of war.

In one form or another, these churches ask the question at baptism: "Do you renounce war as sin and promise to put on only the Scriptural armor of God in waging war against evil?"

The one requesting baptism answers, "Yes!" with a clear understanding that his or her commitment is not a comfortable blending with the world, but contending against the world and its systems of violent power.

How Jesus Combats Evil and Conquers the Enemy

About 1850, in his book, *Training in Christianity*, Soren Kierkegaard wrote,

As soon as Christ's kingdom comes to terms with the world, it is abolished. In this world Christ's church can truly survive only by contending (against the world), that is, by fighting for its survival every instant.

By fighting, Kierkegaard meant contending against evil in a fallen world with weapons of God's Spirit, not of man's sin.

Karl Barth put it like this:

The church exists to set up in the world a new sign which is radically dissimilar to the world's own manner which contradicts it in a way which is full of promise.

While in human form, Jesus fully shared our real struggles with evil and death and overcame them all. He especially shared them on the cross where He experienced the full fury of the Powers and Principalities. In the words of Christian theologian, Walter Wink:

They scourged him with whips, but with each stroke of the lash their own legitimacy was laid open. They mocked him with a robe and a crown of thorns, spit on him, struck him on the head with a reed, and ridiculed him with the ovation, "Hail, King of the Jews!"—not knowing that their acclamation would echo down the centuries. They stripped him naked and crucified him in humiliation, unaware that this very act had stripped them of the last covering that disguised the towering wrongness of the whole way of living their violence defended.

The Law by which they judged Jesus was itself judged and nailed to the cross that conquered violence and death by the

Holy Spirit's power of God's love incarnate in Jesus. The cross, resurrection, and indwelling of Jesus revealed the impotence of violence and death when they were swallowed up in the God of love and peace.

Testifying that his Deliverer was "Jesus Christ, Son of God, Savior", Paul reminded the church:

> For though we live in the world we are not carrying on a worldly war, for the weapons of our warfare are not worldly, but have divine power to destroy strongholds.
> -2 Corinthians 10:3-4

> We are not contending against flesh and blood, but against the principalities, against the powers, against the world rulers in this present darkness, against the spiritual hosts of wickedness in the heavenly places.
> - Ephesians 6:10-12

In sin's warring world, nation-states and their military systems contend against flesh and blood in futile attempts to overcome evil with coercive power which is inherently violent. Nothing is more tragic than to see the church mimic the military might of the state and its manufactured weapons, and, in so doing, fail to witness to God's power to give total peace in the crucified-risen-ascended-ruling-indwelling Christ.

In contrast, Paul describes the redeeming weapons the church is to use in overcoming evil:

> Be strong in the Lord and in the strength of his might. Take the whole armor of God. Stand therefore, having girded your loins with truth, and having put on the breastplate of righteousness, and having shod your feet with

the equipment of the gospel of peace; besides all these, taking the shield of faith with which you can quench all the flaming darts of the evil one. And take the helmet of salvation, and the sword of the Spirit which is the word of God. Pray at all times in the Spirit.
- Ephesians 6:10-18

These are the redemptive weapons Jesus used to overcome the evil Powers and Principalities that cause war (See Colossians 2:15). This is why the New Testament is a victorious gospel of agape and joy, the good news that the Messiah the Old Testament was waiting for HAS COME, and is now the victor over every enemy.

How to Witness to Jesus' Victory Already Won

This was the good news of peace a young man named Luke was proclaiming in a discussion at a Mennonite church conference. The question on the table was whether or not the Mennonite church should continue its historic peaceful position of absolute nonviolence and rejection of all war, or fight in certain circumstances. One elderly gentleman, well-to-do owner of a large farm, thought the Mennonites should not be rigid in rejecting all war. He pointed out there might be circumstances in which Christians should engage in a "just war" to protect property and person.

Pointing out it is not the privilege of Christians to select the kinds of war to kill; Luke stood up and defended the peaceful tradition held by Mennonites since their beginning in the sixteenth century. When Luke finished speaking, the older man quickly responded, "It's easy for you to talk in such a lofty manner, but one of these days an enemy may come and take everything you have." Luke replied, "This poses no problem for me. You see, Sir, when I became a Christian, I gave everything I had to Jesus. If they do come they can only take what already belongs to Jesus. As the sovereign Lord

31

and Ruler of life, I'm sure he can handle the problem."

The older Mennonite responded, "All right, so they can't take from you what you have given to Jesus, but they can kill you." The young man replied, "No, they can't kill me. When I was baptized and became a Christian, my life in this world came to an end. The new and eternal life that I received in Christ is not at the mercy of enemies." In frustration the older man responded, "They may not be able to take what you have given to the Lord, they may not be able to kill you, but let me assure you, young man, they can sure make you suffer." Luke's answer was without hesitation, "If and when that day comes, I hope I will remember the words of Jesus, "Blessed are those who are persecuted for righteousness' sake, for theirs is the kingdom of God." You see, Sir, there is nothing the world can do to a Christian who doesn't own anything, is already dead, and rejoices in sharing Jesus' suffering for the sake of a world redeemed."

Luke was not waiting for Jesus' Second Coming to witness to God's peaceable kingdom on earth. God's word and the young man's experience of truth that came by abiding in the Holy One was enough to assure Luke that God's salvation-peace has been completed in the life and work of Jesus Christ, Son of God, and Savior.

It is finished!
- John 19:30

In every present moment, Jesus calls His church to bear witness to the finished business of His peace so that a God-estranged world may believe He is the Messiah the Old Covenant promised and the New Covenant in the blood of Christ made reality.

Luke was not waiting for the Apocalypse to destroy every enemy when peace will finally prevail at the end of history. Luke was witnessing to the good news that the Messiah's victory at the end of history is reality in our present history as we abide in Alpha and Omega.

By abiding in God's holy Spirit, Jesus conquered sin's world of hate, the world of revenge, the world of anger, the world that wants to dominate and control, the world of insecurity that breeds war through His death on the cross. Sin that causes people to hate and kill to gain power and make them feel important nailed the Nazarene to a cross. The world did everything possible to destroy Him as a person, placing a crown of thorns on His head and mocking Him, saying, "Now King, let's see you save yourself".

Then, the world gambled to see who would get His only material wealth, a few pieces of clothing, and pierced the Savior's body. In short, the world unleashed the worst kind of evil it had in that day.

But on the cross, the nonviolent Messiah triumphed over the worst the world could do to Him, not with more of the same—more hatred, more violence, and more power that kills. No! Jesus conquered by an entirely different power: Abba's reconciling and forgiving love, the Holy Spirit of good that overcomes the world of evil and restores in humans that for which we are created -- a right relationship with our Creator and with each other (See Ephesians 2:1-10). This is why Jesus said, "in me you shall have peace": In me, in my cross, in my resurrection, in my indwelling. He is our peace (Ephesians 2:14). As we lose our life in His Spirit, we fulfill our destiny by becoming what we were created to be, and the Christmas anthem of the angels becomes Reality:

> Glory to God in the highest, and on earth peace among men with whom he is well pleased!
> - Luke 2:14

This must have been what Saint Paul meant when he said

Jesus nailed our sinful nature to the cross and in so doing disarmed the Powers and Principalities, making a public spectacle of them and triumphing over them (See Colossians 2:15).

The church must not continue to wait until Jesus' millennial rule of a thousand years to witness to Jesus' victory over violence. Nor should they wait for His Second Coming. By keeping our attention fixed on the future, false prophets blind the church to the power Jesus has given His disciples to conquer violence and live peaceably in the present, under all circumstances, under any political system.

The revealing vision of St. John makes clear what the entire New Testament makes clear. Listen to Jesus' words the Apostle John hears near the end of his visionary experience on the isle of Patmos:

> Behold, I make all things new. It is done! I
> am the Alpha and the Omega, the beginning
> and the end. To the thirsty I will give from the
> fountain of the water of life without payment.
> - Revelation 21:5-6

Do those words sound like something Jesus is going to do in the unknown future, or what He has already accomplished and continues to do in the present for all who abide in Him?

His words, "It is done" proclaim a mission accomplished. "I am Alpha and Omega" sounds like the I AM THAT I AM God who speaks in every present moment. Jesus' offer to give those who are thirsty water from the fountain of eternal life echoes Jesus' words to the Samaritan woman at Jacob's well:

> Every one who drinks of this water will thirst
> again, but whoever drinks of the water that I
> shall give him shall never thirst.
> - John 4:13

These are the waters of peace present, not peace future. God's gospel would not be good news if it were primarily about a victory at the end of history. The gospel is good news because it applies to every present moment. John's vision of Jesus' victory over the Powers and Principalities gave new courage to the martyrs because they heard it as a message from the Eternal, which applied to their present struggle with the Beast. It was a reminder of Jesus' words to the Apostles as He struggled with the same Beast:

> In the world you have tribulation; but be of good courage, I have overcome the world.
> - John 16:33

> Lo, I am with you always, to the close of the age.
> - Matthew 28:20

Instead of arguing over the precise meaning of apocalyptic symbols and letting them divide the church, this is the good news that should unite Christians universally in witnessing to our total peace in Christ and Jesus' total Victory over sin, including the sin of war. In Jesus Christ, Son of God, Savior, the Messianic Age has begun! In the Messiah, the first-fruit of the kingdom of God has come on earth as it is in heaven (Matthew 6:10) to be consummated, not begun, with His Second Coming.

Growing up on a cotton farm in Alabama, an African-American, John Lewis, was harshly beaten and imprisoned as one of the prophetic voices of the civil rights movement in the 1960's. Since 1987, he has been the Representative for the Fifth Congressional District of Georgia. Recognized by co-members of both parties as the embodiment of the grand legacy of Martin Luther King Jr., John Lewis was asked how he could be nonviolent in the face of the world's hostility.

He replied,

> "Hate, hostility, malice will destroy you; they will eat away at your very soul, your very essence. And it does not help lead toward a greater sense of the Beloved Community, or what Dr. King spoke of as "the world house". You cannot build one house, you cannot build one family, you cannot build one community, if you're not somehow consumed by the spirit of love."

According to the gospel, we do not have the Spirit of Christ if in party-spirit we live like "ordinary men of the flesh" and say, "I belong to Appolos", or "I belong to Cephas", or "I belong to Paul" (See 1 Corinthians 3:21). There is one Spirit who is Christ, and that consuming Spirit is the Eternal's indwelling love (1 Corinthians 13).

My friend, Brian Wilson, lost both of his legs when a train carrying munitions to a repressive government in Central America refused to stop for those standing on the tracks in protest. Although he lost both legs, Brian could say, "I am STILL ME", a person continuing to be loved by Abba. Reflecting on that experience, Brian said,

> I think nonviolence is not so much a tactic as a way of experiencing the world within yourself -- of understanding the sacred connection with all of life.

During those first centuries after Pentecost, people like Brian Wilson, John Lewis, and Luke, did not turn the world upside down because they had their new faith neatly packaged with an abstract theological answer for every question. What they did have was the gift Jesus promised the church on Pentecost: POWER! (Acts 1:8) The power of a Presence so overwhelming they knew they were not alone in their frailty and their daily struggles. The church had the assurance that Abba was with them, sharing a power nothing can destroy (Matthew 16:18). Someone was not only with them in their house, they knew it was not their House. They were living in God's Home of the Spirit, a House no storm can topple, no politician could take from them (See Matthew 7:24-27).

Origen, a teacher in the first theological seminary of the church in Alexandria, lived in Abba's reconciled one Family House built on the Rock of the Risen Messiah. He said to his students, "For we no longer take up sword against nation, nor do we learn war any more, having become children of peace, for the sake of Jesus."

Another one of my heroes, Maximilian, at the end of the third century moved into the Holy One's Place of Peace. About twenty years before Constantine, his father Fabius gathered their whole family together to celebrate the twenty-first birthday of his son, Maximilian. At the high point of the celebration, Fabius announced a surprise birthday gift for his son. "This is for you, my son", he said; "a special coat I had made for you when you enlist in the army," and proudly hung the coat around his son's shoulders.

The guests were so busy admiring the coat they did not notice how quiet Maximilian had suddenly become—no one except his father.

"What's the matter, son, don't you like the coat?" asked his father.

"Yes, yes, of course I do", replied Maximilian." "What bothers me is that you assume I will enlist in the army. As you know, father, I have become a Christian and the Lord Jesus teaches me to love my enemies. How then can I become a soldier? It is impossible."

Fabius was shocked. "I didn't think your being a Christian

would make any difference. I thought you always wanted to become a soldier. As a recruiter for the proconsul's army, I have given Dion your name. You are to report to him tomorrow."

"I will report", Maximilian replied, "but I will not become a soldier." His father knew how dangerous it was to admit being a Christian and refuse to obey the Emperor. It meant death.

The next morning as they walked toward the proconsul's office, Fabius said, "Son, I'm sorry I gave your name to Dion. I would give anything to undo what I did."

"I understand, Father," replied his son. "I do not hold it against you. I hope you understand why I cannot be a soldier." "I do," said Fabius. "If you take seriously Jesus' command to love your enemies, you cannot do otherwise."

After a strong handclasp, they continued on to the proconsul's office where Dion cordially greeted his friend and his son. "Welcome, welcome, Fabius and congratulations on having such a fine son. He will make a fine soldier. Maximilian, here is your badge. Wear it with honor."

"I am sorry, sir, but I cannot serve as a soldier," said Maximilian. "I am a Christian and must obey Christ as my sovereign Lord."

No longer smiling, the proconsul said: "I can't believe my ears. This is ridiculous. To be a soldier and serve your country is the most honorable thing you can do. I have heard about these stupid Christians. Surely you won't let imaginary religious scruples stand in your way of a brilliant military career. Here, take this badge, and I will forget that you are a Christian."

"No", replied Maximilian. "I cannot serve as a soldier. I cannot do evil." At that point the proconsul exploded. "Evil? Evil? What evil do they do who serve their country?"

"You know what soldiers do," replied Fabius' son. "They not only kill one man, as a murderer does, but thousands. A crime multiplied does not become a virtue."

Turning to Fabius, the proconsul said sternly, "Fabius, as a recruiter, you know the law. Persuade your son to change his mind or he must die."

His face now pale, Fabius replied, "Dion, even if I could change his mind, I would not. I am proud of my son."

"Then take him away," the proconsul shouted to the guards. In agony, Fabius walked out alone. "My son, my son," he moaned. The next morning, Maximilian was executed. He died without fear because by abiding in Jesus, the indwelling Holy Spirit had given Maximilian the certainty of eternal life in the deathless and peaceable kingdom of God.

The church in Africa was so deeply moved by the witness of Maximilian that they took his body to Carthage and buried it near that of Cyprian who had been the overseer of Jesus' church in that city. Cyprian had also met a martyr's death in the year 258 A.D. when the persecution of Christians was part of Rome's 1000th Anniversary celebration.

That the congregation in Carthage wanted the body of Maximilian to lie close to the body of Cyprian shows that their beloved bishop believed God's gospel is one of absolute nonviolent agape. Members knew that Cyprian would feel comfortable having such a witness to the Messiah's nonviolent kingdom at his side.

May all of us who profess Jesus Christ as Lord scratch "fish" on our hearts and hands, not as a secret symbol, but as a public witness that our peace and victory over the world is Jesus, who has given us the weaponry of God's Holy Spirit to conquer every enemy.

This is the good news brother Archbishop Desmond Tutu was witnessing to in 1988 when he shouted to the brutal enforcers of apartheid gathered outside St. George's Cathedral in South Africa's Cape Town; "You are not God, you are mortals. You have already lost. Come and join the winning side."

Beloved, join the winning side of Jesus now! Today is the day of salvation!

Chapter 2

When and How
The Church Turned to Violence

> All we like sheep have gone astray; we have
> turned everyone to his own way.
> - Isaiah 53:6

After almost three centuries of witnessing to Jesus'
nonviolent Way of the cross, the church made two tragic
mistakes.

The first mistake was mixing the kingdom of God Jesus
inaugurated with Constantine's political kingdom. In giving
Caesar equal devotion, we forgot that

> No one can serve two masters; for either he
> will hate the one and love the other, or he will
> be devoted to the one and despise the other.
> - Matthew 6:24

The 180-degree turn the church took during the twenty-five
year reign of Constantine began with his military victory in
312 A.D. As Constantine extended a hand of friendship to
Jesus, he put the sword into the hands of Christians. They
have been using it ever since to protect their life and so-
called "Christian" civilization.

Church historian, Roland Bainton, said this about the turning point,

> One cannot but marvel that neither the emperor nor the church felt an impropriety in placing the cross upon the military labarum. Constantine tacitly ranged himself in the succession of the martyrs in that he was the first emperor to bestow upon himself the title "Victor". This designation which the pagans gave only to the gods, and the Christians only to the martyrs, was assumed by the Christian emperor on the ground that what the martyrs had commenced with their blood, he had completed with the sword.

In the century just before his military victory which made Constantine sole Ruler of the West, thirty emperors had made claim to the throne. No longer granted power by the Roman Senate, emperors took power by military might, slaying their rivals. The death of one Caesar was the signal to Roman troops somewhere to acclaim a new ruler. Constantine became Emperor by the power of the sword. Far to the north in Britain, his father, Constantius, was one of the two rulers in the West when his son who had been living in the court of Diocletian, emperor in the East, came to fight by his side. In 306, Constantius died suddenly and his admiring troops kept their promise that they would acclaim his son one of the two emperors in the West.

Not satisfied to rule only Britain, Gaul, and Spain, Constantine had his eye on the entire Empire. By 310, his only rival in the West was Maxentius, the son of one of the two Caesars in the East. Both Constantine and Maxentius had their eye on the same prize and prepared for a showdown. With an army, which seemed much too small for the task, Constantine crossed the Alps and headed for Rome where his rival's larger army enjoyed the fortifications of the Empire's capital city. Hearing that his rival was going all out to win the favor of the gods in their coming battle, Constantine, like his father, believed that victory in battle depended upon divine intervention, so he prayed to the God of the Christians for help.

Constantine Envisions Christ Leading His Armies

The following days changed the history of the church and of the world. Eusebius, Rome's historian, describes what happened according to Constantine's own words:

> Constantine said that about noon, when the day was already beginning to decline, he saw with his own eyes two beams of light in the heavens above the sun forming a cross and bearing the inscription, "By this conquer".

Constantine also told Eusebius about his dream. In it, Constantine said he was directed to construct a military standard with a cross on it and carry the standard into battle to protect his troops from the enemy. With haste, Constantine ordered the standard to be made with a gold-plated spear placed upright. A shorter bar formed the shape of a cross. A gold wreath studded with jewels was laid over the crossbar with the Chi-Rho monogram signifying the name of Christ. Carrying the standard of the cross into battle, the armies of Constantine met the enemy at the Milvian Bridge two miles outside the walls of Rome. Maxentius was killed in the battle, and his military forces were decisively defeated. Constantine became the sole ruler of the West on October 12, 312.

Constantine attributed his success in battle to the god of Christians. To show his gratitude, the new Emperor showered countless gifts on the church and issued the Edict of Milan which said,

We resolve to grant both to the Christians and to all men, freedom to follow the religion which they choose, so that whatever heavenly divinity exists may be favorably inclined to us and to all who live under our government.

An Emperor Grants Favors Instead of Persecution

Constantine favored Christianity, not because of any personal experience of the life-changing power of God's indwelling Spirit, but because he believed a united church would help unify the disintegrating Roman Empire.

Constantine and his father were among the few emperors who believed Rome's persecution of Christians was a failed policy. After each period of persecution, the church continued to grow in numbers and in organization. Although Constantine continued to have the image of the Sun-god engraved on Roman coins, he stopped the persecution of Christians and gave his blessing to Christianity with the hope that his friendship would bring Rome good fortune.

Shortly after his military victory, Constantine paid a visit to the bishop of Rome who was now generally recognized as the chief overseer of the church in the West. Bishop Miltiades had heard about Constantine's victory but could not understand why the new Emperor had come to his small unpretentious home. A man of action, Constantine wasted no words. The sixty-two-year-old bishop was told that the Empire's policy toward the church had been reversed and began to ask Miltiades many questions: "Where are the bones of Peter and Paul? Where is the cross? Where are the nails which fastened Jesus' body to the cross? Who would Miltiades' successor be?"

The next day, Constantine was back again with his wife, Fausta, and his Christian mother, Helena. With Miltiades they rode to the places where Peter and Paul were buried.

The emperor amazed the bishop when he said he planned to build basilica churches in both locations to honor Peter and Paul. Constructing a basilica on the spot where Peter and Paul were executed by Rome was hardly the Christian way to honor the Apostles, whose only basilica had been the open sky and a believer's humble home.

A little later, standing on Rome's Lateran Hill with his wife, Constantine told Miltiades that the largest of the ancient Laterani family palaces was owned by his wife. It had been a dowry gift from her father, Maximilian, and would be given to the church as the bishop's new residence.

Living in such a spacious palace did not help the head of the church obey Jesus' teaching: "Abide in me and I in you" (John 15:3). The palace did not draw the Pope and the church closer to the One, who said,

> Foxes have holes and birds of the air have nests, but the Son of man has nowhere to lay his head.
> - Matthew. 8:20

Sacred Spikes

Later, after Helena returned from a trip to Jerusalem which she claimed was directed by God, Constantine's mother handed her son three spikes she said she found in the tomb where Jesus was buried, and assured her son they were used to nail the Messiah's body to the cross. The warrior-emperor had one spike put in his royal crown to signify that he would rule in the name of Jesus. Another he used as the bit for his horse to signify that he would ride into battle against all enemies as the Lord's representative. Using one of the spikes as a bit in the mouth of the Emperor's war horse was hardly consistent with Jesus riding triumphantly into Jerusalem on the back of a donkey (Mark 11:7-10). Putting another in the Emperor's crown was not in keeping with the risen Lord's word to the martyrs.

> Hold fast to what you have so that no one
> may seize your crown.
> - Revelation 3:11

Then Constantine decreed that all priests would be paid by the state so they could be free to devote all of their time to their priestly duties, and in this way, bring rich blessings on the tottering empire he was trying to restore.

Doesn't paying priests tend to make them ministers of the court? Doesn't this muffle their prophetic utterances just as Judah's king tried to silence Jeremiah (Jeremiah 5:13, 18)?

In the early church prior to Constantine, fighting in war was never approved. Soon Constantine announced that priests should serve in the army to minister to soldiers. Less than a hundred years later, only Christians were allowed to serve in the army they had rejected for more than two centuries.

The weapons Constantine trained his armies to use against enemies were not on this list Paul recommended to the church, as noted in Chapter 1.

Constantine also decreed that anybody involved in a legal case could take his claim to a church court where the bishop's ruling would be accepted as "sacred and honorable", just as it would be by a civil judge.

This hardly agrees with Jesus' answer to the man who asked Him to settle the division of property between him and his brother.

> Man, who gave me the right to judge or to
> divide the property between you two?
> - Luke 12:13-14 TEV

It was the clear teaching of the New Testament church that Christians were never to engage in lawsuits (1 Corinthians 6:7-8).

For more than two centuries, Christians never retaliated with physical force when attacked by mobs or soldiers. They were always willing to suffer at the hands of the enemy rather than inflict suffering. The Apostles gladly and willingly accepted martyrdom and taught their brothers and sisters in the church to endure persecution nonviolently and follow Jesus' example (See 1 Peter 4:9-11). Now, in a church preferred and favored by Constantine, the state began to use the power of the sword to banish those bishops declared to be heretics. The persecuted became the persecutors. It's the age-old story of power. Corrupting and absolute power tends to corrupt absolutely, especially a church that wines and dines with Caesar.

Constantine impressed Christians by declaring that the Day of the Sun be a public holiday in Jesus' honor, although he retained the name "Sunday" in honor of the Sun-god. Though he called himself a Christian, Constantine never completely separated himself from the Roman Sun-god of his father and refused to be baptized until his dying day twenty-five years later.

Postponing baptism until a more convenient time is hardly consistent with the Apostolic Tradition that baptism means dying to a fallen world and being raised to a new self empowered by Abba's indwelling Holy Spirit who cleanses the soul of all sin (Colossians 2:12-15). These were the urgent words of the Apostles:

> Today is the day of salvation. Repent and be
> baptized.
> - Acts 2:38

With today's great emphasis on the family, the question would be asked, what was Constantine's family-life like? Did he set a good example as a Christian father for his subjects to follow? What kind of a father was he? When his first son of his first marriage returned from a great military victory over Licinius, emperor in the East, the crowds were beginning to say, "Constantine has slain his thousands, but Crispus has slain his ten thousands." In a rage of jealousy, Constantine had Crispus put to death without even giving his own son the benefit of his day in court.

Furious over the death of her first and favorite grandson, the emperor's mother, Helena, accused Constantine's second wife, Fausta, of jealously bringing false charges against Crispus to protect the succession of her own three sons to the throne. His mother's charges against Fausta prompted Constantine to order his wife murdered by suffocation while bathing in one of the imperial bathhouses.

It is unbelievable that such an emperor who murdered his wife and son to preserve his crown would be called "Constantine the Great" by the church and honored as the great benefactor of Christians. Why did the church tolerate Constantine's evil and refuse to condemn such violence? Because the throne showered the church with favors and gifts, now bishops and priests were the favored ones, not the persecuted ones.

Hoping the church would unite his disintegrating empire, Constantine was infuriated when he found priests and bishops arguing over the Trinity. Arius, a popular presbyter in Egypt's Alexandrian church had started the dissension in 318 by arguing that the Logos was brought into being by God out of "nonexistence", implying there was a time when Jesus did not exist.

To stop the open warfare, which became more and more

acrimonious, the Emperor took it upon himself to call a church-wide council at Nicea in 325, insisting that the representatives of the church assemble and come to a quick agreement. Constantine himself presided over the first-ever gathering of the Empire's bishops. After two months of debate between the Arius party, which argued Jesus was a created being, and those who insisted Jesus was the eternal Son of God, Constantine brought the controversy to an end by throwing his imperial weight behind the Greek word "homoousios" which means "one substance" with the Father. A non-Scriptural word and open to other possible interpretations, "homoousios" ended the debate to the satisfaction of the Emperor.

The vote of the bishops was almost unanimous. Only two bishops and the presbyter, Arius, voted "No". Because they refused to sign Nicea's creed, Constantine had them exiled with no protest from the other bishops.

The Council of Nicea was an amazing happening. Most of the 300 bishops came with fresh memories of their persecution by Rome. Instead of fearing arrest and traveling in secret, now overseers of the church came openly and proudly, not walking the long miles with tired and sore feet as they used to. They traveled in comfort to the council, all expenses paid as guests of the Emperor.

Eusebius, overseer of the church in Caesarea at that time, described the great banquet Constantine held at the end of the Nicean Council to celebrate the agreement he believed would unite church and state:

> No bishop was absent from the table of the Emperor. Bodyguards and soldiers stood guard around the outer court of the palace with sharp swords drawn, but among them the men of God would walk fearlessly and enter the deepest parts of the palace. At dinner

some of them lay on the same couch as the Emperor, while others rested on cushions on both sides of him. Easily one could imagine this to be the kingdom of Christ, or regard it as a dream rather than reality.

Bishop Paphnutius from Egypt, who had lost one eye during the cruel persecution of Emperor Diocletian, was singled out for special honor. As a sign of the new friendship between church and state, Constantine kissed the bishop's eyeless cheek. The charming ruler of Rome's Empire had the church under his magic spell. Bishops were fast becoming the Emperor's pets.

Fifteen months after Constantine fought his way to the throne and knocked on Miltiades' door to announce Rome's new policy of friendship, the frail bishop died. Christians wondered who would succeed Miltiades as Head-Bishop of the church in the West. Constantine, not a Council of bishops, made the announcement: "Silvester has been chosen as the new bishop of Rome." Enthusiastic about the new alliance between church and state, Silvester was crowned with all the royalty and splendor of a prince by the "king", who saw himself as ordained by God to lead the church on a new way that would bring about the conversion of the world under the emblem of Rome. The world has been converted, not to the nonviolent Way of Jesus' Spirit, but to the warring way of Constantine's sword.

I found myself comparing Paul's vision on the Damascus Road with the vision of Constantine on the road to Rome. There are similarities, but also great differences. Both were persecutors of the church. Both stopped their persecution of the Church.

(1) After his vision, Constantine continued his killing on the battlefield, even killing those of his own family. After his

vision Paul lived and loved nonviolently, teaching,

> Owe no one anything except to love one
> another . . . love does no wrong to a neighbor.
> Love is the fulfilling of the law.
> - Romans 13:8,10

(2) For Constantine, the cross meant being made strong to win battles of the sword and destroy those called barbarians. For Paul, the cross meant reconciliation with barbarians, saying,

> There is no longer any distinction between
> Gentiles and Jews, barbarians, savages,
> slaves, and free men, but Christ is all and in
> all.
> - Colossians 3:11 TEV

(3) Constantine spent the rest of his life ruling Rome by coercive and violent power. Paul spent the rest of his life proclaiming Jesus' triumphant ascension and rule of the Holy Spirit, who must be accepted voluntarily as Lord, saying to Paul,

> My power is made perfect in weakness.
> - 2 Corinthians 12:8

(4) One used the resources of an empire to found a new capital of Rome he arrogantly named Constantinople. The other humbly used the resources of the kingdom of God to found churches in all the cities of the empire his weak body could reach while being stoned, shipwrecked, lashed with a whip, and imprisoned.

(5) After his vision and hearing Jesus' voice speak to him on the Damascus Road, Paul could not wait to be baptized and let the world know to whom he belonged. After his vision, Constantine put off baptism until his dying day.

(6) Constantine used the church to unify a crumbling empire to satisfy his own self-pride and ambitious lust for power. Paul served the church to unify a divided world in the peaceable kingdom of God.

(7) After his vision of the cross and military victory, one of the spikes that supposedly fastened Jesus to the cross became a part of the crown Constantine wore on his head. Just before another emperor of Rome had Paul's head chopped off, Paul wrote from his prison cell:

> I have fought the good fight, I have finished the race, I have kept the faith. Henceforth there is laid up for me the crown of righteousness on that Day, and not only to me but to all who have loved his appearance.
> - 2 Timothy 4:7

Comparing the visions of Constantine and Paul helps us understand the irreconcilable difference between the civilization of the Holy Spirit in the early apostolic church, and the civilization of nation-states and their self-preserving law enforced by violence to which all mainline "just war" churches are still attached.

I recall two lines of a hymn I have often sung, especially on the day commemorating Jesus' death on the cross:

> O dearly has he loved, and we must love him, too;
> And trust in his redeeming blood, and try his works to do.

The redeeming blood of Jesus' cross is very different from the vengeful blood Constantine was responsible for shedding in his family, in the halls of government, and on the battlefield. Trust in the Lord's redeeming blood inspires works of agape and peace Jesus embodied, not the works of war Constantine embodied.

The cross confronts every human with a choice between the vision of Paul and the vision of Constantine. It is Either-Or, not Both-And. It's either Constantine's way of the Sword, or God's Way of the Spirit whose fruit is "love, gentleness, and peace" (Galatians 5:22).

Constantine's offer of partnership with the state in place of persecution by the state was accepted by most Christians because they sincerely, but blindly, believed the power of the state can be harnessed to God's gospel of the kingdom and go forth to fulfill the Great Commission (Matthew 28:19) and establish the kingdom of God on earth as it is in heaven.

To be violently coercive and lovingly Christ-like at the same time is impossible. The power Constantine represents corrupts. It does not cleanse. The nature of coercive power that forces persons to yield to another's will is evil, not only in dictatorships, but in every form of human government, including democratic republics whose legal, judicial, legislative, and military systems, are also based on coercive and dominative power inherent in every nation-state. When the state speaks, Jesus is silenced. The name "Jesus" is never mentioned when matters of state are discussed. The state's "God in general", is popular, but "Jesus in particular", never. The God in which the state trusts is a catch-all God who is used to support the political rhetoric of the moment. The fatal flaw in the Constantinian compromise is the illusion that the nature of God revealed in Jesus is compatible with the nature of the state that they can coalesce and become one in mission to the glory of God. They cannot. As human history shows, they do not.

As Paul made clear to Timothy, there can be only one sovereign ruler in the life of a Christian:

The blessed and only Sovereign, the King of
kings and Lord of lords, who alone has
immortality and dwells in unapproachable
light, whom no man has ever seen or can see.
To him be honor and eternal dominion.
Amen.
- 1 Timothy 6:15-16

The early church echoed Paul's words,

We must obey God rather than men.
- Acts 5:29

Only the Holy God and Creator of life is worthy of the soul's
absolute allegiance.

The state represents the rule of coercive law, not the rule of
the Spirit in the peaceable kingdom of God. Constantine was
a mere man like all mortals named Clinton, Bush, Reagan,
Carter, Nixon, and the like.

When John fell down at the feet of the angel bringing the
good news, the angel objected,

You must not do that! I am only a fellow
servant like you. Worship God!
- Revelation 22:8-9

God is Spirit, the Spirit Jesus enfleshed. As God's nonviolent
Messiah, He has come to share with His disciples the Spirit
who came to dwell with the church on Pentecost and make of
us one people who speak and understand the language of
God's Holy Spirit (Acts 2:5-13).
Peace is not a political achievement of man's power and
genius. Peace is repenting of our pride in power and yielding
to the Eternal's kingdom of the Holy Spirit in whose image
we were created, and then walking each step of the Way in

54

the light of His glorious Resurrection (See Galatians 5:16; Ephesians 5:2,8).

How It All Ended

The end of Constantine's life shows how passing is the political parade of the power Jesus rejects. Constantine died on May 22, 337, leaving behind many relatives with whom he planned to divide the wealth and power of the Empire. However, the army had other plans. The military massacred all of Constantine's family, except his three sons, Constantine II, Constans, and Constantius, and the Emperor's two nephews, Gallus and Julian, who were brothers.

The cake of the Empire was carved into three pieces and handed to the three surviving sons. Gaul, Britain and Spain were on the plate of Constantine II; Italy and Africa were passed to Constans; Egypt, Syria and the other Eastern Provinces were given to Constantius.

None of Constantine's three sons enjoyed their piece of cake. They all died of metaphoric food poisoning: the poison of political power and its inherent violence. Before long, Constantine's sons were at each other's throats. All three were either slaughtered in battle fighting each other, or died during a military campaign fighting to consolidate or expand their political kingdom.

Did Constantine confess any regrets for all the blood shed in battle; for killing his son Crispus and his wife Fausta; for the executions and exile of all those the church and state accused of heresy? Those close to Constantine say that he expressed regrets that he had waited until the last day of his life to be baptized. Just before the Emperor died, he was heard to say: "Not the sword, knowledge."

Paul would have said, "Not the sword! . . . Love! As for

knowledge, it is imperfect and will pass away. . . The greatest of all is love" (1 Corinthians 13:8, 13).

The lesson the church must learn from this episode is crucial.

When Christians accepted the favors of Constantine and became partners with the state in using the dominative power of the law enforced by the sword to protect their life, the church of the crucified-risen-ascended-ruling-indwelling Spirit took a one-hundred-and-eighty-degree turn.

The weapons of God's Holy Spirit became the old and familiar weapons of the world. In accepting the friendship of Constantine, a church that was willing to suffer in witnessing to Christ's kingdom born of the Spirit, became a church that was willing to make opponents suffer in the spirit of a fallen world. A nonviolent church became a violent church and, in so doing, lost the unique sign of the church as the Body of Christ, a redeemed community that has been delivered from sin's violence and death (John 1:29).

Baptism became acceptable to the world, rather than reflecting a dying to the world to become acceptable to God in the life of the Spirit. More and more the Constantinian church became its own norm based on what seemed to be in the best interests of what was mistakenly seen as a "Christian" society. This is in sharp contrast to the church of the Apostles, who believed Jesus was their only criterion of good and evil, the power seated at the right hand of God who had come to fulfill every promise and prophecy of a Messiah who had come to inaugurate the New Age of peace (See Acts 2:22-36). It was not necessary to wait for anything else or anyone else. God's plan of salvation was complete in Christ (Matthew 11:2-6).

Today, the great need of the church is not to enter more deeply into the world and its politics, but to be born again of the Spirit and, abiding in Christ and His word, rediscover who we are: a new counter-culture community liberated from the Powers and Principalities who control the systems of the world and living as the peaceable kingdom of God the New Testament proclaims.

The violent church of Constantine must again become the nonviolent community of Christ; not by human striving, but by dying to our false self-centered humanity and being raised to our true Spirit-centered humanity. It is this humanity that Jesus made flesh 2000 years ago for His church in every age.

Amen. So let it be.

Chapter 3

The Bogus "Just War" Theology Of Mainline Churches

> See to it that no one makes a prey of you by philosophy and empty deceit, according to human tradition, according to the elemental spirits of the universe, and not according to Christ.
>
> - Colossians 2:8

Becoming partners with Constantine and the violent power of the state was the first big mistake of the early church. A century after Constantine, the church made the second tragic mistake by adopting Bishop Augustine's "just war" theology used to validate the mixing of church and state to protect what are called "Christian values".

In this chapter, we will see how Augustine misused Jesus' parables to teach an amalgamation of the church with a fallen world, and the specific "just war" doctrine which resulted. Then we will look at the way Catholic, Orthodox, Protestant, and Pentecostal churches express this heresy at the present time.

How did Augustine reach the flawed conclusion that the church should mix the kingdom of God Jesus inaugurated with the violent life of the world and its nation-states?

In the Upper Room on the night of His betrayal and arrest, Jesus said to the Apostles,

> If you were of the world, the world would love its own; but because you are not of the world, therefore the world hates you . . . They *(the Apostles)* are not of the world, even as I am not of the world.
> - John 15:19; 17:16

When Jesus stood before Pilate on trial for His life He said to the governor,

> My kingdom is not of this world. If it were, my disciples would fight to defend me from my enemies.
> - John 18:36

Jesus' teaching is clear. In God's peaceable kingdom, there is no place for fighting and killing enemies to be safe and secure. In the new and eternal life Jesus came to give us, the Christian's security is guaranteed. Jesus' resurrection is our victory over all evil and death (John 11:25-26).

The theme of the New Testament is Paul's admonition to the church,

> Do not be conformed to this world, but be transformed by the renewal of your mind that you may prove what is the will of God, what is good and acceptable and perfect.
> - Romans 12:2

How could Augustine possibly formulate a theology of justified violence that goes against the grain of Jesus' life and teaching, and have it accepted by the early church of which the historian, Roland Bainton wrote:

The age of persecution down to the time of Constantine was the age of pacifism to the degree that during this period no Christian author to our knowledge approved of Christian participation in battle.

Augustine's "Just War" Theology and Jesus' Gospel

In 410 A.D., Bishop Augustine was fifty-six years old when the Eternal City of Rome was sacked. The fall of Rome led the Bishop to wrestle with the question of the contrast between earthly cities like Rome, which rise and fall and have their little day, and the eternal kingdom of God. The question occupied Augustine for sixteen years and produced his famous work, *The City of God.*

In it, Augustine compares the entire history of human life on earth to two cities: the "City of Man", which he said consists of the mass of godless people bound together by a love of this world's pleasures and possessions; and the "City of God", made up of people born of God's Spirit and bound together by their love of God.

According to Augustine, the two cities represent two kinds of love. The City of God is produced by the love of God, the Creator, whereas the City of Man is the result of the idolatrous love of created beings. One love is holy; the other, unholy. One is social; the other, individualistic. One is subject to God; the other sets itself up as a rival to God. One is serene; the other, tempestuous. One is peaceful; the other, quarrelsome. One prefers truthfulness to deceitful praise; the other is always looking for applause. One is friendly; the other, jealous. One directs its efforts to the neighbor's good; the other, to its own welfare.

Augustine concluded that Rome was destroyed because it was driven by self-love and the pride and praise of men. By its nature, such human love is destined to fail. In contrast, the Heavenly City of God outlasts the glory of Rome because its victory is truth, its standard is holiness, and its life is eternal. The Bishop's description of the City of God and the City of Man are convincing. Where did Augustine go wrong?

According to Augustine, the church represents the City of God and the state, such as Rome represents the City of Man. Significantly, however, Augustine said that so long as the visible church is in the world, it is impossible to know precisely who are in the City of God and who are in the City of Man. Until they put off the flesh and reach their Heavenly destination, redeemed Christians in the holy City of God are mixed with unredeemed non-Christians in the unholy City of Man. Only God knows what is in the human heart and can determine which of the two cities a person truly lives in. It is self-righteous to claim to be in the eternal City of God and put others in the City of Man because God alone is Judge.

Since we cannot tell who is of the world and who is of God, the Bishop concluded that it is the duty of everyone, including Christians, to be involved with the affairs of the world and its politics and work together for a common good.

It is the duty of those in the church to participate fully in human government and its systems of violence, even though flawed, and strive with everyone to achieve the best possible peace and good for humankind. This means Christians must be ready to join the state in fighting to defend the common good when the reason for doing so is perceived to be "just".

Augustine wrote,

> The earthly City of Man does not live by faith. It seeks only an earthly peace and limits the goal of its peace to the voluntary and collective attainment of objectives necessary

to mortal existence. The Heavenly City, on a pilgrimage in this mortal life, living by faith, must use this earthly peace until such time as our mortality has passed away. Therefore, so long as her life in the earthly city is that of a captive and alien, she has no hesitation about keeping in step with the civil law which governs matters pertaining to our existence here below. For, as mortal life is the same for all, there ought to be common cause between the two cities in what concerns our purely human living.

This was Augustine's conclusion based on human reason and logic which he taught and in which he had been steeped for many years prior to his conversion.

Augustine agreed that the ultimate goals of those in the City of Man and those in the Heavenly City of God are different. Because all mortals have a common life in the flesh, however, the Bishop said Christians and non-Christians alike are duty-bound to obey the civil law and, with everyone, work for the best possible common life, prepared to defend it when threatened.

To be sure, Augustine had a brilliant mind, but the New Testament is not the record of brilliant reasoning. The gospel is based on God's Self-Revelation in Jesus (See John 1:1-18). The way of the cross is foolishness to the world but to those being saved, it is the wisdom of God (1 Corinthians 1:19). The Scriptures of the church say nothing about the church joining the world to achieve a "common good" and then killing enemies to protect that "common good", in order to enjoy what the Bishop calls an "earthly peace".

God's gospel in Christ proclaims an unearthly peace; a peace which this world can neither give nor take away (John 14:27); a peace which the world does not understand (Philippians

4:7); a peace achieved through Abba's crucified-risen-ascended-ruling-indwelling Spirit (Colossians 1:20), not through the state, its military power, and political alliances, which shed blood to protect the "common good".

The New Testament puts the emphasis on keeping Jesus' kingdom and the kingdoms of the world separate (John 15:19), not on mixing them. In the Gospel of John, we hear Jesus pray,

> I have given them thy word; and the world has hated them because they are not of the world, even as I am not of the world.
> - John 17:14

In his first letter, John wrote,

> Those false prophets speak about matters of the world, and the world listens to them because they belong to the world. But we belong to God. Whoever knows God listens to us; whoever does not belong to God does not listen to us. This, then, is how we can tell the difference between the Spirit of truth and the spirit of error.
> - 1 John 4:6 TEV

Not one of the Apostles advocated a mixture of the kingdom of God with the kingdoms of the world to achieve a "common good". On the contrary, referring to Jesus, Paul wrote,

> He has delivered us from the dominion of darkness and transferred us to the kingdom of his beloved Son . . . For in him all the fullness of God was pleased to dwell, and through him to reconcile to himself all things, whether on

earth or in heaven, making peace by the blood
of his cross.
- Colossians 1: 13, 19-20

The only "common good" the Apostles knew and proclaimed
was the kingdom of God—the New Creation—God's perfect
gift in a crucified-risen-ascended-ruling-indwelling Messiah.
The gospel's "common good" is not the result of solidarity
with the world and joining in a common human undertaking
with the state; it is all about "overcoming" the world in
solidarity with the Holy One of Israel. Jesus' "overcoming
the world" is the good news.

To be sure, like all humans, we are born into sin's world
which is subject to violence and death. In this way,
Christians are mixed with the City of Man and a very
imperfect world. But in repentance and baptism, the
Christian is given newness of life and shares Jesus' victory
over the world (John 16:33). It is to this victory over fallen
Babylon that the church is called to witness and be Jesus'
embodiment of God's peace.

The gospel which Paul proclaimed called for witnessing to
the Christian's new life in "heavenly places", not mixing
with the world and postponing the good news until we die to
enter a future life of peace. Paul's new creation led him to
testify,

> Far be it from me to glory except in the cross
> of our Lord Jesus Christ, by which the world
> has been crucified to me and I to the world.
> - Galatians 6:14

In the world, Paul became all things to all people, not to
work for a common cause, but to make Jesus known, loved,
and obeyed.

Augustine's Misuse of Scripture

To make his case, Augustine clearly misused two of Jesus' parables. One was Jesus' Parable of the Tares and the Wheat, the story of an enemy who comes in the night and sows weeds in a farmer's field of wheat. Later, when the seeds mature, the farm workers ask the manager if they should pull out the weeds to prevent them from taking over and destroying the wheat. The workers are told to let them grow together until harvest time, lest in destroying the weeds they damage the wheat. Then, at the end of the growing season, they can separate the tares and burn them and gather the wheat and store it in the barn (Matthew 13).

According to Augustine's logic, keeping the parable's bad tares and good wheat together until harvest means that those in the church should remain mixed with non-believers until the End, the final Harvest, when all will be separated. In the interim, they are to be totally involved with the state in seeking a common good, defending it in war whenever the cause is "just." We shall examine the Bishop's criteria for what is "just."

Let's look at the Augustinian "just war" teaching as taught in the *Catholic Catechism* approved by Pope John Paul II on October 11, 1992:

> Each human community possesses a common good which permits it to be recognized as such; it is in the political community that its most complete realization is found. It is the role of the state to defend and promote the common good of civil society, its citizens, and intermediate bodies. (1910)

> This good calls for an organization of the community of nations able to provide for the different needs of men. (1911)

It is necessary that all participate. (1913)

The Catholic Catechism echoes Augustine's teaching of mixing church and state in slaughtering enemies to defend a common good. This is the Augustinian teaching of mainline churches, which, as we shall see, has perpetuated the "just war" heresy for centuries.

What does the Parable of the Tares and Wheat teach? Certainly it teaches not mixing church and state in killing enemies. Jesus would have made this clear if this were His plan. He did not. In symbolic language, which Jesus used throughout His public ministry, the parable's lesson in keeping with His life and the New Testament gospel is as follows:

(1) The church lives in the midst of hostile powers always trying to uproot the kingdom of God (See Romans 7:14-20). The church must be aware of the Enemy and be on guard.

(2) The mission of the church is not to act as judge and separate the tares from the wheat, bad people from good people. As Jesus said to the Pharisees: "You judge according to the flesh. I judge no one." (John 8:15), I say to you, "Judge not, that you be not judged" (Matthew 7:1). The role of the church is to love as Jesus loves (John 13:34), not to judge as the world of nation-states judge- separating, and punishing those perceived to be wicked (Romans 12:19).

(3) The church is to remain in the world, side by side with all of God's children to serve as Jesus served, to witness as Jesus witnessed to God's grace and gift of eternal life, not to strive for a common good determined by the latest poll of the people, defending it at all costs. In fallen Babylon, the will of the people is not the will of God (See John 7:14-24).

If Jesus wanted His church to mix with the world in working

67

for the best possible good based on self-interest and defending such good to the death, He had the vocabulary and the intelligence to say so. He did not. In fact, Augustine's partnership with the state and its systems of coercive power is on a collision course with the New Testament. Bishop Augustine constructed his "just war" theology on man's sin-corrupted human reason, not on God's Self-Revelation enfleshed in Jesus Christ (John 10:30, 38).

Augustine also used Jesus' Parable of the King's Banquet to justify the church mixing with the state in using military power to protect and promote the "common good" of nation-states. When Augustine became Bishop of Hippo, he inherited the controversy with the Donatists, the predominant church in his jurisdiction in North Africa. The followers of Bishop Donatus refused to recognize reinstated priests and bishops who had not stood firm and faithful during times of persecution. Augustine insisted the authority of the priest who administers the Sacraments does not reside in his moral nature but in God's nature and authority in Christ.

At first, Augustine tried to use peaceful persuasion to get the Donatists to return to Mother Church, which had ordained him. He wrote many articles to try to convince the Donatists they were wrong in refusing to recognize priests who had been reinstated and pleaded with them to return to the fold. When peaceful persuasion failed, like Constantine a century before, Augustine resorted to imperial law enforced by the state's police power to compel these "heretics" to return to what Augustine considered to be the one true church. To justify the use of violence to compel them to return, Augustine made use of Jesus' Parable of the King's Banquet. When the king was told that all of the seats at the banquet table were not filled, the king said to his servant,

> Go out to the roads and to the hedges and
> compel them to come in so that my house
> may be filled.
> - Luke 14:23-24

Augustine reasoned, if in His parable, Jesus tells about a king who compelled his subjects to come to his banquet table, certainly the church of Jesus has the right to compel dissidents to obey.

There is one flaw: Augustine's reasoning does not square with the nature of the Holy Spirit who does not coerce or compel. Love cannot win by forcing subjects to act against their will. The peace of God cannot be forced on a violent world.

A careful reading clearly shows this parable was directed particularly to the Pharisees (Luke 14:1) to let them know that God's Banquet of Eternal Life is open to the whole world, that Jesus was not a Jewish Messiah for the Jews, but a Messiah for all who repent and believe (John 3:16). In God's family there are no favored children. Every soul is invited to come to God's Banquet. The purpose of the parable was to teach the Pharisees they had no exclusive claim to the kingdom of God; on the contrary, God invited every soul to enter (Matthew 28:19).

For hundreds of years, the Catholic church misused these same words, "Compel them to come in", to justify the horrible torture of the Inquisition and the persecution of those called "heretics" to force rebels to return to Mother Church.

In the same misuse of Scripture, Augustine turned to one of the Old Testament Psalms to prove that it is permissible for the church to violently persecute and punish enemies of God. He wrote:

Again I ask, if good and holy men never
inflict persecution on anyone, but only suffer
it, whose words do you think those are in the
Psalm where we read:

I have pursued my enemies and overtaken
them. I did not turn again until they were
consumed.
- Psalm 18:37

This is precisely the way mainline Christians put the Old
Testament and its violence on the same level of truth with
the New Covenant, even though the Scriptures tell us that
the New Covenant makes the Old obsolete (Hebrew 8:13).
Jesus is the way, the truth, and the life (John 14:3), not
Abraham, Moses, and David.

It must be noted that persecution of "heretics" was not
limited to the Catholic Church. Protestant churches have
also engaged in the same use of violent force to compel.
This is reflected in Calvin's theocratic Geneva, Cromwell's
England, and Winthrop's New England. In addition,
Protestant reformers Luther and Zwingli's persecution of
Anabaptists is well documented.

Such was Augustine's misuse of Scripture to prop up the
teaching and practice of wars considered good enough for
the church to fight.

Augustine's Rules to Justify an Acceptable War

Now let's look at the criteria used by Augustine to decide
whether a particular war is the kind Christians should
support. Note that not once is Jesus' name or gospel
mentioned in the criteria. As we shall see, the origin of the
"just war" criteria is the reasoning and logic of the Greek
philosophers, not the power and God's wisdom of the cross
needed to redeem a violent world. Building on the reasoning

70

of his mentor, Bishop Ambrose, Augustine gave the church seven criteria to determine when a war is "just" and which Christians should fight to defend the "common good". As I list them, I will answer them by referring to the life and teaching of Jesus.

First Rule: To be "just", the war must be declared by a legitimate head of state, such as a prince, king, or president.
Just because the head of state authorizes a war does not make it right. Based on the New Testament, Christians believe Jesus is their only sovereign authority, not the king in the White House, not Congress whose members spend their time warring among themselves, not any Parliament of fallible and mortal humans. Jesus is the one and only Ruler whose life and teaching determine right and wrong for the church (See John 14:6; Matthew 18:18). Jesus is the supreme authority for the church (Matthew 18:18). Christians are baptized in the Name and Spirit of Jesus Christ, not in the name and spirit of any human or collection of humans (Acts 5:29).

Second Rule: For Christians to kill, Augustine said the intention of the war must be based on justice and the establishment of peace and order, not on revenge or a desire to dominate and destroy others.
Every nation believes the intention of every war it declares is "just". Sin always justifies itself. In the United States the only time the President and Congress agree unanimously is when they declare war on an enemy, who is always regarded as a monster the nation must unite to destroy. Whoever heard of ruling authorities saying, "The cause for which we are fighting is unjust"? Corrupt humans always see their side as civilized and the other side as barbaric. Like beauty, justice is in the eye of the beholder. The only impartial determiner of good is God (Mark 10:18).

Third Rule: to be legitimate, the war must be waged only as a last resort. Every other solution must have been tried and failed.

71

Who can honestly say all other solutions have been tried and failed before declaring war on an enemy? The fact is, Jesus' answer of overcoming evil with good is never even considered by the state, let alone tried. Said G. K. Chesterton, "Christianity has not been tried and found wanting; it has not been tried." Who decides how long a solution other than war has been tried? How many times are we to forgive? Seven times? Seventy times seven? How long does love suffer wrong rather than inflict suffering on others? Where is the Solomon so wise as to say, "We have tried all other solutions than war and they have failed. Now we must resort to war."

Fourth Rule: for Christians to fight, the war must accomplish some good purpose that will outweigh the evil of the war and its result.

With modern weapons of mass destruction, it is impossible to calculate the precise evil a particular war will inflict, and then compare it to the precise good the war will accomplish in the end. Once the passions of war are unleashed, there is no predicting what evil will result. At the beginning of the Second World War, rulers had no idea that before the war ended, atomic bombs would be invented and dropped on Japanese cities. The evil of war is incalculable.

Fifth Rule: Augustine said a "just war" must have a reasonable chance of success.

That such a criterion should even be considered by Christians shows how far mainline churches have departed from Jesus' Sermon on the Mount. In war, success means killing more of "them" than more of "us" will be killed. The Rules of Augustine go from bad to worse when the success of a war is measured by the greater number of people the winner is able to kill. Jesus has come as God's life-giver, not as the world's life-destroyer (John 10:10).

Sixth Rule: The "just war" must follow a code of moral law that protects noncombatants and prisoners and does not engage in indiscriminate killing and destruction of property.

Modern warfare does not discriminate between those who wear a military uniform and those who do not; between soldiers and civilians. Who can forget the faces on television of old couples and parents with their children forced to leave their burned out homes in Kosovo, trudging in lines a mile long toward another country with nothing except what they could carry? These were civilians—noncombatants—who found no protection from Augustine's moral code. The six million persons executed in the Holocaust were civilians, not soldiers.

To these six criteria, Augustine tacked on a <u>Seventh Rule</u> which stated that *before engaging in killing, the Christian should repent of what he is about to do and then go into battle with God's love for the enemy.* Supposedly, the inner love of the killer will cancel the outer act of killing. This new way of loving one's enemies is not mentioned in the New Testament. This is the same as saying, before you rape or steal, first repent of what you are about to do and have love in your heart for your victim, then the act of rape or stealing will be acceptable in the sight of God. Little wonder the church has lost all credibility in the public domain.

Such are Bishop Augustine's seven criteria of a "just war" used first by the Catholic Church and later inherited by mainline churches. Listing four of them, the Catechism of the Catholic Church states: "These are the traditional elements enumerated in what is called the "just war" doctrine." (2309) When the Catholic Catechism calls these "the traditional elements" in the "just war" doctrine, we must ask, <u>which tradition</u>? It is not the tradition based on Jesus' life and teaching recorded in the New Testament. Standing before Pilate and the Roman state, Jesus testified:

My kingdom is not of this world. If it were, my disciples would fight to defend me.
- John 18:36

Nor is it the tradition of the Apostles. Peter testified,

Christ left you an example that you should follow in his steps. When he was reviled, he did not revile in return; when he suffered, he did not threaten; but he trusted to him who judges justly.
- 1 Peter 2:21-23

The tradition of the Apostles is nonviolent. As the Book of Acts clearly shows, the Twelve did not resort to violence on a single occasion when they were attacked by a mob.

Nor is it the tradition of the early church whose practice, preaching, and pronouncements for more than two hundred years reflect Jesus' teaching that the meek, not the mighty of the military (Matthew 5:5) shall inherit the earth. Justin Martyr, a Roman philosopher converted to Christianity and executed by the state in 165 because of his faith, testified, "We who formerly murdered one another now refrain from making war on our enemies."

The "just war" tradition is the human Tradition formulated by the mind of bishops such as Ambrose and Augustine, not the Tradition of what Saint Paul called "the mind of Christ" (1 Corinthians 2:16).

A Schizophrenic Church

Mainline churches try to have it both ways. For example, on the one hand Article 2305 of the Catholic Catechism clearly states God's authentic gospel of peace:

Earthly peace is the image and fruit of the peace of Christ, the messianic "Prince of Peace." By the blood of his cross, "in his own person he killed the hostility," he reconciled men with God and made his Church the sacrament of the unity of the human race and of its union with God. "He is our peace." He has declared, "Blessed are the peacemakers."

But then, after teaching that the blood of Jesus has broken down the walls of hostility which separate those within the warring human race, the Catholic Catechism adds,

However, as long as the danger of war persists and there is no international authority with the competence and power, governments cannot be denied the right of lawful self-defense, once all peace efforts have failed. (2308)

Public authorities, in this case, have the right and duty to impose on citizens the obligations necessary for national defense. (2310)

In this "however", we see the schizophrenia, the split life of the church, one part contradicting the other. On the one hand, the "just war" church teaches that the risen Christ is our peace, that His perfect sacrifice on the cross and indwelling have given the church a new life of peace, becoming a sacrament of humankind's unity in the Christian's new union with God. But, at the same time, the Catechism teaches the sacred duty of Christians to obey their government's call to fight and kill in defense of their country, if the danger of war persists and there is no international authority and military power such as NATO to deal with enemies.

In a fallen world, the danger of war will continue. What is

also overlooked is that the military might of NATO is exactly the same as that of individual nation-states. An individual evil does not become a collective virtue. This is the two-pronged peace of mainstream Christianity which teaches a nonviolent peace for one's personal and heavenly life and a violent earthly peace for one's socio-political life. Conversely, the Bible teaches that there is one Spirit who claims our whole life (See Ephesians 4:4-6). There are not two gospels, one for the Christian's personal and private life and a different gospel for one's public life.

> BVB In him *(Christ)* all things hold together.
> - Colossians 1:17

We have examined the rational "just war" theology of Bishop Augustine and its influence on Catholic doctrine. Now let's see how this bogus teaching has been perpetuated by mainline churches.

Orthodox Churches Perpetuate "Just War" Heresy

The various branches of the Orthodox Church in the world—Russian, Greek, and ethnic Eastern Orthodox churches in the United States—do not have a catechism which spells out a "just war" doctrine in the precise way the Catholic Church does, but they teach the same dogma.

In formulating its theology through the centuries, the Orthodox Church has been more mystical and less legalistic than the Catholic Church. This is evident in a new catechism published by St. Vladimir's Seminary in 1989. Written by a number of teachers of catechism in several Byzantine Rite parishes in France, it follows the fifty-day festivals of the Orthodox Church calendar from Good Friday to Pentecost.

In beautiful poetic and mystical language, this "Living God" Catechism of the Orthodox Church celebrates Jesus' death on the cross, resurrection from the dead, ascension and rule at the right hand of the Father, and His gift of the Holy Spirit to the church on Pentecost. There is not one word of instruction to Orthodox members on what this redeeming work of God has to do with the participation of disciples in war.

The Preface of the Catechism states that "the genius of the Orthodox church lies in its attraction to spiritual beauty . . . perceived in the light of the Cross and experienced in tears by which the person opens himself before God and joins himself to his brethren, to become wholly filled with peace as a foretaste of the experience of the Kingdom of God" (The Living God, p. X11). From this preface, one might expect a clear and powerful statement on the Christian's newness of life in the kingdom of God, which has no place for killing and war. Not so. It only assures the reader that the "uniqueness and strength of this catechism lies in the way it draws together musical themes and reproduction of icons".

Even though the Orthodox Church differs from Rome on issues such as the authority of the Pope and the use of icons, when it came to Catholic Croatians and Orthodox Serbians killing each other in what was once Yugoslavia, both branches of the church were one in their obedience to the same "just war" Tradition. It is this Tradition that seeks ethnic cleansing, not by the blood of Jesus (Ephesians 2:15-17), but by bombs and tanks. It has left the Balkans in shambles, battlefields red with the blood of its victims.

Did anyone hear Catholic and Orthodox church authorities condemn the human butchery of their members and declare unequivocally that those who engage in such human slaughter have no place in the church? Neither Catholic Pope nor Orthodox Patriarch stated that the deliberate massacre of men, women and children in the name of "ethnic cleansing" is incompatible with Jesus' life and teaching. Neither church announced publicly that those who deliberately participate in such wanton violence cut

77

themselves off from membership in the Body of Christ. Why do we wait in vain for such a pronouncement? The reason is that both Catholic and Orthodox churches teach their people to participate in "just wars". The church cannot excommunicate members for doing what they are taught to do.

Though persecuted by Russia's atheist Stalin, the Russian Orthodox Church gave complete and absolute loyalty to Stalin's atheistic state in fighting Hitler. This war cost twenty million Russian lives, to say nothing of the countless maimed and homeless. The persecuting Communist state of Russia and the persecuted Orthodox Church in Russia joined hands in killing the enemy whom Jesus teaches His disciples to love. Russian church and Russian state reacted to the enemy in exactly the same way. When the chips are down, Nationalism is a fallen world's other religion.

Protestant Reformers Continue the Heresy

Five centuries after the final break between Eastern Orthodoxy and Western Catholicism in 1054, the Protestant Reformation spawned autonomous denominations. These denominations were similar in their disagreements with Catholicism and Orthodoxy, but united in teaching the duty of Christians to destroy enemies of their nation when their particular nation-state declares a war defined as "just".

Among them was the Reformation's Church of England. Its *Thirty-Nine Articles* affirm that "it is lawful for Christian men, at the Commandment of the Magistrate, to wear weapons and serve in the warres." The lead reformers, Martin Luther, Ulrich Zwingli, and John Calvin, rejected the infallibility of the Pope, celibacy, and the Eucharist's miracle of transubstantiation, but they did not reject the Catholic Tradition that mixes church and state in killing enemies.

The Lutherans

How Luther applied the "just war" code is seen in his reaction to Germany's Peasants' War in 1525. When armed bands of peasants broke loose and ravaged the country, these peasants were sure that Martin Luther would see their cause as "just"—one of the criteria of a legitimate war.

Instead, Luther harshly condemned the peasants' revolt because the war was not legally declared by a governing Magistrate and, therefore, broke one of the "just war" rules. Luther saw it as an irresponsible uprising which should be stopped. When Prince Frederick hesitated to do so, Luther informed the Magistrate that it was his duty to use his soldiers to "smite, stab, slay and kill" the peasants whom he considered enemies of the state because they were causing chaos and disorder. The state's law and order took precedence over the Christian's trust in God's Spirit of love.

Perpetuating the "just war" heresy, the Lutheran Augsburg Confession states,

> It is taught among us that all government in the world and all established rule and laws were instituted and ordained by God for the sake of good order, and that Christians may without sin occupy civil offices or serve as princes and judges, render decisions and pass sentence according to imperial and other existing laws, punish evil doers with the sword, engage in just wars, serve as soldiers, etc. (XVI Civil Government)

Evidently bishops consider civil order to be more important than God's love reflected in the incarnated Jesus.

The Presbyterian Church

The Presbyterian attitude toward war continues to reflect the mind and action of their well-known first leader, John Calvin. He advocated a "church restored" based on the kingdom of God, expressed on earth in theocratic commonwealths like the one Calvin tried to establish in Geneva. Calvin believed Geneva's civil government was ordained by God, not only to protect the good and punish the bad, but also to support and defend true religion, which he identified with his restored church in Geneva.

In the militant spirit of a holy crusade, Calvin's theocracies fought to gain a foothold in France, the Netherlands, Scotland, and England. A Calvinist theocracy was based on God's elect, whose faith was expressed in reasonable charity, the preaching of the Gospel, and the proper administration of the Sacraments, all protected by the world's sword of steel. Apparently, God's sword of the Spirit was considered too weak.

Today, supporting democracy of equal justice under law rather than Calvin's theocracy, the Constitution of the United Presbyterian Church, U.S.A. echoes the "just war" doctrine of all Presbyterian bodies, stating,

> It is lawful for Christians to accept and execute the office of a magistrate (appointed or elected political office) when called there unto; in the managing whereof, as they ought especially to maintain piety, justice, and peace, according to the wholesome laws of each commonwealth, so, for that end, they may lawfully, now under the New Testament, wage war upon just and necessary occasions.
> Westminster Confession, Ch. XXIII, Sec. 2

The Methodist Church

Methodists are more restrained in their teaching on war. The 1992 Book of Discipline of the United Methodist Church declares:

> We believe war is incompatible with the teachings and example of Christ. We therefore reject war as an instrument of national foreign policy.
> (War and Peace, p. 105)

Based on that statement, we might conclude that Methodists refuse to join the violent Armed Forces of their country. But the Methodist churches I know are certainly not "peace" churches, whose members are known for their rejection of war. No one was ever more positive than the founder of Methodism, John Wesley, who taught that the Christian life is a disciplined life in accord with Jesus' person and teaching. Wesley believed in seeking perfection and loving enemies as the gospel teaches. He wrote,

> Do all the good you can,
> By all the means you can,
> In all the ways you can,
> In all the places you can,
> At all the times you can,
> To all the people you can,
> As long as ever you can.

Those are words from a nonviolent heart.

Although opposed to war in principle, the most recent Methodist Book of Discipline supports those who fight as well as those who refuse to fight, stating,

> We support and extend the ministry of the Church to those persons who conscientiously

oppose all war, or any particular war, and who therefore refuse to serve in the armed forces or to cooperate with systems of military conscription. We also support and extend the Church's ministry to those persons who conscientiously choose to serve in the armed forces or alternative service ministry. (G, p. 75)

The reader may ask, should not Jesus' church minister to all Christians in the same loving way? Certainly! All of God's children should be ministered to by the church; prostitutes, law-breakers, students, soldiers, those who refuse soldiery, every one. But in church ministries of comfort and compassion, the challenge of Jesus' nonviolent cross should never be omitted. It should be made clear in ministering to prostitutes that the church does not approve prostitution; to rapists that the church does not approve rape; to students that cheating is forbidden, etc.

In the same way, chaplains to the nation's armed forces should be free to discuss with soldiers the evil of war. They are not. They too, must wear a military uniform and defend the war system. Clergy who reject war are not appointed chaplains to minister to those who wage war. Christian ministry should not only comfort sinners with the assurance of God's unconditional love and forgiveness; the ministry of the church should also seek to correct sin and call for repentance. If the Methodist Church really believes that "war is incompatible with the life and teachings of Jesus" as stated in their Book of Doctrine, the ministry of Methodist clergy to those in the Armed Forces should make this clear. A ministry which comforts the sinner without correcting the sin is not the Holy Spirit's comfort. It is cheap grace.

In 1968, the Methodist Church merged with the United Brethren in Christ. One of their founding fathers was Martin Boehm who in 1780, testified, "We believe war and

bloodshed are contrary to the gospel and spirit of Christ."
But, by 1968, after mingling with other Protestants and their
"just war" thinking, the nonviolent Tradition of the United
Brethren in Christ had eroded. In spite of their earlier
declaration that "war is incompatible with the example and
teachings of Jesus", the merged United Brethren Church
now reflects mainstream "just war" Christianity, another
example of the world converting the church, rather than the
church converting the world.

The Episcopal Church

Designed to make plain the doctrine of the Episcopal
Church in the United States, in 1987, Beverly D. Tucker and
William H. Swatos published *Questions of the Way: A
Catechism Based on the Book of Common Prayer*. Question
140 asks:

> Does the Church have an absolute and
> "official" answer for all moral questions?
>
> Answer: No. . . . because there are differences
> of opinion within the Church. For example,
> the Church has not reached unanimous
> agreement on whether war is sometimes
> justified as a means to an end . . .
> Circumstances in which we live change and
> our understanding changes. (p. 54.)

This sounds like opinion-poll faith. After 2000 years, the
Episcopal Church is still waiting for their members to come
to a unanimous decision that Jesus and war are
incompatible. If Jesus did not make this clear when He
walked and taught in Galilee, why should we believe the
Messiah will make the answer any clearer today or next
month? Do changing circumstances change the word of
God? Is the truth the church is to live by determined by the
unanimous agreement of the members?

Jesus did not say, "I am the truth under certain circumstances." He said, "I am the truth." Period. The history of a sinful world reflects changing cultures, but the word of God Jesus enfleshed is the "same yesterday, today, and forever (Hebrew 13:8). Jesus is a reflection of Eternity, not today's media coverage of a fallen world's violence and death.

The Baptists

What about the Baptists, growing so fast some say there will soon be more Baptists than people? The heritage of the Baptist Church is one of autonomy. Therefore, there is no one official Baptist statement about war which applies to all local congregations. The best way to discover what Baptists think about war is to read the statements of their Annual Conventions, Minutes of Association meetings, articles of magazines and books by Baptists.

In his book, *Social Ethics Among Southern Baptists*, George Kelsey has researched the largest body of Baptists. Like all mainstream Christianity, Southern Baptists believe that for Christians there is an <u>individual</u> ethic which forbids taking revenge and killing a personal enemy, and there is a <u>public</u> ethic which makes it the duty of the Christian to join the state in punishing enemies who threaten the life and welfare of the state. Kelsey uses this quotation from one Baptist publication:

> According to the Scriptures, a nation is not only permitted to go to war against another nation that attacks it. Under such circumstances the attacked nation is held responsible for its own defense, under a penalty of a curse. "Curse ye Meroz, said the angel of the Lord, curse ye bitterly the inhabitants thereof; because they came not to

the help of the Lord against the mighty"
(Judges 5:23). Again, "Cursed be he that
keepeth back his sword from blood."
(Jeremiah 44:10).

How does all this apply to a soldier who kills
another man in battle? It applies in this way:
The soldier is not acting from his own
initiative and as an individual. He is the
servant of, and under authority from, his
government, which, as we have seen, derives
authority from God. Therefore the soldier,
who is a representative of and in service for
his government, is an instrument of God,
NOT a murderer. <u>He is a messenger and
servant of his country and his God</u>. His
position is stated in a nutshell in Romans
13:4: "For he is the minister of God to thee
for good. But if thou do that which is evil, be
afraid; for he beareth not the sword in vain;
for HE IS THE MINISTER OF GOD, A
REVENGER TO EXECUTE WRATH
UPON HIM THAT DOETH EVIL."
Is Man A Murderer Who Kills Another in
Battle?
(Western Recorder, Sept. 13, 1942)

Romans 13:1-5 is the passage of Scripture used most often
by mainline churches to justify Christians joining the state
in war. Later, we will examine these words of Paul to the
church in Rome.

The United Church of Christ

We haven't mentioned the United Church of Christ, the
denomination of my parents and family. As a result of
merging with several other denominations in the last fifty
years, the United Church of Christ is now the sixth largest

church body in the United States. In an unusual way, the merger combined Zwingli's 16th century German Reformed Church and its Heidelberg Catechism with the Puritan Congregationalists who came from England with no fixed creed except the New Testament.

Considered by Luther to be too liberal in his theology and tainted by the pacifism of Erasmus, Zwingli in his earlier years wrote,

> Our honor stands on blood and war
> Nature's rights are drowned in gore,
> With all the furies loose from hell.
> How could anybody tell
> That we are Christian save by name,
> Without patience, love, and shame?
> If God grant not that wars have ceased
> We shall have turned from man to beast.

A different Zwingli emerged in his organizing Reformed churches in Switzerland in opposition to the papal church. Now Zwingli engaged in fighting armies because they were closely connected to the Pope's foreign mercenaries who came into Switzerland on the side of the Catholics. In the battle of Kappel in 1531, Zwingli was in the thick of the battle and died killing Catholics. Zwingli opposed war in general, but not particular wars such as war against Catholics and those who opposed his reformed church. Zwingli found war incompatible with Jesus' life and teaching, but somehow, he did not eschew wars favorable to his party.

Crossing the Atlantic to escape religious wars, the Congregationalists who were to merge with the reformed church of Zwingli, also believed in theory that they should be faithful in living by the standard of the Sermon on the Mount, but, faced with real wars being waged by their new homeland, they too, joined the other mainline churches in taking up arms to fight: in the American Revolution to be saved from taxation without representation; in the Civil War to free the slaves and preserve the Union; in the Spanish-American War to save Cuba and the Philippines from misrule by Spain; in the First World War to make the world safe for democracy; in the Second World War to save the world from German Nazism, Italian Fascism, and Japanese treachery; in the Korean and Vietnam wars to stop atheistic Communism; and in the Gulf War to prevent Saddam Hussein from making and using chemical and atomic weapons.

This is the familiar story of Christians who insist they are against war and in favor of peace, BUT when a real war breaks out, they go along with their fellow citizens to safeguard their country from whoever the politicians say is the monster of the moment. With such patriotic fury and fervor, Mark Twain was inspired to compose his satirical wartime prayer:

> O Lord our Father, our young patriots go forth to battle. Be Thou near them. We also go forth from the sweet peace of our beloved firesides to smite the foe. O Lord, our God, help us to tear their soldiers to bloody shreds with our shells. Help us to wring the hearts of their unoffending widows with unavailable grief. Help us to turn them out roofless to wander with their little children, unfriended in the waste of their desolated land in rags and hungry and thirsty. . . Blast their hopes, blight their lives, make heavy their steps, water their way with tears, stain the white snow with the blood of their wounded feet. We ask it in the spirit of Love, of Him who is the source of Love who is the ever-faithful Refuge and Friend of all that are sore beset and seek His aid with humble and contrite hearts. Amen.

Mark Twain's prayer expresses the complete contradiction between praying in the Holy Spirit of God who is love, and killing in the unholy spirit of war which is sin.

The Pentecostal Church

Founded at the beginning of the 20th century, Pentecostals originally opposed the military establishment. The founder of the Pentecostal Movement, Charles F. Parham, married a Quaker and taught that war is sin from which Christians have been delivered, that the Christian life is rooted in the holiness of God, and that the unholy nature of war contradicts the holy nature of God. Generally, this was the attitude toward war among Pentecostals prior to 1917 and the First World War.

At first, Pentecostal leaders had the courage to reject all war. Bishop Charles H. Mason was jailed and sent to prison for teaching members to love their enemies instead of slaughtering them. The Espionage and Sedition Act, which made it a crime to cause another person to refuse military duty, tested the depth of the Pentecostal's conviction on the issue. By the end of World War I, their conscientious objection to war shifted to non-combative service and permitted members to fight if it did not violate their conscience.

The period between the two World Wars heard a few Pentecostal voices upholding Jesus' Sermon on the Mount, particularly from New York's Broadway Tabernacle, saying, "We cannot reconcile the way of Christ with the way of war." But these were voices crying in the wilderness. When the United States declared war on Japan and Germany, all but a handful of young Pentecostals obeyed the command of the state and enlisted to kill the enemy. Pentecostals joined the other mainline churches in supplying chaplains to the armed forces. This brought to an end their official position which, in the beginning, had called war "sin". Again, Nationalism, man's other religion, prevailed. The *Dictionary of Pentecostal and Charismatic Movements* concludes:

> Thus, while some Pentecostals retained residues of the general pacifism of an earlier era, others had even gone beyond nonpacifism and had hardened into an antipacifist position, continuing to merely reflect, rather than to instruct, public opinion.

This, in brief, is the story of mainline churches and their centuries old "just war" doctrine based on the human wisdom of Greek and Roman philosophy, not on the Christians' new creation in their crucified-risen-ascended-ruling-indwelling Lord.

The Error

The one basic error behind all "just war" doctrine is the church's allowing what the world calls "practical solutions" to human problems to replace the gospel's solution of the kingdom of God revealed to the Apostles and practiced by the early church. Over a period of time, "reasonable solutions" of humans have become sacred traditions, placed on the same level of truth as the Word of God Jesus embodied (John 1:14).

The Catholic Catechism reflects the error,

> Sacred Tradition and Sacred Scripture, then, are bound closely together and communicate one with the other. For both of them, flowing out from the same divine well-spring, come together in some fashion to form the one thing and move toward the same goal. (80)

As a result the Church, to whom the transmission and interpretation of the Revelation is entrusted, does not derive her certainty about all revealed truths from the holy Scriptures alone. Both Scripture and Tradition must be accepted and honored with equal sentiments of devotion and reverence. (81)

The error of giving <u>both</u> Scripture and Tradition equal devotion and reverence has led mainline churches to give <u>equal devotion</u> to the state's violence of "just wars" and to the nonviolence of Jesus' Way of the cross. One contradicts the other. Killing in the wars of a fallen world completely nullifies the witness of the church to the peace of God Jesus enfleshed and offers to sin's sick world of violence and death.

Taking the military for granted, members of mainline churches join the Armed Forces the same way non-Christians do. Because they are taught no alternative, God's nonviolent Messiah and His peaceable kingdom are almost a non-thought in mainstream Christianity. What is not thought cannot be taught. What is not thought or taught cannot be practiced. What is not thought, taught, or practiced, is a non-entity.

The mistake of Catholic theology à la Augustine, from which the "just war" doctrine comes, stems from a peculiar brand of optimism. This non-biblical optimism is in <u>untainted</u> human reason's ability to define a common good realized by the political process and defended by the military power of the state. In a fallen world of sin, reason is always tainted by pride and self-interest. Saint Paul questioned such optimism in human wisdom and the ability of human reason to provide the solution to human problems. In his first Letter to the Corinthians, Paul wrote,

Has not God made foolish the wisdom of the world? For since, in the wisdom of God, the world did not know God through wisdom, it pleased God through the folly of what we preach to save those who believe . . .For the foolishness of God is wiser than men, and the weakness of God is stronger than men.
- 1 Corinthians 1:20-25

Referring to his own life and experience, Paul testifies that with all his learning and ability to think reasonably,

I do not understand my own actions . . . I do not do the good I want, but the evil I do not want, that is what I do.
- Romans 7:13

Separated from God, decisions based on reason are always tilted in favor of the decision-maker. In the Second World War, the Germans used human reason to define their "common good" as their right to have access to basic human needs such as food, clothing, and shelter, and the right of human dignity, which the church and state in Germany insisted had been denied them by the injustices of the Versailles Treaty. The German nation and the German church allowed Hitler to take them into what they called a "just war" to correct the injustice of Versailles. Although they were right about the injustices of the Versailles Treaty, they were wrong in their devotion to Hitler and use of violence to achieve what their sin-corrupted reason defined as Germany's common good. Blinded by self-concern, Germany, the home of Luther, accepted whatever Hitler said was their common good.

At the same time, Italy's disordered economy and general unrest moved the Italian state, with the support of the Catholic Church, to accept the Fascist dictator, Mussolini. He led them into a "just war" as partners with the Nazis to defend their "common good", which their human reason defined as an orderly and properly disciplined society.

The architect of Communism, Karl Marx, used reason not only to define Russia's "common good", but the "common good" of the whole world. This world would reflect a classless "just" society in which all human beings would have equal access to food, clothing, and shelter, with equal opportunity to work with dignity. Guided by reason, the "just" society defined by Karl Marx looked so promising that it convinced half of the world's people that it was worth fighting in order to achieve it. Communism is a reasonable solution in theory, but diabolical when practiced by a self-addicted world separated from God.

Likewise, democratic capitalism is a reasonable political and economic system based on a free flow of trade and ideas, but the reasoning of every trading nation and its various groups of workers and entrepreneurs is corrupted by the same sin of self-interest. "Hot money" speculators quickly move their capital in and out of developing countries for only one reason: to make a profit. Wall Street reflects the same reasoning tainted by sin.

John Steinbeck wrote about a fallen world's reason which is never pure and untainted from sin's self-interest. In his novel, *The Grapes of Wrath*, the 'owner men' confess to the tenant farmers that they don't like money's banking system. They confess that this system lives by peasant's labor and sweat, the foreclosing of mortgages of poor families, putting them out on the streets with nothing, as they did during the Great Depression. "We're sorry", says one of the owner-men. "It's not us. It's the monster. The bank isn't like a man." "Yes, but the bank is only made of men," a squatting tenant farmer replies. "No, you're wrong there—quite wrong there," says the owner-man. "The bank is something else than men. It happens that every man in a bank hates what the bank does, and yet the bank does it. The bank is something more than men, I tell you. It's the monster. Men made it, but they can't control it."

Steinbeck's novel is about a world created for a common good in God, but in our self-will, we redefine the world which God has already defined in his self-giving way. The result of sin's redefinition is a monster of violence which the world cannot control.

Who is the monster? It is Steinbeck's banker who hates what the bank does but does it anyway; the Wall Street broker who knows he is gambling with other people's life savings but does it anyway; the politician twisting words to make him and his party look good, but does it anyway; the salesman giving his prospective buyers a line with no connection to the truth but does it anyway; the scientist producing a nuclear monster with enough power to destroy life on the planet but does it anyway; people toying with sex outside the God-intended family structure based on married love, but doing it anyway. It's the Beast mentioned thirty-eight times in John's Revelation. The Bible calls it sin and identifies it with this world's "powers and principalities" (Ephesians 6:12) which are not fallen angels flapping their wings somewhere in the heavens. These are the self-willing "elemental spirits of the universe" (Galatians 4:3); hostile to God's Spirit of agape, righteousness, and peace; never letting up on the human race; deceiving the world that self-will is God's will, that national glory is God's glory, that, under certain circumstances, slaughtering our neighbors in war is necessary to preserve "our way" of life.

This is God's word:

> My thoughts are not your thoughts, neither are your ways, my ways, says the Lord.
>
> Beloved, never avenge yourselves, but leave it to the wrath of God; for it is written: Vengeance is mine; I will repay, says the

Lord". Do not be overcome by evil, but overcome evil with good.

Have this mind among yourselves, which is yours in Christ Jesus.
- Isaiah 55:8; Romans 12:19,21; Philippians 2:5

The crucial question is this: abiding in Christ, can we or can we not overcome the evil powers and principalities which constantly beset us, and live a Christ-like life in the midst of evil?

This is the gospel according to Jesus:

In me you may have peace. In the world you have tribulation; but be of good cheer, I have overcome the world.
- John 16:33

In our own power, we cannot overcome a fallen world of violence and death, but in Christ and the power of the Holy Spirit, we can say with Paul,

I can do all things in him who strengthens me.
- Philippians 4:13

The revolution of peace God has wrought for us in the church through Christ is wrapped up in Paul's teaching,

If any one is in Christ, he is a new creation; the old has passed away; behold, the new has come. All this is from God who through Christ reconciled us to himself and gave us the ministry of reconciliation. So we are ambassadors for Christ, God making his appeal through us.
- 2 Corinthians 5:17-20

If we are not able to live the peaceable life Jesus enfleshed and teaches, then we are of all people most miserable and hopeless. As the Master asks, "Are ye able to be crucified with me?" We answer, "To the death we follow Thee!" Why? Because we know that in Christ, death-resurrection is one word. Dying in the flesh with Jesus to sin's warring world, we continue to walk in the Master's Resurrection-life of the Eternal's Holy Spirit. This is the certainty given by the Father's indwelling Spirit in Christ. (2 Corinthians 1:22; 5:05)

For Christians, peace is no longer a mystery (See Ephesians 1:9-10). Peace has become reality in Christ who expects every church to be a "peace church." It is our privilege to be a part of such a church, precisely in the circumstances we are in at this moment, no matter what the political system under which we live. With God it is possible to fulfill His plan for our life when we abide in Christ as the branch abides in the vine. This is God's plan for your life and mine:

> to unite all things in him(Christ), things in
> heaven and things on earth.
> - Ephesians 1:10

Amen. So let it be.

Chapter 4

Understanding Violence in The Old Testament

> You search the scriptures because you think
> in them you have eternal life; and it is they
> that bear witness to me; yet you refuse to
> come to me that you may have life.
> - John 5:39-40

Until we understand the reason for violence in the life of Israel, mainstream Christians will continue to use Old Testament violence and war to justify legalized mass homicide perpetrated by the church.

Considered the most successful military leader of the Civil War, Confederate General Stonewall Jackson was motivated by the conviction that the Lord Jesus wanted him to follow in the footsteps of the Old Testament warriors in fighting a holy war led by Jehovah-God. Jackson's mistaken reading of the Old Testament led him to order that no prisoners of wars were to be taken alive. Every man, woman, and child were to be killed because this is the way God commanded David to deal with enemies (See 1 Samuel 27:8-9). If it was right for David, it must be right for Stonewall Jackson and the church. Here we see the tragedy of placing Old Testament wars and warriors on the same level of truth as the New Testament gospel of total peace that has come in Jesus and those who abide in His living Spirit and word.

97

Two Different Realities

We must recognize the difference between the Old and New Testaments just as Jesus did. Four times, Jesus contrasts His teaching with that of Moses and the Old Testament patriarchs (See Matthew 5:27-29; 5:33-36; 5:38-41; 5:43-48). The Old and New Covenants represent different life-styles. The Old is of the Law. The New is of the Spirit who fulfills the law.

The Old Testament wistfully promises God's new age of the Spirit in a coming Messiah. The New Testament joyously proclaims that the new age of the Spirit has come in Christ:

A new birth of the Spirit living in the person who begins to walk in the light of Jesus (John 3:1-21).

A new creation of the Holy Spirit in whom "the old has passed away, and the new has come" (2 Corinthians 5:17).

A new Spirit-ruled person reconciled to God through the cross, thereby bringing sin's hostility between Jew and Gentile to an end (Ephesians 2:15-16).

A new Christ-nature that is being renewed in knowledge after the image of the creator (Colossians 3:9-10).

A new baptism that dies to the flesh and is raised to a resurrection-life of the Spirit (Romans 6:5-10).

The new and living way God opens up for sinners by Jesus' death on the cross when the temple-curtain separating worshipers from the Holy One is torn down (Hebrew 10:19-23).

A new Way of life that turns the world upside down(John 14:6; Acts 17:6).

The new garment of life from which one does not cut a piece to patch life's old worn-out garment (Luke 5:36). The Christian life is completely new in Christ, not of the old (Matthew 9:16).

So it is. The reader of the Bible should recognize that going from the Old Testament to the New is entering a new and different world. This is why it is called the New Testament, or the New Covenant in Jesus' blood which is renewed every time we partake of the Bread and Wine (Luke 22:20).

The New Testament has a new standard of life for the church (Romans 6:17); one not found in the Old. The Old is still bound to sin's world of war; the New has moved into the Promised Land of the Spirit's peace.

This does not mean discarding or denigrating the Old Testament. Because the New Testament is deeply rooted in the Old, it is impossible to understand the New apart from the Old. The Creator in the Book of Genesis is the same Holy One who gave His Christ-Spirit to the church on Pentecost. The God of Abraham, Isaac, and Jacob, is the God of Matthew, Mark, Luke, and John.

The New Rooted in the Old

The Holy Spirit of Jesus is rooted in the Old Testament's foundation in the holiness of God:

The name of Israel's God is "holy" (Psalm 105:3).
Their Creator and Maker is the Holy One (Isaiah 43:3).
Israel's new homeland is holy to the Lord (Jeremiah 48:14).
The covenant that binds Israel to God is holy (Luke 1:72).
Israel is called "the holy people" (Isaiah 63:12)
The priests, even their garments, are holy (Exodus 28:4).
The Ark and its contents are holy (2 Chronicles 25:3
The Sabbath is holy (Exodus 10:8).
The Way is holy (Psalm 77:13).

99

The Hebrew root for the word holy is "kds" and implies that which is separate. To be holy is to be set apart for God; holiness describes what every part of Israel's life was meant to be. And what every part of the life of the church is meant to be—set apart to make known the life, work, and teaching of Jesus so that in Christ, the world God loves shall not perish in its blinding idolatry (See Jeremiah 50:38).

The only recognized Scriptures the early church had for more than a century were the Old Testament's Hebrew writings, which were translated into the Greek language so the disciples could read and understand them. About A.D. 140, Marcion and the Gnostics discarded the Old Testament because they mistakenly regarded Hebrew Scriptures as the story of a different God than the God of Jesus.

The early church recognized the difference between the Old and New Testaments, but reconciled the difference between the two by regarding the Old as the beginning of God's plan of salvation, and the New as the completion of that plan (See Ephesians 1:3-20).

How the Early Church Interpreted the Old Testament

The early Christians saw the blessing God promised to all of earth's families through the descendants of Abraham (Genesis 12:3) as fulfilled in Jesus (See Acts 3:18-25). They saw in the Old Testament the seed of salvation planted in Israel (John 4:26) and harvested by the church on Pentecost (See Acts 2:22-42).

The pattern of interpretation was promise and fulfillment. Following Pentecost, the church heard God speaking through Ezekiel, saying,

> I will take you from the nations, and gather
> you from all the countries, and bring you into

my land. I will sprinkle clean water upon you, and you shall be clean from all your uncleannesses and from all your idols I will cleanse you. A NEW HEART I WILL GIVE YOU and a NEW SPIRIT I WILL PUT WITHIN YOU and I will take out of your flesh the heart of stone and put my spirit within you. You shall be my people and I will be your God.
- Ezekiel 36:24-28

For Israel, Pentecost was the holy festival when the people assembled joyfully to celebrate the harvest of crops the twelve months of the year had produced according to God's good creation. It was on Pentecost, fifty days after the Messiah's Resurrection, that Israel and the world received the Spiritual harvest of almost 2000 years of God's clearing, planting, and cultivating the chosen fields of Israel.

When an amazed and perplexed people asked about the meaning of what was happening on Pentecost, Peter replied,

These men are not drunk, as you suppose. This is the fulfillment of what was spoken by the prophet Joel: "And in the last days it shall be, as God declared, I will pour out my Spirit upon all flesh" . . . This Jesus delivered up according to the definite plan of God, you crucified, but God raised up Jesus, and of that we are witnesses. Being exalted at the right hand of God, and having received from the Father the promise of the Holy Spirit, he has poured out that which you see and heard.
- Acts 2:15-24

The New Testament's Peace-Pentecost was the <u>destination</u> toward which the Holy One was taking Israel during their Old Testament <u>upward journey</u> of almost 2000 years.

Christians should read the Old Testament with eyes fixed on the destination in Christ toward whom the Holy One is leading Israel. Israel's current violent and unredeemed behavior is not to be emulated.

The Old Testament cannot stand alone as a religion without anticipating the Holy One of Israel acting in the future to fulfill the promises of a New Age of Peace. Chapters 40 to 55 in Isaiah illustrate this. Whether or not this is Deutero Isaiah of the 6th century B.C., or the same 8th century B.C. prophet enabled to see two hundred years down the line, does not matter. This is the typical Old Testament message of great expectations, as God speaks to His Chosen People:

> I, the Lord, have called you in righteousness. I will keep you and make you to be a covenant for the people and a light for the Gentiles, to open eyes that are blind, to free captives from prison and to release from the dungeon those who sit in darkness . . . .
>
> Do not be afraid, for I am with you; I will bring your children from the east and gather you from the west. I will say to the north, "Give them up!" and to the south. "Do not hold them back." Bring my sons and my daughters from the ends of the earth- everyone who is called by my name, whom I created for my glory, whom I formed and made.
> - Isaiah 42:6-7; 43:5-7

No doubt this is the prophet's vision, which has woven together the Holy One's use of Cyrus and the Persian armies to release the Hebrew exiles from their captivity in Babylonia, with the coming of God's Messiah to release all of God's children from the bondage of evil and death. Just as Isaiah heard Yahweh's voice in these words, saying He was using Cyrus to release Israel from their exile and rebuild

Jerusalem, so Christians are to read these words in the Old Testament as the good news of our release in Christ from our sin's fallen world of violence and our death.

Christians are to read the Old Testament as both Israel's and humanity's upward journey from Babylon's self-centered world to the New Jerusalem, where man/woman's self-pride and prejudice have been conquered by the sword of God's self-giving Spirit (Ephesians 6:17) enfleshed in Jesus. In other words, violence in the Old Testament is the <u>old</u> nature of Israel's unredeemed life, and that of <u>every human</u> the Holy God of love would lead us <u>away from</u>. Our common destiny is Jesus, His indwelling Presence given on Pentecost. Unless we understand the Scriptures as such an UPWARD JOURNEY from sin's death to God's eternal life, the Old Testament's unredeemed sinners become false heroes who only perpetuate the sin of violence and leave a warring world and church in the same unredeemed condition.

The Holy One chose Israel through whom He would come to a world that had lost its oneness with Eternity. The Old Testament is a dialogue between the Divine Lover and a people being prepared for the Lover's enfleshment in "Jesus Christ, Son of God, Savior." Israel's story is one of preparation, not fulfillment.

According to the Old Testament prophets and psalms, Israel was thankful for being chosen by Jehovah-God as "children of the covenant" and realized they were called to entrust their life to the Holy One, but over and over their desired trust in the Lord turned to trust in their own human devices, a common trait of humankind. Repeatedly, the prophetic voice of a psalmist tells the tale:

> They did not keep God's covenant. They
> forgot what He had done. He divided the sea
> and let them walk through it.. In the daytime
> he led them with a cloud, and all the night

with a fiery light. Yet they sinned still more against him, rebelling against the Most High they had no faith and did not trust His saving power.
- Psalm 78:11-22

The Old Testament is a Christian Book of Scriptures for the church only when it is read as the Upward Journey of a people whose loving Father is leading Israel and a fallen world-way from our God-rebellion, with its violence and death toward a cross on which Jesus has overcome the world and restores us to our destined at-homeness in the Spirit. Jesus' resurrection and indwelling enable every troubled and repentant soul to experience the first-fruit of a transformed life of rest and peace in the here and now peaceable Home of the Eternal's reconciled family. This is the Spirit's guarantee (2 Corinthians 5:5).

An example of the need to understand the vast difference between the Old and the New Testaments might be Brazil's nation-wide prayer movement called "Desperta Debora", Portuguese for "Wake up, Deborah." The name for this prayer movement was based on Judges 5:12: "Awake, awake, Deborah! Awake, awake, utter a song!" The words are part of the Song of Deborah (Judges 5:1-31), which tells about Deborah leading Israel's army of 10,000 against the Canaanites commanded by Sisera. During the battle, Sisera sought refuge in the tent of Jael, one of the Hebrew women. When General Sisera asked her for a refreshing drink, Jael, "the most blessed of women", gave him milk. Then the Book of Judges says,

> Her hand reached for the tent peg, her right hand for the workman's hammer. She struck Sisera, she crushed his head, she shattered and pierced his temple. At her feet he sank; there he lay. At her feet he sank and fell- dead.
> - Judges 5:26

The Song of Deborah ends with these vindictive words,

> So may all your enemies perish, O Lord.
> - Judges 5:31

Unless Christians of Brazil read this Old Testament story of revenge as God's leading Israel and Deborah away from their bondage in violence to the New Testament's reconciling love, joy, and peace, Brazil's prayers will be to a God of War. This god glories in crushing the head of his enemies; it is not to the God who glories in Jesus' love on the cross that has:

> broken down the dividing wall of hostility . . .
> that he might create in himself one new man in place of the two, so making peace, reconciling us both to God in one body through the cross, thereby bringing the hostility to an end.
> - Ephesians 2:14-16

Reading the Old Testament as Israel's Upward Journey from sin's violence to the Lamb of God who delivers a violent world from evil, the church will see Deborah and all of Israel, not as they were, but as the people God was preparing them to become. Not persons who pound stakes in the heads of opponents in sin's spirit of violence and revenge. Instead, they will be a people empowered by the Holy Spirit to overcome the evil of fallen Babylon with God's good agape. Jesus will overcome Satanic Evil—our real Enemy (John 16:33). The glorious victory over evil the church is called to demonstrate is life in a warring world as the living Body of Christ. Just before His crucifixion, He said:

> Now shall the ruler of this world be cast out; and I, when I am lifted up from the earth will draw all men to my side.
> - John 12:31-32

In Christ, the satanic ruler of this world has been cast out!

The Difference

A common trait from which Israel rarely rose above was their request that God wipe out the wicked, their enemies they made synonymous with the enemies of God, but to show favor to them:

> O God, insolent men have risen up against me; a band of ruthless men seek my life, and they do not set thee before them. But thou, O Lord, art a God merciful and gracious . . . return to me and take pity on me; give thy strength to thy servant . . . show me a sign of thy favor that those who hate me may see and be put to shame.
> - Psalm 86:14-17

How different are the New Testament disciples of Jesus who pray for their enemies and include them in God's plan of salvation for a world reconciled to Him and to each other.

Another common strand runs all the way through the Old Testament to show the difference between the seeking people of Israel and the finding people of Jesus. This strand is Israel's lack of joyful certainty of at-one-ment with God, who had called them into a covenant relationship, and the joy and certainty of the Father's Presence in Christ experienced by the church of the New Testament. This is illustrated in the 22nd Psalm:

> Why art thou so far from helping me, from the words of my groaning? O my God, I cry by day, but thou dost not answer; and by night but find no rest... my heart is like wax... thou dost lay me in the dust of death.
> - Psalm 22:1-2,14-15

We have heard for ourselves, and we know
indeed that this is the Savior of the world.
- John 4:42

To be sure, before Jesus' resurrection and Pentecost's
indwelling, there were times of doubt and despair in the
hearts of the Apostles, but never after Jesus' victory over
death and God's gift of the fullness of His Holy Spirit. Then
the cry of the New Testament church was not, "Oh that I
knew where I might find him (Job 23:3), but "We have
found the Messiah! (John 1:41).

The passion of the New Testament is sharing the good news
of God's coming in Christ and His deliverance from sin's
violence and death with the whole world. Old Testament
Israel as a people never got far beyond their waiting for God
to come and fulfill His promised blessing. Nothing like the
Great Commission (Mark 16:15) is to be found in the Old
Testament. God's gift of eternal life's peace in Christ is the
good news the church was called to share with the whole
world.

Israel's First Lesson about God's Way of Deliverance

When the Holy One called Israel to prepare the way for His
coming, the very first lesson He taught was trust in His
power to deliver from every enemy.

Trapped at the edge of the Red Sea with Pharaoh's army
closing in, the Hebrew slaves saw their plight as hopeless.
They wanted to return to slavery where, at least, they would
stay alive. In the face of what they believed was certain
annihilation, this was God's word from the lips of Moses,

The Lord will fight for you, you have only to
be still.
- Exodus 14:14

This is not the Eternal's instruction to the world's military generals who laugh at such a non-sensical command. This is God's word to Moses and the Chosen People, whom God is preparing for the coming of His new nonviolent kingdom, a kingdom of the Holy Spirit.

The Lord said to Moses,

> Lift up your rod and stretch out your hand over the sea and divide it, that the people of Israel may go on dry ground through the sea.
> - Exodus 14:16

Moses believed and obeyed a command which would seem foolish to a fallen flesh-bound world. The slaves followed the leader God had provided. At the end of the day, the fleeing Hebrews had been delivered from the Egyptian warriors and shouted with joy,

> The rider he has thrown into the sea. The Lord is my strength and my song, and he has become my salvation; this is my God and I will praise him.
> - Exodus 15:1

It was the same lesson the Liberator was teaching Israel when they crossed over Jordan (See Joshua 3:7), and His same instruction to King Jehoshaphat when he found himself surrounded by hostile forces:

> Fear not, and be not dismayed at this great multitude; for the battle is not yours, but God's; take your position and stand still, and see the victory of the Lord on your behalf.
> - 2 Chronicles 20:15-17

Victory was given by the Hand of God who is Spirit (John 4:24), not by the hand of man who is flesh. Peace is grace,

God's gift of His Holy Spirit, not the misguided effort of sin's unholy military might, which led the prophet Jeremiah to cry out,

> They have healed the wounds of my people lightly, saying, "Peace, peace," when there is no peace.
> - Jeremiah 6:14

What the world calls peace by political diplomacy and military victories, is not peace at all. It is only a temporary lull in the fighting, leaving both sides exhausted and still bitter. This is not the peace the Old Testament calls "shalom", which means a new life of righteousness (right-relationships) in which everyone is part of a sharing and caring community.

In 600 B.C., the Babylonian army invaded Judah and took people of Israel into captivity. It was in these circumstances that Jeremiah wrote to those languishing in exile this message from the Lord.

> Seek the peace (shalom) of the city where I have sent you into exile, and pray to the Lord on its behalf, for in its peace (shalom) you will find your peace (shalom).
> - Jeremiah 29:7

Israel Failed to Follow the Prophet's Vision

Despising their captors, yearning to return to Jerusalem and their homeland, and resenting God's failure to save His Chosen People, they couldn't believe what Jeremiah was saying. This crazy man of God was telling them to pray for their enemies, that in living for the peace and welfare of their Babylonian foes, they would find their shalom. Jeremiah's letter was not a best-seller. Exile was not accepted as an opportunity to submit to God's teaching to love as He loves, giving the people of Babylonia a clue to what it means to be redeemed from sin's violence and death.

Israel was never an apt pupil of nonviolence. Following their deliverance at the Red Sea, we read of savage wars led by Joshua and Gideon, who used the hand of flesh to gain possession of Canaan and the Promised Land. We should know that God's original instruction to Israel was not to fight their way into the Promised Land. The Books of Exodus and Deuteronomy both tell how the Holy One offered to give Israel their new homeland without using sword or spear:

> When my angel goes before you and brings you in to the Amorites, and the Hittites, and the Perizittes, and the Canaanites and the Hevites, and the Jebusites . . . I will send my terror before you, and I will throw into confusion all the people against whom you shall come, and I will make all your enemies turn their backs to you. And I will send hornets before you which shall drive out Hivite, Canaanite, and Hittite from before you. I will not drive them out from before you in one year, lest the land become desolate and the wild beasts multiply against you. Little by little I will drive them out before you, until you are increased and possess the land . . . They shall not dwell in your land, lest they make you sin against me; for if you serve their gods, it will surely be a snare to you.
> - Exodus 23:23-33; Deuteronomy 7:17-26

This was the plan of I AM THAT I AM to deliver the people of Israel from their enemies and give them the Promised Land without killing. God had the power to accomplish it, but like a fallen world, Israel did not have the faith to allow God to do it.

This nonviolent story of God's original plan for Israel to enter the promised Land is not highlighted by the "just war" church, only the great military victories of Joshua, Gideon, and the other warriors. They are featured in sermons and Sunday-School lessons to perpetuate the "just war" heresy. If Israel had waited patiently and trusted in the Lord's power to give them the victory as He did at the Red Sea, the Old Testament would describe Israel's nonviolent victories of faith and trust, not self-willed bloody victories of war.

The lifestyle of the cross (outlined in Matthew 5, 6,and 7) is the way of God's Suffering Servant Messiah prophesied in Isaiah 53. It is radically different from the old Way of the Mosaic Law outlined in the Torah (the first five books of the Bible).

The Reason for Old Testament Law

Abba's love, which is willing to suffer to save all of His children from perishing in their idolatry of the flesh, does not contradict the old way of equal justice under law. Jesus' new way of suffering love, demonstrated on the cross, <u>fulfills</u> the old way of the law. This is necessary in Babylon's fallen world to establish some degree of stability to prevent sin's self-centered world from self-destruction. Jesus made this crystal clear:

> Think not that I have come to abolish the law
> and the prophets; I have come not to abolish
> them, but to fulfill them.
> - Matthew 5:17

Jesus has come, not to give us more and better laws to break, but rather to give us His holy Spirit. This Spirit empowers us to fulfill the law and its purpose, inspiring us not to kill, not to steal, not to commit adultery, but to walk in the Eternal's Spirit of holiness.

Paul asks the question, Why the law? (Galatians 3:19). This is the evangelist's answer:

> Now before faith came, we were confined under the law, kept from restraint until faith should be revealed. So that the law was our custodian until Christ came. But now that faith has come, we are no longer under a custodian; for in Christ Jesus you are all sons of God through faith. For as many of you as were baptized into Christ have put on Christ. There is neither Jew nor Greek, there is neither slave or free, there is neither male nor female; for you are all one in Christ Jesus.
> - Galatians 3:23-29

Instructed thoroughly in the Old Testament, Saint Paul understood the reason why God called Israel. It was to ground a particular people in God's holy law; to prepare them for His Self-gift to the world so that we may abide in His gracious love and peace.

God's Ten Commandments were necessary to make us aware of three realities: the reality of God's holiness; the reality of our sin; and the impossibility of sharing God's holy life for eternity apart from repentance and a new birth.

The purpose of God's holy law is to lead the soul to repentance and submission to the rule of God's Holy Spirit of love. Herein lies our peace. Jesus' self-giving on the cross makes the sinner aware of our need to repent. In our crucifixion with Christ to the flesh and its violence and death, we are raised to our new God-self in Christ and eternal life.

The Bible is one story which begins with the problem of our separation from holy God and ends with the holy Person in whom the separation and its violence and death have been overcome. The purpose of this chapter is to teach how to read the Old Covenant of God's restraining law within the context of the New Covenant of God's redeeming Spirit. The Old leads to the New. The old law is not on a par with the Spirit who makes all things new.

When we read the Old Testament correctly, we become aware with Isaiah of our alienation from our Creator-Source and our need to return to the Holy One of Israel:

> We have all become like one who is unclean, and all our righteous deeds are like a polluted garment. There is no one that calls upon thy name, that bestirs himself to take hold of thee; for thou hast hid thy face from us, and hast delivered us into the hand of our iniquities.
> - Isaiah 64:6-7

Genesis, the first Book of Scripture, is the story of humanity's idolatry and the resultant flood. The story of a disobedient people continues to the last Book of the Old Testament where we hear Malachi say,

> Have we not all one Father? Has not one God created us? Why then are we faithless to one another, profaning the covenant of our fathers?
> - Malachi 2:10-11

From Genesis to Malachi this is God's word,

> My people are bent on turning away from me.
> - Hosea 11:7

It's the story of Israel's life, and ours, outside a redeeming relationship with Abba.

Israel's Demand to be Ruled Like Other Nations

There is no more important story depicting Israel's disobedience and ours, than Israel's demand to have a king like the other nations of the world. The eighth chapter of First Samuel is crucial in understanding Israel's violence and our sinful reliance for security on the state and its military might. The elders of Israel came to Samuel demanding to have a king and be ruled like the other nations of the world. Since the time of Moses, the twelve tribes of Israel had no political rulers to govern them, only leaders called judges; charismatic leaders whose primary purpose was to point Israel to Elohim and his holy and righteous power revealed to Moses on Mount Sinai. The very meaning of the word Israel means "let El rule" or "let El shine". This was the command of the judges: "Let Elohim rule over Israel. He is our king. We have no other ruler." (Puritans were often heard to shout, "We have no king but Jesus!")

When Samuel took Israel's demand for a king to God in prayer, this was the answer he received, "They have not rejected you. They have rejected me. They have forsaken me to serve other gods."(See 1 Samuel 8:7 - the story of a fallen world) Samuel was told to warn Israel what the consequences of their decision would be; their sons would be forced to operate the military system and serve in the king's army. Some would be forced to make weapons for the soldiers (1 Samuel 8:8-12).

In their self-will, Israel made the mistake of thinking the goal God had in mind for them was to become a super political and military power to rule by God's law over all other nations.

> They all were looking for a king
> To slay their foes and lift them high;
> Thou cam'st, a little baby thing
> That made a woman cry.

Isaiah had it right:

> For to us a child is born . . . and the
> government will be upon his shoulder . . . a
> bruised reed he will not break, and a dimly
> burning wick he will not quench.
> - Isaiah 9:6; 42:3

The Holy One was calling Israel to prepare the world for a
Suffering Servant Messiah (See Isaiah 53) who would
conquer by "a sword not of man" (Isaiah 31:8). Jesus is that
sword.

Why should we be shocked by Israel's wars, which led
God's chosen but unredeemed people to wipe out an entire
village, town, tribe, including women, and children? The
terrible violence of Israel's nation-state was no more cruel
than today's warfare of fallen nation-states, which annihilate
every human in the path of their bombs and missiles.
Nothing in the Old Testament is worse than Hiroshima and
Nagasaki.

In fallen Babylon, unredeemed human nature and its wars
never change. The only thing that changes in the world's
warfare is the method and the weapons. Whether in 1000
B.C., 1000 A.D., or in 2000 A.D., war is sin's twisted
apprehension of God's will. Hosea warned,

> Israel has forgotten his Maker and built
> palaces;
> Judah has multiplied fortified cities . . .
> You have trusted in your chariots . . .
> Israel has gone up to Assyria,
> A wild ass wandering alone . . .
> They hire allies among the nations . . .
> But they are not able to cure or heal your
> wound.
> -Hosea 8:14; 10:13; 8:9-10; 5:13

115

Outside the indwelling of the Holy Spirit, Israel's conception of God as a warrior was like that of other nations. In the words of the psalmist,

> Blessed be the Lord, my rock, who trains my hands for war and my fingers for battle; my rock and my fortress, my stronghold and my deliverer, my shield and he in whom I take refuge, who subdues the people under him.
> - Psalm 144:1-2

We should tremble, not exalt, when we hear the Psalmist shout,

> Happy shall he be who takes your little ones and dashes them against the rocks.
> - Psalm 137:9

If it is true that God is love (John 4:16), and that Jesus is the incarnation of the Holy One's Spirit (John 10:30), then it is not God's nature to train the hands of His children for war and make happy those who slaughter tiny babies. Calling the children to His side, the Good Shepherd says to His flock:

> It is not the will of my Father who is in heaven that one of these little ones should perish.
> - Matthew 18:14

In the Old Testament God Plays Down Violence

As sin's violence runs through the Old Testament, we must see it within the context of the Holy One continually playing down Israel's weapons of violence and showing his Chosen People that their victories were of the Spirit, not the flesh.

An example of this is God's instruction to Gideon as he prepared for battle. Gideon was all set to go into battle against the Midianites with 32,000 soldiers when the Lord said, "Wait a minute, Gideon. Your army is too big. With that size army, Israel will get the idea that it's your plan and power that gives the victory, not God." So Gideon pared his army down to 10,000 and again was ready for battle when the Lord said, "Still too many, Gideon. Take your soldiers down to the river. Eliminate those that lap like a dog. Keep those that drink from their cupped hand." From 32,000 soldiers at the beginning, Gideon's army ended with 300. (See Judges 7). Military commanders laugh at the weapons God told Gideon to use: jars. When Gideon gave the command, they smashed their jars, blew their trumpets, and in panic, the Midianite raiders fled (Judges 7:20). It was God's strategy, not Gideon's, which gave Israel the victory.

Here we see the Sovereign Ruler taking a war-minded people where they were in time and space and, in his own way, teaching them that:

> A king is not saved by his great army; a
> warrior is not delivered by his great strength.
> The war horse is a vain hope for victory, and
> by its great might it cannot save.
> - Psalm 33:16-17

It's the truth Abba was teaching Israel all the way through the Old Testament:

> Not by might, nor by power, but by my
> Spirit", saith the Lord.
> - Zechariah 4:6

This is what we mean by Israel's Upward Journey toward a cross and resurrection-life Abba would make possible in Jesus. Before that goal was reached, Gideon was to take revenge on two cities of the Midianites and slaughter the people because they would not feed his army. He captured two of their kings and killed them because they had killed his brothers (Judges 8:10-21). This is Satan's hell, not God's holiness.

When Gideon died, his seventy sons from his many wives were slaughtered by Abimelech, his son from a concubine. Abimelech incited his mother's clan to a rebellion and had himself made their king. When many refused to accept his rule, especially in the city of Shechem, Abimelech destroyed the city. In the bloody battle, a woman crushed Abimelech's skull with a stone. Near death, the king said to his armor-bearer, "Draw your sword and kill me, lest men say of me, 'A woman killed him'" (Judges 9:53-55). Such was Israel's mad machismo.

Because of Israel's idolatry and desire to live as other nations of the world, the Lord continued to call his Chosen People to repent and walk in the way of holiness and peace, saying,

> Even though you make many prayers, I will not listen; your hands are full of blood. Wash yourselves and make yourselves clean; remove the evil of your doings from before my eyes; cease to do evil; learn to do good; seek justice, correct oppression; defend the fatherless, plead for the widows. If you refuse and rebel, you shall be devoured by the sword.
> - Isaiah 1:15-17, 19-20

Those who look to the Old Testament for military mentors do not hear the message of the many guides Abba sent to warn that:

> The haughty looks of a man shall be brought low, and the pride of men shall be humbled; and the Lord alone will be exalted. Turn away

from the man in whose nostrils is breath, for of what account is he?
- Isaiah 2:11, 22

The prophets pleaded with Israel to turn away from a lost world's trust in military might and surrender completely to the Eternal who was saying,

> In returning and rest you shall be saved; in quietness and in trust shall be your strength. And you would not, but you said, "No! We will speed upon our horses. We will ride upon swift steeds"; therefore, your pursuers shall be swift. A thousand shall flee at the threat of one, till you are left like a flagstaff on the top of a mountain.
> - Isaiah 30:15-17

This is to say that David is to be emulated, not because of his military courage and skill, but only because of his contrite spirit and readiness to repent, crying out to the Lord for mercy and forgiveness.

As the people of the Old Testament matured in their understanding of the holy nature of Abba, more and more they came to understand their own sinful nature and need to repent and to cry out with the psalmist,

> Have mercy on me, O God. Create in me a clean heart, O God, and put a new and right spirit within me.
> - Psalm 51:1-10

The Need to Keep Our Eyes on The Upward Journey's Goal

This is the main point: when we read the Old Testament, we are to keep our eyes focused, not on the violence, but on the

Victor toward whom the Holy One of Israel was leading his
Chosen People. This was the goal Isaiah envisioned,

> It shall come to pass in the latter days that
> they shall beat their swords into plowshares,
> and their spears into pruning hooks; then
> nation shall not lift up sword against nation,
> neither shall they learn war any more.
> - Isaiah 2:2, 4

The goal Micah prophesied,

> They shall learn war no more . . .Every man
> shall sit under his own fig tree, and none shall
> make them afraid . . . In that day, says the
> Lord, I will cut off your horses from among
> you and will destroy your chariots and throw
> down all your strongholds . . . and you shall
> bow down no more to the work of your hands
> . . . The nations shall see and be ashamed of
> all their might.
> - Micah 4:3,4:10,13; 7:16

The victor Nahum envisioned,

> Behold, on the mountains the feet of him who
> brings good tidings, who proclaims peace!
> - Nahum 1:14

Jeremiah must have been aware of Israel's ultimate destiny
when the southern kingdom of Judah decided to take up arms
against Nebuchadnezzar. When he attacked Babylonian
armies, King Zedekiah heard God's word from the lips of
Jeremiah,

> Behold, I will turn back the weapons of war
> which are in your hands and with which you
> are fighting against the king of Babylon and

against the Chaldeans who are besieging you outside the walls . . . I set before you the way of life and the way of death. He who stays in this city shall die by the sword . . . but he who goes out and surrenders to the Chaldeans shall live. I am against you who say, "Who shall come down against us, or who shall enter our habitation? (Jeremiah 21:4, 8-9) The land is full of adulterers. Their course is evil, and their might is not right.
- Jeremiah 23:10

Because of the guilt of Judah and the holy city of Jerusalem, Jeremiah not only said God would destroy their nation and allow Nebuchadnezzar to carry them into captivity, he counseled them to accept their chastening and not resist the enemy. Moreover, foreshadowing the coming of the nonviolent Messiah, Jeremiah counseled Judah in exile to love their enemies, to do good to their persecutors and pray for them:

Build houses and live in them; plant gardens and eat their produce. Take wives and have sons and daughters; multiply there and do not decrease. But seek the welfare of the city where I have sent you into exile and pray to the Lord on its behalf, for in its welfare you will find your welfare . . . For I know the plans I have for you, says the Lord, plans for welfare and not for evil, to give you a future and a new hope. Then you will call upon me and pray to me, and I will hear you. You will seek me and find me; when you seek me with all your heart.
- Jeremiah 29: 5-7, 11-13

Jeremiah was on the Upward Journey, becoming more and more aware of the Christ-like nature of the Eternal with the assurance that there is an imperishable future for all who abide in the Lord's Spirit and word. In the day of God's indwelling, each of us, from the least to the greatest, will know the God of Peace in whose kingdom violence and death are no more (See Jeremiah 31:31-34).

The only thing that saved the Old Testament prophets from utter despair was their vision of a nonviolent Messiah who would come and, in a New Israel, establish his holiness on earth as it is in heaven. The ripened fruit of New Israel is the Beloved Community of Jesus.

When we read the pages of the Old Testament, therefore, let the eyes of our soul focus on the Lamb of God who takes away the sin of the world, (John 1:29):

> Despised and rejected by men,
> He has borne our griefs and carried our sorrows,
> Wounded for our transgressions,
> Upon him was the chastisement that made us whole,
> By his stripes we are healed.
> Oppressed and afflicted, yet he opened not his mouth,
> Stricken for the transgression of God's people.
> The righteous one shall make many righteous,
> They made his grave with the wicked although he had done no violence.
> - Isaiah 53

The author of Hebrews summarized it when he wrote,

> These *(in the Old Testament)* all died in faith, not having received what was promised . . . acknowledging that they were strangers and exiles on earth, seeking a better country.

Therefore, since we are surrounded by so great a cloud of witnesses, let us lay aside every weight and sin which clings so closely, and let us run with perseverance the race that is set before us, looking to Jesus the pioneer and perfected of our faith who for the joy that was set before him endured the cross, despising the shame, and is seated at the right hand of the throne of God.
- Hebrews 11:13-16; 12:1-2 *(emphasis added)*

Jesus gives His church THE KEY to reading the Old Testament in this one verse of Scripture:

You search the scriptures, because you think that in them you have eternal life; and it is they that bear witness to me; yet you refuse to come to me that you may have life.
- John 5:39-40

Symbolically, the Old Testament is the crib in which the New Testament Jesus is laid. He is our peace who fulfills Israel's longing for peace when we abide in His Spirit and His word. Abba calls each and every soul to be a peace-person and every church to be a peace-church by demonstrating to sin's fallen world of violence and death what Jesus has done to deliver us from evil.

Amen. So let it be.

Chapter 5

The Misuse of the New Testament To Justify War

> Do your best to present yourself to God as
> one approved, a workman who has no need to
> be ashamed, rightly handling the word of
> truth.
> -2 Timothy 2:15

We have already seen how Augustine misused two of Jesus'
parables to justify the use of violence by the church. In this
chapter, we will examine the five New Testament passages
most often misused by mainstream Christianity to show that
in certain circumstances, Jesus advocates the use of violence.

The Cleansing of the Temple

The first is the account of Jesus' cleansing the Temple in
Jerusalem, which appears in all four Gospels: (Matthew
21:12-17; Mark 11:15-17; Luke 19:45-48; John 2:13-22).

The four Gospels agree that Jesus "drove" from the Temple
the money-changers and those who bought and sold, warning
them that the Temple is God's house of prayer, not a house
of merchandise to buy and sell. Only the Gospel of John
mentions a whip.

Making a whip of cords, Jesus snapped it at the animals. It

was the only language they understood at that moment. The animals ran amok to get out of the Temple as though they knew it was their last chance to escape the butcher's knife at their throat.

The sellers of animals and the money-changers were well acquainted with Scripture and knew they were breaking God's Law by making our Father's House a place of business (See Zechariah 14:21). It was their deep guilt that drove them out of the Temple, not a whip.

None of the four Gospels says anything about battered and dead bodies lying around. If there had been wounded victims of Jesus' violence, with human blood splattered, we can be sure the priests and Pharisees would have exclaimed that Jesus was savagely violent, just another impostor instead of the gentle Messiah of whom Isaiah said,

> He will not cry or lift up his voice, or make it heard in the street; a bruised reed he will not break, and a dimly burning wick he will not quench.
> - Isaiah 42:3

Neither Jesus' physical prowess, nor the whip, cleansed the Temple of greed. It was the sovereign and purifying power of Abba's Holy Spirit who convicts the heart of sin. The Father's House of Prayer for all people would have been the last place in the world to use violence. When David wanted to build a Temple to replace the Tabernacle Tent, God forbid him, saying,

> You have shed much blood and have waged great wars; you shall not build a house to my name, because you have shed so much blood before me upon the earth.
> - 1 Chronicles 22:8

A fallen world's violence is a complete contradiction to God's holy Temple built in the name of the Holy One of Israel who is love (1 John 4:16).

In refusing to allow David to build a new Temple in Jerusalem, the Holy One was telling a world of war that in no way can His House of Prayer be connected with violence. Why, therefore, does any church say that Jesus used violence to cleanse the Temple? Violence and God's Temple are as far apart as the East is from the West.

In cleansing the temple, the Prince of Peace was fulfilling the messianic prophecy of Malachi,

> The Lord whom you seek will suddenly come
> to his temple . . . he will purify the sons of
> Levi.
> - Malachi 3:1,3

And the messianic prophesy of Zechariah,

> And there shall no longer be a trader in the
> house of the Lord of hosts on that day.
> - Zechariah 14:21

Of one thing we can be sure; that particular act of Jesus in Abba's House was not to justify Christians butchering Christians as they have for centuries.

Instead of searching fruitlessly for bloody violence in Jesus' use of a whip in cleansing the Temple in Jerusalem, the church should be teaching the central meaning of the story: Jesus' Resurrection-Victory over evil, the foundation for the theology of Christian nonviolence.

The central truth in this incident is about the risen Christ, the new temple, in whom the church will worship the Father, not in Jerusalem in a Temple made with hands, but anywhere and everywhere in Spirit and in truth (See John 4:21-24). The temple's curtain separating the worshiper from God was torn to shreds when Jesus hung on the cross (Matthew 27:51).

In the risen, triumphant Christ, the repentant, believing soul abiding in Christ and His word would have access to Abba. The resulting relationship no longer depended upon any particular time or place (See Romans 5:2, Ephesians 2:18). A living relationship with a living Lord was now possible. Jesus Christ, Son of God, Savior, would now be the new temple, the God-Person in whom is our peace (Ephesians 2:14).

When the Pharisees expressed fear that Jesus was threatening their Temple, which took forty-six years to build, He replied, "Destroy this temple and in three days I will raise it up" (John 2:19).

In cleansing the Temple, Jesus was announcing to a fallen world that His indwelling Presence would become the new and living Temple for anyone who repents and abides in Him as a branch abides in the vine (John 15:3).

This is the significance of the removal of the symbolic Temple curtain separating God's people from the "Holy of Hollies", which could be entered only by one High Priest on one special day of the year. Now, Abba would be ever-present, everywhere, to every soul who seeks first God's peaceable kingdom established in Christ.

The crucified-risen-ascended-ruling-indwelling Lord of Life is the fulfillment of Ezekiel's vision of a new and living temple; not made with hands, in whose indwelling humankind's true nature is restored:

> I will make a covenant of peace with them. I
> will put my Spirit within you and will set my

sanctuary in the midst of them for evermore. My dwelling place shall be with them, and I will be their God, and they shall be my people. Then the nations will know that I the Lord sanctify Israel, when my sanctuary is in the midst of them for evermore.
- Ezekiel 36:27; 37:26:26-28

Instead of supporting the "just war" heresy, Jesus' cleansing of the Temple points to the coming of God's kingdom of peace to a warring world. As Paul explained it,

Now in Christ Jesus you who were once far off, have been brought near in the blood of Christ. . . For through Him we both have access in one Spirit to the Father. So then you are no longer strangers and sojourners, but you are fellow citizens with the saints and members of the household of God, built upon the foundation of the apostles and prophets, Christ Jesus Himself being the chief cornerstone, in whom the whole structure is joined and grows into a HOLY TEMPLE in the Lord.
- Ephesians 2:13-22

So, instead of justifying violence by the church, Jesus cleansing the Temple in Jerusalem is the gospel's good news that the crucified Jesus will be raised from the dead as the conqueror of evil and death and become God's living temple of the Holy Spirit whose fruit is shalom, the fulfillment of God's promise:

Steadfast love and faithfulness will meet; righteousness and peace will kiss each other.
- Psalm 85:10

Referring to this incident in the temple in his book, *Jesus*

129

Before Christianity, Albert Nolan argues that an organized group acted with Jesus to help Him clear the temple by stationing a peoples' army at the gates to prevent the merchants from continuing their business. The premise assumes Jesus did not disassociate Himself from the five thousand men who had gathered to hear Him on the day He fed them with a lad's two fish and five barley-loaves and wanted to force Jesus to become their king (John 6:15). He allowed these men to make Him their king and help drive from the Temple those who were using their religion for profit. This is Liberation Theology which makes of Jesus the leader of violent revolutions designed to throw off the yoke of political and economic bondage.

Two things are wrong with such a premise which has the five thousand following Jesus, not hesitating to use the sword against enemies. One, the story in the four Gospels does not say this. In the Temple Jesus acts alone. And, two, it contradicts the Spirit of the cross whose fruit of meekness and gentleness (Galatians 5:22) is the exact opposite of such violence. It manipulates the cleansing of the temple to fit the "just war" thesis of Liberation Theology. The purifying of God's House of prayer for all people cannot be used to justify human butchery. Never! No matter how "just" the cause.

According to Nolan, the only reason why Jesus did not lead His followers in a war against Rome was that He was a realist who knew that in the particular circumstances of that day, "war with Rome could only end in a wholesale massacre of the people". The circumstances Jesus found Himself in did not lend themselves to using the strategy of violent revolution. Against the power of the Roman Empire, there was no chance of success.

In different circumstances, Nolan states that Jesus probably would have acted differently to free the oppressed to establish justice in a society of equal opportunity for all the people. Nolan wrote,

> We do not know what he would have done in other possible circumstances. But we can surmise that if there had been no other way of defending the poor and the oppressed, and if there had been no danger of an escalation of violence, his unlimited compassion might have overflowed temporarily into violent indignation. He did tell his followers to carry swords to defend themselves, and he did clear the temple courtyard with some measure of violence (we have dealt with both of these). However, even in such cases, violence would have been a temporary measure with no other purpose than the prevention of some more serious violence. The kingdom of total liberation for all men cannot be established by violence. Faith alone can enable the kingdom to come.

This is the "just war" heresy that accepts and rejects violence at one and the same time. The "just war' church admits violence is wrong, but under certain conditions, permits whatever killing is necessary to right a wrong. This is the false doctrine that we are saved by faith in Jesus Christ; that the teachings of Jesus are true; that Jesus is the way, the truth, and the life, BUT that in certain circumstances, when evil no longer can be tolerated, the power of violent weapons must be used by Christians to resist the enemy.

This is not the gospel of "Jesus Christ, Son of God, Savior", whose kingdom is not at the mercy of evil and death. This is the gospel of loopholes, which gives Christians a way to ignore the commands of Jesus unless they are applied in the best of times. This is the GOSPEL OF BUTS, which theoretically accepts Jesus as Lord, BUT when the going gets rough, God's power of suffering love that Jesus enfleshed and teaches in His Sermon on the Mount is temporarily by-passed. God in Christ is not up to dealing with the really bad people like Hitler. Now, governing authorities in Christian nations must take over and call the shots aimed at the really wicked enemies. And the shots are as lethal as they can possibly be.

This is Augustine's Constantinian church mixing with the world and using the state's legalized mass murder to stop evil when the cause is "just"(good). Of course, in the eyes of the state which commands the killing, the cause is <u>always</u> considered "just". In Christendom, the church agrees with the state since ruling authorities that call the war "just" are almost always on the membership rolls of the church. In Christendom the people of the church and people of the state are almost always one and the same.

Luke 22:36
Why Jesus Told the Apostles to Buy Swords

Just before His arrest in the Garden of Gethsemane, Jesus asked the Twelve if they lacked anything when He sent them on their first mission without purse, bag, or shoes. When they answered, "Nothing, Lord," Jesus said to them, "But now whoever has a purse, or bag, must take it; and whoever does not have a sword must sell his coat and buy one" (Luke 22:36 TEV).

A quick and casual reading of these words does make Jesus appear to be advocating the use of the sword. Since the Scriptures are their own best commentary, let's examine Jesus' next words, which give us a clue to their meaning:

> For I tell you that the scripture which says, "He was counted among the outlaws" *(Isaiah 53:12 NEB)*, must come true about me, because what was written about me is coming true.
> - Luke 22:37

These words of Scripture Jesus was quoting, "He was counted among the outlaws," are part of the twelve verses in the 53rd chapter of Isaiah, the Old Testament's clearest picture of the promised Messiah. From the beginning of Jesus' public ministry until that very hour, friend and foe alike were comparing the Lord's life and teaching to such messianic prophecies to determine whether Jesus was the true Messiah the Old Testament promises, or whether they would have to look for another (See Mark 13:21-23). The Twelve were well acquainted with this messianic prophecy which linked the Messiah with outlaws and swords. So, in those last moments, wanting to reassure the Twelve that He was the Messiah Isaiah prophesied would come, Jesus said they should sell their coats and buy a sword. The reference to swords fulfilled the words of Isaiah's prophecy, "He shared the fate of evil men" (Isaiah 53:12 TEV).

On the cross, Jesus did share the fate of evil outlaws who had used swords to steal and kill. He did this not to teach His disciples the way of violence, but to teach his church that the Father receives into his Paradise all who repent and surrender to the rule of His Spirit, even thieves and murderers (See Luke 23:43).

The Lord's very next words to the Apostles clearly confirm the fact that Jesus was not urging His disciples to rush out and arm themselves with swords. When Jesus told the Twelve to buy a sword, they responded, "Look, Lord, here are two swords." Jesus answered, "That is enough." (Luke 22:38)

Obviously, two swords would not have been enough for a band of twelve men to defend themselves if their trust for security had been in violent power.

If Jesus had really wanted Peter and the others to go forth on their mission with swords flashing, instead of two swords,

133

He would have said, "Buy ten more. Stockpile as many swords as you can get your hands on. You will need them to combat evil." A few minutes later, the Good Shepherd illustrated that He does not want His flock to use the weapons of the world, when one Apostle, panic stricken, used a sword to protect Jesus. They all heard the Master's sharp rebuke:

> Put up your sword. All those who take the
> sword will perish by the sword.
> - Matthew 26:52

The sword is part of a perishing world of violence, not a part of our Father's imperishable kingdom of reconciling love. At best, a sword may temporarily restrain evil. Man's sword does not redeem or reconcile. Only the power of the cross accomplishes this purpose to which the church is called to witness.

Again, a few hours later, Jesus' words to Pilate should leave no doubt whatsoever about the nonviolent nature of God's peaceable kingdom:

> My kingdom doesn't belong to this world. If
> it did, my followers would have fought to
> keep me from being handed over to our
> leaders.
> - John 18:36 CE

If Jesus wanted His church to fight, He would have said so, just as Mohammed told his followers in the Koran. Over and over again in Islam's Scriptures, Mohammed speaks as he does in Surah II, 191:

> Persecution is worse than slaughter. If they
> attack you, then slay them. Such is the reward
> of disbelievers.

Jesus had the intelligence to make His instructions clear. His teaching of nonviolence is perfectly clear to all who abide in Abba's Holy Spirit. The problem is not a lack of clarity; it is a lack of trust and obedience. That the Apostles understood Jesus' clear teaching which has no place for lethal weapons, is clear both from their nonviolent lifestyle and their writings. Paul wrote,

> For though we live in the world we are not carrying on a worldly war, for the weapons of our warfare are not worldly but have divine power to destroy strongholds.
> - 2 Corinthians 10:4

Peter wrote,

> Christ suffered for you, leaving you an example that you should follow in his steps. When he was reviled, he did not revile in return, but he trusted in him who judges justly.
> - 1 Peter 2:21-23

John wrote,

> God is love. We love because God first loved us. If someone says he loves God, but hates his brother, he is a liar. For he cannot love God whom he has not seen, if he does not love his brother whom he has seen.
> - John 4:16,19-20

James wrote,

> What causes wars, and what causes fighting among you? Is it not your passions that are at war in your members? You desire and do not

have, so you kill. And you covet and cannot
obtain, so you fight and wage war. Unfaithful
creatures! Do you not know that friendship
with the world is enmity with God?
- James 4:1-6

The Apostles were faithful in teaching what they had learned
from their Teacher, not only in words, but also in the Spirit
and deeds Jesus lived. As we have seen, the apostolic church
consistently responded nonviolently to those who physically
attacked them.

In turn, the pupils of the Twelve such as Ignatius, Overseer
of the church at Antioch, and Polycarp who shepherded the
Lord's flock at Smyrna, and Irenaeus who served the church
in Lyons, all willingly suffered and died at the hands of
enemies <u>without ever raising a fist or using a sword to
defend themselves</u>. Their security was the Eternal's sword of
the Spirit, walking in the Messiah's Resurrection-Life that
has overcome sin's world of violence and death

Hippolytus, a pupil of Irenaeus and a pastor in the early
church, instructed catechumins for church membership in
these words:

> The soldier who is of inferior rank shall not
> kill anyone. If ordered to, he shall not carry
> out the order, nor shall he take the oath. If he
> does not accept this, let him be dismissed.
> Anyone who has the power of the sword, or
> the magistrate of a city, who wears the purple,
> let him give it up or be dismissed. The
> catechumin who wishes to become a soldier
> shall be dismissed, because this is far from
> God.

Pastors in the early church did not need one official
catechism to spell out Jesus' nonviolent Way of the Cross.

Given His Sermon on the Mount (Matthew 5-7, His New Commandment (John 13:34), and their New Creation in Christ (2 Corinthians 5:17), Jesus' nonviolent Spirit was taken for granted, like the rising and setting of the sun.

Justin Martyr was on his way to his accustomed place of meditation on the Mediterranean coast when his path crossed that of an old and venerable Christian, who explained to Justin the futility of searching for God with the mind. This elderly saint led Justin from Plato to the prophets and from the prophets to Jesus. Said Justin, "Straightway a flame was kindled in my soul; and a love of the prophets and of those men who are friends of Christ."

After his conversion, Justin Martyr went about teaching that Christians are "purified by the blood of Christ of all that makes for war and violence". In one of Justin's sermons, they heard him say:

> From Jerusalem twelve men went out into the world, unlearned, unable to speak; but by the power of God they told every race of men that they had been sent by Christ to teach all the world of God. And we, who were formerly slayers of one another, not only do not make war upon our enemies, but for the sake of neither lying nor deceiving those who examine us, gladly die confessing Christ.

In defending the church from the charge that their refusal to bear arms would leave the Empire weak and defenseless, Justin told the emperor that Christians were the best allies and helpers Rome could possibly have. He compared what the state offers its citizens to what God offers citizens of his kingdom. Emperors can offer their soldiers "nothing incorruptible; but, we," said Justin, "loving what is incorruptible, endure all things for the sake of receiving what we long for from Him who is able to give it." Justin knew that he was part of an imperishable kingdom, greater than the temporary Roman Empire; that the victory he shared with Jesus' church was greater than any victory the soldiers of Rome could win on the battlefield. Loving his enemies as Jesus did, Justin Martyr was executed by the Roman state in 165, as his Teacher had been put to death more than a century before.

The practice of nonviolent love by these pupils of the Apostles is undeniable proof that the New Testament church did not sell their coats to buy swords and use them in combating evil. These disciples of Jesus knew that their crucified and risen Lord had already defeated the enemy. To this truth the church witnessed then, and is called to witness now, that the world may believe that Jesus is the Lamb of God who takes away the sin of the world (John 1:29), including the sin of war.

One of the main reasons why ordained pastors and priests do not witness forthrightly to the gospel's clear teaching of nonviolence is that the membership of their local congregations has become so diverse in its thinking. Pastors know that to reject all war as the early church did for centuries would alienate most of their members who would demand their resignation. It's much easier not to rock the boat and let the "just war" institutional church sail in quiet waters with the national and Christian flags side by side, giving them equal devotion. In this way, pastors rationalize drifting with the world's "just war" political-patriotic currents. In so doing, the shepherd offers little help to the flock when it comes to the congregation's understanding and practice of Jesus' Way of nonviolent agape, the best kept secret of "just war' mainline churches.

It's a kind of vicious circle. To understand Christian nonviolence, the congregation must be thoroughly instructed about the nonviolent nature of the crucified-risen-ascended-ruling-indwelling Spirit. But immediately such teaching becomes suspect by members who have imbibed from birth the "just war" gospel of Nationalism. In their mind, faith in God and fighting their country's wars are one and the same.

The peaceable kingdom the Lord Jesus said is "at hand"(Mark 1:14) is postponed until Heaven, hardly a challenge since only angelic saints dwell there. Whatever is not willingly desired on earth cannot be forced in Heaven. Contrary to Bishop Augustine, God's Spirit of agape cannot be compelled. Satan does not deny the truth of the Holy One's nonviolent Way of the Cross. He only deceives the church that loving enemies must wait until Jesus comes again and we enter Heaven. Killing people here and now in a less than perfect world hardly prepares the saints to love enemies in heaven's perfect future where only the saints abide.

Matthew 10:34
The Sword of Jesus Divides

> Do not think that I have come to bring peace
> on earth; I have not come to bring peace, but a
> sword.
> - Matthew 10:34

Lifted out of the paragraph in which they occur, these words of Jesus could support the "just war' teaching of mainline Catholic, Protestant, Orthodox and Pentecostal churches. However, their meaning could not be clearer when read within the context of the whole paragraph in which they were spoken. These words follow:

> For I have come to set a man against his
> father, and a daughter against her mother, and
> a daughter-in-law against her mother-in-law;
> and a man's foes will be those of his own
> household. He who loves father and mother
> more than me is not worthy of me; and he

139

who loves son or daughter more than me is not worthy of me; and he who does not take up his cross and follow me is not worthy of me. He who finds his life will lose it, and he who loses his life for my sake will find it.
- Matthew 10:35-39

Obviously, Jesus is not talking about the violent sword of the military that kills. The God-Revelation He incarnated does not run parallel with the world and its systems. Life in the Holy Spirit of God's kingdom on earth creates a counter culture hostile to our self-centered desires and demands. This is why the Christian life necessitates a NEW BIRTH, which the world cannot understand and therefore opposes.

The sword of Jesus' Spirit does separate His disciples from those family members who are all wrapped up in family fame and name. Their lesser loyalties clash with our citizenship in the kingdom in which Jesus is in all and above all (Colossians 3:11). There is no sweet peace in a family whose loyalties and loves crisscross between love of Jesus and love of the world. Lifestyles clash. Although the fruit of the Spirit is patience and gentleness and will try to make life in the family as pleasant as possible, the Christ-Spirit does not compromise convictions just to have peace and cheery conversation in the home. If witness for Christ does not begin in the home, it soon ends. Jesus relates to us as friend, but true friends put truth before cheery froth.

This was St. Paul's counsel to the church. "Whatever is true, whatever is honorable, whatever is just, whatever is pure, whatever is lovely, whatever is gracious, if there is any excellence, if there is anything worthy of praise, think about these things and the God of peace will be with you" (Philippians 4:8-9). Such thinking will be expressed within the family and it will always separate believers from those whose minds are bound by the world (See 2 Corinthians 4:2-6).

Mark 12:17
What Belongs to God?

> Render unto Caesar the things that are
> Caesar's, and unto God the things that are
> God's.
> - Mark 12:17

It is difficult to understand how serious readers of the gospel could use these words of Jesus to give their absolute allegiance to the state when ruling authorities declare war and give the command to take up arms and slaughter. This mirrors the opposite of Jesus' teaching in His Sermon on the Mount. In a time of national crisis, does the authority of Caesar's command suddenly supersede that of "Jesus Christ, Son of God, Savior"? It is this Jesus who said,

> A new commandment I give to you, that you
> love one another, even as I have loved you.
> -John 13:34

Christians love as Jesus loves, not as Caesar loves. Jesus' love is unconditional, and includes enemies. Caesar's love is quid-pro-quo conditional love that loves only those who have something considered good to give back. For the church to equate what is given to Caesar with what is given to the Creator is nothing less than blasphemy.

Again, it is necessary to examine the context in which Jesus spoke these words:

The Herodians and Pharisees were trying to set a trap for Jesus, asking Jesus whether it is in keeping with the law for Jews to pay taxes to a foreign power? If Jesus answered "No", He would be in trouble with Caesar. If He answered, "Yes", He would be in trouble with the people who were already overburdened with heavy taxes levied by an occupying tyrant.

Jesus requested that they bring Him a coin, the kind used to pay taxes to Rome. Looking at the money, Jesus asked, "Whose image is on the coin?" When they answered, "The image of Caesar", Jesus told them to "render unto Caesar the things that are Caesar's and unto God the things that are God's." The question being discussed is about the authority of rulers to levy taxes to pay the state's bills for building roads and water systems and the like. It is not about the authority of rulers to declare war and demand citizens to join in the mass killing. Jesus not only failed to command His church to kill for the state; He told Pilate His followers do not fight (John 18:36).

Those who set the trap were amazed at Jesus' answer and say no more. No long debate ensues. The issue is over and done with. There is not the slightest hint that "render unto Caesar the things that are Caesar's" means blind submission to ruling authorities who demand that everyone – even members of the Body of Christ – defend the state by taking up arms and killing those they are told to kill.

Dorothy Day, founder of the Catholic Worker movement, said, "If you render to God the things that are God's, there will be nothing left for Caesar." Dorothy was a Christian who understood that when she put Jesus and His kingdom on one side of the scale and Caesar and his kingdom on the other, the weighed value of God's side was infinite, whereas the weight of Caesar's side of the scale was insignificant. What we are to render to the Lord Jesus is absolute!

> You shall love the Lord your God with ALL your heart, and with ALL your soul, and with ALL your mind. This is the first and great commandment. And a second is like unto it, You shall love your neighbor as yourself.
> - Matthew 22:37-39

When God's ALL is on one side of the scale, how can there be something equal on the other side? Caesar is a mortal and sinful man. God is the Eternal who redeems us of sin. If we render to the Creator and Redeemer what belongs to Him, there can be very little left to render Caesar, except a few dollars for labor and material.

Mainline churches disagree, saying there is much which is left for Caesar, and they use as support Romans 13:1-5. Let's now look at this classic "just war" proof text.

Romans 13:1-5
To Submit is Not to Conform

> Everyone must submit himself to the governing authorities, for there is no authority except that which God has established. The authorities that exist have been established by God. Consequently, he who rebels against the authority is rebelling against that which God has instituted and those who do so will bring judgment on themselves. For rulers hold no terror for those who do right, but for those who do wrong. Do you want to be free from fear of the one in authority? Then do what is right and he will commend you. For he is God's servant to do good. But if you do wrong, be afraid, for he does not bear the sword for nothing. He is God's servant, an agent of wrath to bring punishment on the wrong doer. Therefore, it is necessary to submit to the authorities, not only because of possible punishment but also because of conscience.
> - Romans 13:1-5 NIV

More than any part of the New Testament, these words of

Paul are used by the church to justify engaging in wars that kill, maim, rape, lie, steal, destroy homes, hospitals, schools, cause disease and sickness—the very opposite of the abundant life Jesus offers a sick world (John 10:10). Why would Paul, the foremost evangelist of the Apostolic church, insert these several sentences in his letter to the church at Rome to proclaim a completely different gospel of violence and war, contradicting the whole gospel he proclaimed. In the preceding chapter of this same letter, he wrote:

> Do not be conformed to this world . . . Let love be genuine; hate what is evil, hold fast to what is good. . . be aglow with the Spirit. Bless those who persecute you . . . Repay no one evil for evil . . . so far as it depends upon you, live peaceably with all. Beloved, never avenge yourselves, but leave it to the wrath of God; for is it written, "Vengeance is mine, I will repay, says the Lord." No, if your enemy is hungry, feed him; if he is thirsty, give him drink; for by so doing you will heap burning coals upon his head." Do not be overcome by evil, but overcome evil with good.
> - Excerpts from Romans 12

To go from this Spirit of Christ on one page to the spirit of the world on the next does not reflect Paul's thinking. Of one thing we can be sure; after his conversion, Paul refused to conform to the world which Rome represented. We can also be sure that in these five verses, Paul was not formulating a doctrine of church-state relations for the next two thousand years. With the other Apostles, Paul was expecting the Lord's return within his own lifetime (See 1 Thessalonians 4:13-18; 1 Corinthians 7:29-31). Paul believed the time was short when the Lord would return. For this reason Paul concluded it would be better for single persons not to marry (See 1 Corinthians 7:29), a teaching the church soon had to discard.

In Romans 13:1-5, Paul is dealing with the members of a particular church in Rome and their attitude toward particular ruling authorities in light of their special circumstances. As in all of his letters, Paul was dealing with thorny specific questions a church faced. Nothing is as irrelevant as answers to questions which are not being asked. Paul was dealing with questions he knew the church in Rome was troubled about.

We can also be certain of this: Paul's answer to every question was always illuminated by the eternal light of truth that shines in Jesus Christ. There are many questions, but only one gospel and one Lord who does not change with the questions asked (See Ephesians 4:4-5). For Paul every passage of Scripture had to be interpreted within the context of God's self-revelation in Christ (John 5:39).

Each verse and chapter of Scripture does not have its own truth. In fact, the division of books of the Bible into chapters and verses is relatively recent. Stephen Langton, a professor in Paris who later became Archbishop of Canterbury, is said to be the first to make such divisions in the thirteenth century.

In Christ, all verses and chapters of the gospel hold together (Colossians 1:17). The gospel has the same meaning from Matthew to Revelation.

What, then, was Paul counseling the church in Rome to do when he wrote, "Everyone must submit himself to the governing authorities."? (Romans 13:1)

In Rome's political center, Christians were not sure what their relationship to governing authorities should be. Located in the capital of the Roman Empire, the church in Rome where the Emperor was enthroned was undoubtedly wrestling with the question, What should our attitude and relationship be toward the ruling authorities?

Only twenty-five years old, the church was spreading like wildfire across the Roman Empire. The more the Way spread, the more Caesar saw the church as a threat. No longer regarded by Rome as a tiny insignificant Jewish sect, the Way of Jesus was now looked upon with growing suspicion.

To understand the climate of the time, it was only five years after Paul wrote this letter to the church in Rome that the most serious fire ever to afflict that city raged for more than a week. Nero blamed Christians and persecuted them as the madman that he was. Many of Jesus disciples were put to death to provide the Romans with entertainment. Christians had become a marked people, Number One on Rome's "hit list". How should Christians react? Should they submit peacefully or offer violent resistance to such ruling authority? This was the question to which Paul was speaking.

We can understand how members of the church in Rome must have been strongly tempted, not only to defend themselves against such political madness, but also to join forces with the Zealots and others. These people were urging Christians to follow their strategy to remove the tyrant from the holy land. In this geographical area, their Lord and Savior had His public ministry, died on a cross, left behind an empty grave, and ascended into heaven. It was here that the church was born on Pentecost and housed their central headquarters in Jerusalem.

Simon, one of the Twelve had come from the Zealots, a militant group that regarded Jesus' mission and their task almost entirely as the recovery of Palestine's political independence. They were convinced that acceptance of foreign domination and paying taxes to Caesar must end. In

146

the eyes of the Zealots, Rome's occupation of Palestine was blasphemy against the Holy One of Israel. Less than eight years later, their armed rebellion against Rome's ruling authorities broke out in fury. The rebellion went on for four years, resulting in the devastation of Judea and Galilee, the burning of the Temple in Jerusalem, and the near destruction of the entire city.

It was in this climate of uncertainty that Paul counseled the church in Rome to "Submit!" and not to take it upon itself to be the instrument of God's wrath. This was not the role of the church. Paul wrote these words to keep the newly born church from moving toward anarchy and becoming completely contemptuous of the state, wasting time and energy as a revolutionary sect fighting the state and Rome's authorities. Paul understood that the Zealots merely wanted a change of government—from Roman to Jewish. Jesus wanted a change of one's total life—from self-centered to God-centered, from flesh-centered to Spirit-centered; a new creation in a totally different kingdom.

Paul was counseling the church to submit to the Roman government, just as Jesus had submitted to Pilate. He was saying, "Do not resist violently when the ruling authorities treat you harshly as public enemies. Submit. Do not join the rebellion to drive Rome from Jerusalem and the Homeland of the church. Submit. The church of Jesus has a different mission with different weapons than the world uses to fight and conquer" (See 2 Corinthians 10:4; Ephesians 6:10-20). Submit! God is in control. The victory is already ours in Christ.

For Paul to "submit" was totally consistent with Jesus, who in submitting to Pilate, trusted wholly in the power of God to overcome evil in sin's fallen world. To make "submit" to the state mean fight alongside the state and its armed forces of violence is heresy! Such teaching is not in harmony with the gospel of the New Testament. It is a wrong handling of the word of God Paul warned the church to avoid.

Looking back, we now know from history that Christians <u>did not</u> join the rebel movement that went to war against Rome. The church did not fight to defend Jerusalem. The church submitted nonviolently. That no Christian joined the rebellion (A.D.66-70) to free Jerusalem is evidence that the church in the city of Rome and throughout the Empire obeyed Paul's counsel to <u>submit and not fight</u>.

To submit is not to conform. Jesus submitted. He did not conform, saying,

> My kingdom is not of this world. If it were
> my servants would fight.
> - John 18:36

Paul submitted to Rome, but he did not conform to Rome. This is why Rome finally executed Paul. They feared his counter-culture lifestyle.

To submit and refuse to kill and destroy is not to do nothing. Rather is it to confront the evil Powers and Principalities with the weapons of Abba, who has <u>already triumphed</u> over sin's world of violence and death (See Colossians 2:15) and calls His church to witness to His victory by refusing to use a fallen world's weapons to combat evil. Paul recognized that in a fallen world there is a role for government. <u>Where sin abounds</u>, law is necessary to restrain. But Paul knew that law and its coercive power is never redemptive.

A Jew, Paul was a student of the Old Testament, a child of Israel that had demanded a king in order to be ruled like all other nations. Paul knew the Holy One's answer to Samuel whose instruction to Israel had always been "Let El rule! Only God is our Ruler."

If they demand to be ruled by the authority of
a king, so let it be. They have not rejected
you, they have rejected me.
- 1 Samuel 8:7

The rule of the Eternal Spirit in the kingdom of God cannot
be forced. Israel rejected the rule and authority of God's
Spirit, demanding to be ruled by the authority of man's law
enforced by coercive power. God permitted Israel to be ruled
by the authority of human government and its military force
(See 1 Samuel 8:6-18), but because of their decision, Israel
experienced the wrath of God like all other nations. For this
reason it was taken into captivity. As we shall see, God used
pagan rulers and armies of state to accomplish this.

Then Paul added these words which certainly tend to
confuse: "He who rebels against the authority is rebelling
against what God has instituted, and those who do will bring
judgment on themselves. For rulers hold no terror for those
who do right, but for those who do wrong" (Romans 13:2-3).

How is the church to interpret these words of Paul? Jesus did
no wrong, but ruling authorities executed Him. The Apostles
did no wrong, but, except for John, they were all put to death
by the ruling authorities of Rome. And John was a prisoner
of Rome when he put in writing his vision of Jesus' victory
over sin's violence and death to encourage a host of others
who were being persecuted and put to death by the state
(Revelation 13:10, 14:12). The history of nations is largely
the history of war and the brutality of ruling authorities, even
in a democracy. How could Paul tell the church that "rulers
hold no terror for those who do right?" History proves
otherwise. In a short time Paul, himself, would be executed
by the state, but not for doing wrong.

Paul's statement, "Rulers hold no terror to those who do
right" may have been linked to his plan to visit Rome which
he announced in his letter (Romans 16:22-33). Paul knew his

149

letter would certainly come to the attention of the ruling authorities in Rome and wanted them to see him as he truly was: a peace-maker, not a trouble-maker. Paul wanted the authorities in Rome to see his visit to the empire's capitol as a journey of peace—as a leader counseling submission—not political revolution. Paul did not want his visit to add fuel to the fire of political strife, so he pictured the ruling authorities as benefactors, not beasts. Moreover, Paul had an inkling that he would be arriving in Rome as a prisoner to be put on trial for his life. If so, as a citizen of Rome, he hoped for a fair trial, that his life would be spared for a few more years of witnessing and proclaiming the gospel of God's peaceable kingdom (Romans 15:30-33).

As the evangelist of the Spirit's agape who "bears all things, believes all things, hopes all things, and endures all things" (1 Corinthians 13:7), Paul hoped his optimistic description of Rome's ruling authorities as "rulers who are not a terror to good conduct . . only God's servants for your good", would hold true when he stood before his judges. He would face them, not in terror and in fear, but in the confident hope that they would act as God's servants, concerned only for his good. Therefore, in his letter, Paul described ruling authorities as God intends them to be, as friends and not foes, in terms of their best, not their worst.

From the Book of Acts, we know that, at first, the ruling authorities were friendly to Paul. His optimism was justified. They allowed him a private residence for two years, during which time he had the opportunity to argue his case and welcome visitors who came to hear him teach the kingdom of God and proclaim the gospel (Acts 18:23-31). But then there is a sudden turn of events. The state acts as the Beast in Revelation, executing Paul as Rome did to Peter and countless others in the Apostolic Church. Paul's optimistic hope in the goodness of the state was not fulfilled.

Should we conclude that the State is always a mixture of the

Benefactor and the Beast? A mixture, yes, but the mix is always self-protecting and self-serving. The State is always the authority of law enforced by police and military power to preserve and protect its own national welfare. Soldiers and police are never absent from the State. The state cannot survive apart from coercive force which can temporarily restrain, never eternally redeem, which is the mission of Jesus and His church.

Also, we must ask what Paul meant when he called ruling authorities "God's servants who do not use the sword in vain" (Romans 13:4), again words often used to justify war? The answer to this question is found within the Bible itself. In the Old Testament Scriptures in which Paul had been thoroughly trained, God called Nebuchadnezzar, the pagan king of Babylonia, "my servant" (Jeremiah 27:6). Why? Because the Holy One of Israel made use of this pagan ruler's sword to punish Jerusalem and Judah because of their idolatry. Pagan Nebuchadnezzar <u>was acting as God's servant</u> by taking the Israelites into exile in a strange land, not to destroy them, but to "put them in fire to refine them as one refines silver, and test them as gold is tested" (Zechariah 13:9).

In the same way, Isaiah saw Cyrus, the Persian ruler, as God's servant who allowed the Jews to return from exile and rebuild the walls of Jerusalem. Indeed. The pagan ruler Cyrus is pictured as more than God's servant. The Holy One of Israel says of Cyrus,

> He is my shepherd and will accomplish all that I please; he will say of Jerusalem, "Let it be rebuilt," and of the temple, "Let its foundation be laid." This is what the Lord says to his anointed, to Cyrus, whose right hand I take hold of.
> - Isaiah 44:28; 45:1

So it is. The Sovereign One can, and does, use the sword of ruling authorities to serve His purpose, even when they are totally unaware of His existence and peace-plan in Christ. It is in this sense that Paul refers to the ruling authorities as "servants of God", even though they do not know God. In fallen Babylon in which the human race is born and in which ruling authorities are always present, the Ruler of the universe uses the sword of the state to chastise and lead to repentance those whom He loves, longing to lead them out of Babylon into his kingdom the Book of Revelation calls "New Jerusalem" (See Revelation 3:12).

Paul knew that God uses the sword of the state to restrain and punish evildoers and, for this reason, called ruling authorities "servants of God who do not use the sword in vain." However, it is crucial to understand that the church of Christ is God's servant in a different sense, not to restrain evil, not to condemn and punish, but to be the Lord's instrument of reconciling love that overcomes evil (2 Corinthians 5:18-20) with good, called to witness to Jesus' victory over violence and death and to walk in the Spirit.

Nebuchadnezzar was a "servant of God" in expressing God's wrath. We of the church are called to be servants of God to demonstrate Abba's unconditional love; it is the love which Jesus revealed on the cross and which fleshed out God's victory over sin's violence and death by the glorious resurrection of Jesus. It is imperative not to get the two mixed, as the "just war" church does.

The difference between church and state should be as different as day and night. Part of a fallen world, the state is a nation whose laws are designed to promote the welfare of its people and do what is necessary to survive. The church is the self-giving body of God's redeemed people from every nation-state (Galatians 3:13), a new breed of humans called to witness to Jesus' Resurrection-Victory over the power of

Evil and share God's eternal life by abiding in Jesus and His word. This is in contrast to the fallen body of nation-states whose power mimics and mirrors the very same self-concern and spirit of self-determination, which drove Adam and Eve from the peace of Paradise. There is no peace in the body of law enforced by coercive power, at best only partial justice which leaves people as far apart as ever.

The authority of the nation-state that Israel hankered to be represents a different authority and ruling power than the power of God's Holy Spirit Israel was called to be and rejected. As all the prophets reminded Israel, they were a chosen people called to trust the Holy One to save them from evil and death, not to put their trust in human power for their security and well being (Isaiah 31:1).

The psalmist cried out,

> Put not your trust in princes, in a son of man, in whom there is no help. Trust in the Lord and do good, so you will dwell in the land and enjoy security.
> - Psalm 146:3, 37:3

Isaiah shouted,

> Woe to those who go down to Egypt for help and rely on horses, who trust in chariots because they are many, and in horsemen because they are very strong, but do not look to the Holy One of Israel or consult the Lord.
> - Isaiah 31:1

Jeremiah warned,

> Cursed is the man who trusts in man and makes flesh his arm, whose heart turns away

153

from the Lord. Blessed is the man who trusts in the Lord.
- Jeremiah 17:5,7

The Apostles and early church were of one heart and mind in saying with Saint Paul:

> If then you have been raised with Christ, seek the things that are above, where Christ is, seated at the right hand of God. Set your minds on things that are above, not on things that are on earth. For you have died and your life is hid with Christ in God. When Christ who is our life appears, then you also will appear with him in glory.

> Put to death therefore what is earthly in you: fornication, impurity, passion, evil desire and covetousness which is idolatry. On account of these the wrath of God is coming. In these you once walked. But now put them all away: anger, wrath, malice, slander and foul talk from your mouth. Do not lie to one another, seeing that you have put off the old nature with its practices, and have put on the new nature which is being renewed in knowledge after the image of the creator. Christ is all and in all.

> Put on then as God's chosen ones, holy and beloved, compassion, kindness, lowliness, meekness, and patience, forbearing one another, and, if one has a complaint against another, forgiving each other as the Lord has forgiven you. And above all these, put on love which binds everything together in perfect harmony. And let the peace of Christ rule in your hearts, to which indeed you were called

as one body. And be thankful. Let the word of Christ dwell in you richly. And whatever you do, in word or deed, do everything in the name of the Lord Jesus.
- Colossians 3: 1-17

This is the gospel Paul proclaimed. Romans 13:1-5 and our life as the church must be in harmony with it. There is no place in it for violent thoughts and actions. Therefore, as Christians, let us be true to our mission, and stop mimicking a fallen world and its nation-states. Let every church be the peace church Jesus intends us to be. Let us submit to the state as servants of Jesus and His peaceable kingdom, not as slaves of the state and its systems of violence. Let us handle the word of God in the Spirit of the Prince of Peace who calls us to be His ambassadors of reconciliation.

Amen. So let it be.

Chapter 6

The Peace Church That Continues to Live in Christ

> That through the church the manifold wisdom
> of God might now be made known . . . Christ
> himself being the cornerstone, in whom the
> whole structure is joined together and grows
> into a holy temple in the Lord; in whom you
> also are built into it for a dwelling place of
> God in the Spirit.
> - Ephesians 3:10; 2:20-22

According to a legend, when Jesus ascended to the "right hand of God", He was asked by the angels what other plan He had to carry on His mission if the Apostles failed. Jesus replied, "I have no other plan. I'm counting on them."

Jesus is counting on His church, on ordinary people like you and me, to enflesh God's peaceable kingdom on earth and make known His agapic kingdom to a fallen world of violence and war. He has no back-up plan.

We have seen how the church went from a lowly servant church meeting in homes to a powerful imperial church of cathedrals and state-paid priests; from a persecuted to a persecuting church; from a nonviolent free church to a violent state-linked church; from a Christ-like to a world-like church. Now we will see how some in the church protested and retained a life-style more consistent with Jesus' life and teaching and live as a community molded by the power of agape, not by the economic forces of the market place and the violent systems of the state.

This chapter will help us see various forms of the alternative to the "just war" state. We will see the church seeking to love as Jesus loves by living, moment by moment, in a community shaped by mutual loving care and sharing life; living as the Family of God, envisioned to include all of God's children. None of them is the perfect answer to the question, what is the alternative to life shaped by the politics of the state? But we will see the direction in which the Holy Spirit moves and would direct the church.

The Monastic Movement
A Protest within the Established Church

One protest movement to the imperial church was monasticism, which brings Jesus' disciples together in community where each day they share their whole life as a family of God. So many were attracted to monastic life that it threatened to create a separate church within the church. The threat was resolved only as bishops themselves became sponsors and organizers of monasteries. In this way, the movement was kept under the control of the established church, which prevented a complete rejection of the Catholic "just war" doctrine. In the fifth and sixth centuries, every leader in the church was either a monk himself or was closely linked to monasticism.

Women were not involved in the beginning when monastic life in the desert was completely solitary and marked by extreme individualism. Hermits often competed with each other to see who could stand longest on one leg without food. Simeon Stylites lived for thirty years on the top of a stone column.

From Solitary Life to Solidarity

Because God's Holy Spirit leads to solidarity, not solitary life, the monastic movement soon became cenobitic which comes from the Greek, "koinos bios", which means "common life". In 320, the Holy Spirit led Pachomius to establish the first cenobitic monastery in southern Egypt. A converted soldier, Pachomius went to the desert to live a solitary life as a hermit, but ended up founding the first cenobitic monastery in which hermits enjoyed a common life: working, eating, and praying together as a family. Because the cenobitic experience is more in keeping with the deepest human needs, the movement flourished.

It was about this time that women were attracted to the movement. By the end of the Middle Ages, there were almost as many nuns as monks. Eventually, all of the major monastic Orders had nunneries.

Wearing a common garb, living in adjoining rooms, and taking the vow of poverty, chastity, and obedience, monks performed worthwhile tasks, which included excellent translations of the Bible and the development of self-supporting communities with the best of farms, schools, and libraries. Monks wove their own cloth, constructed whatever buildings were necessary, grew their own food, and with their own water supply, fishpond, poultry yard, and the like, the community accepted full responsibility for their common life. Idleness was not permitted.

As monastic communities spontaneously spread throughout the Roman Empire, different leaders wrote different Orders for their communities. In 529, on the heights of Monte Cassino, Benedict, after a time of trial and error, initiated what was to become the model monastery for all of Europe.

Calling for a well-balanced life with discipline for hands, mind, and soul, and with fixed times for each, the monastic community was looked upon as a spiritual fortress in a hostile world. It was a rigorous life, and no one could enter its service until he or she had tried it for at least a year.

Relaxed Discipline

Though strenuous, monastic life was also relaxed. The Benedictine Order allowed seven twenty-minute periods in the day's schedule for quiet prayer and meditation. Monasteries had a great attraction because they provided the best opportunity for study, for worker's protection, for mutual care and social inter-action, and for respite from a fallen world's constant warfare.

Monks and nuns also had social concerns for people outside the monastery. For example, about a hundred years after the church made its tragic alliance with Constantine and the state, Telemachus, a monk who lived in Asia Minor, laid down his life to stop the bloodshed in the popular gladiatorial games which had been going on for centuries to entertain pagans. Many of the church flocked to the public arena to enjoy these bloody spectacles. Not only animals were brought to the arena to fight each other until one was dead, human gladiators were pitted against each other. Usually they were prisoners who had already been condemned to death. This was their "fighting chance" to escape death by killing their opponents. As the gladiators walked to the center of the arena, the excited spectators thirsted for blood.

Telemachus the Martyr

That Christians enjoyed watching such violence disturbed Telemachus so deeply that one day Abba's Spirit of agape led him to the Colosseum, where he took upon himself the suffering and death of the victims. Just as the deadly combat between two young men with swords was about to begin, Telemachus ran into the arena. Holding the cross above his head, he threw himself between the two combatants and shouted,

"In the name of Jesus, our Master, stop fighting!"

Nothing like this had ever happened before. The spectators were furious. This man with the cross was interfering with their sport. They became a screaming mob and stampeded into the arena. With sticks and stones, they pummeled Telemachus to death.

There at the center of Rome's Colosseum lay the little battered body of the monk. Suddenly the mob grew quiet. They had come to watch gladiators butcher each other. Now they had battered a human being to death because he had protested their degraded entertainment. The Roman Emperor, Honorius, rose from his elevated chair and left the Colosseum. Slowly the people followed. The bloody sport ended abruptly for that day. In 404, it ended for all days by imperial decree because a monk had the courage to expose its evil.

Monks Try to Stop Killing

Needed in our age of brutal killing are not more abstract discussions on the subject of violence so much as millions of Christians crying out with Telemachus, "In the name of God, stop the killing," and refusing to participate in the war system.

In the tenth century, Cluny monks devised a plan called "The Peace of God" which tried to limit the frequent violent conflicts between feudal princes. It forbade the army of a prince from attacking priests, nuns, merchants, farmers and their animals, and "women traveling without their husbands, unless they were to blame." Saying it's OK for Christians to kill, so long as they kill the right people, "The Peace of God", though with good intentions, was not, and is not, the solution of the church to the problem of war.

The Cluny monks also devised another plan to control feudal warfare called the "Truce of God". This law forbade fighting from sunset on Wednesday to sunrise on Monday morning, and on holy days. Even if the feudal lords had abided by that rule, there were still a lot of days left on the calendar for killing each other. To restrict killing to certain days on the church calendar is like saying that stealing and raping are permissible on Mondays, Wednesdays, and Fridays, but are forbidden by the church on all other days.

Violence can no more be controlled by law limiting war to certain days or certain people than a bag of feathers thrown into the wind can be controlled. The Cluny Order tried to enforce the "Truce of God" by using the power of excommunication within the sacramental church system, which had been woven into the fabric of the monastic movement, and by using church-state soldiers as peacekeepers. This Cluny peace-plan did not succeed either. Feudal lords quickly took the vow to obey the law but just as quickly broke their vow, whereupon Cluny bishops organized their own armies to stop the armies of the feudal lords. In punishing the oath-breakers, the armies of the church often got out of hand and did their own looting. Armies of civil authorities had to be used to put down armies of the church which were supposedly enforcing God's peace on earth.

Saint Patrick

Another monk who witnessed to God's peace in Christ Jesus was Patrick who had a dream in which the babies of Ireland pleaded with him to come back to their country and tell them about the Son of God they had heard about but did not really know in Spirit and in truth.

Patrick was not Irish. Nurtured as a Christian in England

162

where he was captured during a pirate raid and taken as a slave to Ireland, Patrick prayed to be free. After six years he managed to escape and find his way to the coast where a ship with a cargo of dogs was about to sail for France. Patrick was taken aboard to look after the hounds. After many hardships he arrived back in England, his homeland, where Patrick would gladly have remained. But his dream consumed him and changed his life.

Before going to Ireland as Jesus' missionary, Patrick realized that he needed to be trained for such a mission. To prepare for his adventure, Patrick went to the monastery in France that had once befriended him. From there he went out to become the patron saint of Ireland.

Legend has it that when Patrick arrived in Ireland, he started to walk through the country to tell everyone he met about his nonviolent Lord. One day as he drew near the city of Tara, he found excitement everywhere. That night the king and the people were to honor their fire-god.

After all fires in the town were put out, the king of Tara lit the one symbolic fire outside the palace where the people gathered to worship their god of fire. Across from the palace, there was another fire that Patrick had lit. Soldiers of the king mounted their horses to arrest the defiant one who dared disrupt their sacred ceremony. The people of Tara expected to see a proud and powerful nobleman brought before the king. Instead, they saw a humble but stately man dressed as a peasant. who carried no sword or spear.

"My name is Patrick," he told the king. "I have been sent to you by my Lord Jesus from a far country to tell you that fire is no god." Patrick proceeded to tell an angry king and an amazed people the story of the God who loved them so much that he shared their death by dying on a cross and three days later was raised from the dead. He explained that in God's peaceable kingdom of light and love, citizens have turned away from their old gods of fire and war in order to receive God's Son as their light in a sin-darkened world.

The people crowded around Patrick to hear more. The next morning some of the nobles accompanied Patrick for a few miles to see him safely on his way. About to turn back and bid Patrick farewell, they offered him a sword and breastplate for protection from enemies.

He smiled and thanked them for their love and concern. "I have my own armor and breastplate to protect me," said Patrick. As he disappeared around the bend, they heard their new friend singing about his Protector,

> I bind unto myself this day
> The power of God to hold and lead,
> God's eye to watch, God's might to stay,
> God's ear to hearken to my need.
> Christ be with me, Christ within me,
> Christ behind me, Christ before me.
> Christ beside me, Christ to win me,
> Christ to comfort and restore me.

Patrick introduced a form of communal and ascetic life to Ireland which shaped the Irish church for centuries. Following Patrick's passing in the flesh in 461, the flowering of monastic communities in Ireland spilled over into neighboring lands such as Wales. With them came centers of learning and education for the mind, healing for the body, and peace for the soul.

As for the monastic movement as a whole, over the centuries it has been a mix of fresh air and foul. Often one new monastic Order would come into existence to correct the mistakes of an old one. Such were the Cistercian monks whose Rule dominated the twelfth century to reform Cluny monasteries which had become lax.

The purpose of the Cistercian monastics was to cultivate a more strenuous and self-denying life. Buildings, utensils, food, clothing, forms of worship, all were of the plainest character.

The Baffling Bernard

Much of the early success of the Cistercian monastic movement was due to Bernard, a monk who became more powerful than any pope of the 12th century. Along with a gift for preaching, Bernard gained a reputation as a person gifted with moral insight. He was often called from his cell at Clairvaux to settle disputes within the church, the most famous being the eight-year contested papal election in 1130 with Anacletus II and Innocent II contending for the office. Lining up bishops, kings, and dukes on his side, Bernard managed to get his candidate elected to the papacy.

There is no greater paradox on the pages of church history than Bernard's reputation as the greatest churchman and moral force of his time and this monk's letter to the Knights Templar urging them to join the Second Crusade to drive the infidels out of Jerusalem.

Bernard wrote:

> The soldier benefits himself if he dies, and Christ if he kills. To kill a malefactor is not homicide but "malicide", the killing of the bad. In the death of the pagan, the Christian is glorified because Christ is glorified.

The stated purpose of the Crusades was to free Palestine from the Muslims and to unite the Catholic Church in the West with the Orthodox Church in the East. The "holy wars" made the breach wider than ever, and drove out Islam only for a short time in a victory described by one Crusader in these words,

> Some of our men cut off the heads of their enemies; others shot them with arrows so that they fell from the towers; others tortured them longer by casting them into the flames. It was necessary to pick one's way over the bodies of men and horses. It was a just and splendid judgment of God that this place should be filled with the blood of unbelievers since it has suffered so long from their blasphemies.

Bernard's gift of moral discernment should have led him to condemn the Crusades, not to encourage such bloody butchery.

The monastic church has not been without its flaws simply because it still is the church in the flesh. Nevertheless, monastic communities produced many of the best spiritual leaders the church has ever had.

Let's leave the monastic movement when it was at its best in Francis of Assisi and look at one episode in this monk's life which typifies his Christ-likeness.

Monasticism at Its Best

After two failed attempts to go to the Middle East to convert the Muslims—once because of storms at sea and another because of illness—Francis finally made his way to Syria, and thence to Egypt to observe first-hand the Pope's Crusade against the Saracens.

Arriving in Egypt, Francis went to Cardinal Pelagius, commander of the Christian army, and pleaded with him to stop the Crusade. "We are killing these people so the church will be powerful," the Cardinal told Francis. "When the church is strong it will be able to conquer an evil world."

"The Lord Jesus does not ask us to strive for worldly power," Francis replied "God uses the weak, not the powerful." While on the battlefield, he and his little group bound up the wounds of survivors.

Francis walked miles over hot desert sand to the enemy camp to meet Sultan Al-Kamil face to face and persuade him to stop the war. The Sultan's greeting was as gruff as his person: "Don't you know it's death for a Christian to come here?", he shouted.

Francis pleaded with the Sultan to stop the massacre and amazed Al-Kamil by inviting the Sultan and his people to become Christians.

"For that I should kill you", shouted the Sultan, "but . . .". He paused. There was something about this man that was different. After a long conversation in which Francis told the Sultan how Jesus suffered and died on a cross to reconcile him and his people to the God of perfect love, Al-Kamil bid Francis to leave and take with him all the gold he could carry.

"I do not want your gold. Only permit me to visit the Holy Land within your borders," said Francis. The Sultan sent Francis and his three Little Brothers on their way with a Christian slave to guide them to Jerusalem.

"You will never see that slave again", Al-Kamil was told by his friends. Much to their surprise the slave returned. Francis had kept his promise.

Much later, the Christian army was defeated and Cardinal Pelagius stood before the Sultan in bitter humiliation, begging that his 12,000 men be spared and allowed to return to their homes. "I vowed to kill all of you," the Sultan angrily told the Cardinal. "And nothing you have said has changed my mind. But some time ago, a man by the name of Francis of Assisi came to me from your camp. He is the one and only man whose deeds showed me that the words of your faith are true. For his sake I will spare your lives. You may all go—you as well as all my Christian slaves. I want Francis of Assisi to remember me well."

During the journey of Francis to stop what he considered to be an unholy crusade of killing, his leadership back home waned. From 1221, he retired more and more from the scene where the Franciscan Order he founded, now controlled by the hierarchy of the Catholic Church, went through radical change. The change accommodated those who wanted to be followers of Francis but who wished not to renounce all possessions and "just" war.

The last days of Francis were given to prayer, singing, and meditation. On September 14, 1224, at the close of a long prayer vigil at the Order's hermitage on Mount La Verna, Francis received the stigmata—wounds in his hands, feet, and side like those of his crucified Lord, whose passion had become his passion. At last, feeble in body, totally blind, and suffering greatly from his wounds, Francis died in a little hut on October 3, 1226, as a flock of larks took to the skies. Meeting what a fallen world knows as death, Francis continued his walk with his risen Lord in a glorified body of the Spirit's resurrection-life.

In his book, *The Monastic Journey*, another monk, Thomas Merton, wrote this about the peace of Jesus souls of the church are called to enflesh:

> Christ alone is able to bring true peace to the hearts of men, and it is through the hearts of other men that he brings it. We are all mediators with Christ by our humility and love in taking upon ourselves the sins of the world without condemning sinners, placing

ourselves below others and forgiving all. By our humility and charity Christ lives in the world, and prepares the consummation of his kingdom.

THE ANABAPTISTS
A Protest Movement Outside the Established Church

Let's look now at another movement that has protested the Constantinian church for the last half millennium: the Anabaptists, whose vision of the kingdom of God led them outside the Catholic and Reformed churches to form agape and koinonia communities. Unlike the monastic movement, these communities were not celibate; the entire family could be baptized and become members of this church.

Led by the Eternal Spirit Jesus enfleshed, and with the New Testament as their only creed, they were nicknamed "Anabaptists" because they believed baptizing babies a few days old is not the kind of baptism the gospel teaches and does not lead to the radical discipleship Jesus calls His church to follow.

Anabaptists viewed the reforms of Luther, Calvin, and Zwingli as good, but they believed these reforms did not go far enough to restore the church of the New Testament. Protestant reformers did their best to wipe out the Anabaptists, and in 1529, the Catholic-supported imperial Diet of Speyer declared them to be heretics. Because every court in Europe was obliged to arrest Anabaptists and execute them, thousands were put to death by fire, water, and sword.

Why were Anabaptists persecuted both by Protestant and Catholic churches? Not only because they questioned infant baptism, which was practiced by Catholics and Protestants, but, on the basis of Jesus' Sermon on the Mount, they refused to undertake any form of military service or swear public oaths. In the eyes of Luther and the Pope, therefore, they were anarchists. The first to practice complete separation of church and state, Anabaptists were seen as a threat to a stable and orderly society. As we shall see, such faith does not lead to anarchy.

The Birth of a Peace Church

On the night of January 21, 1525 in Zurich, Switzerland, about a dozen men emerged out of the darkness and, one by one, entered a house close to the Great Munster church where Zwingli served. Earlier that same day, Zurich's City Council had passed a law forbidding Anabaptists to assemble or preach. Exile would be the penalty for any who disobeyed. Four days earlier, another civil law declared that parents who refused to have their babies baptized within eight days after birth would be banished from Zurich and their property confiscated. On this cold winter night, they were meeting to decide how to respond to the action of Zurich's political leaders.

Some of the group had been close friends of Zwingli. For five years they had been part of Bible study groups Zwingli had encouraged to discern God's will for the church. There had been long and stimulating discussions on the nature of the church, its relationship to the state, the meaning of baptism, and the Christian life. At first there had been a spirit of enthusiastic unity among them, but as Zwingli allowed the civil authorities of Zurich to make decisions about how the church should worship and function, disagreements increased. Zwingli's Reformed church was turning out to be a church in partnership with the state just like the Medieval state-church they were opposing.

The group that appeared out of the darkness that night firmly believed that the church of Christ represents a separate and holy people who are ruled only by the Word of God Jesus enfleshed. Consequently, partnership with governing

170

authorities was wrong. Submit nonviolently to ruling authorities, "yes", but to be one of them in ruling with coercive power, "no"! It was the way the early church lived for more than two centuries, and the way Anabaptists believed all Christians should live.

Some Members of the Memorable Meeting

One member of the group gathering that night to pray and seek the Holy Spirit's guidance was Felix Manz, once a faithful supporter of Zwingli. It was at his mother's house in Neustadtgasse where they were meeting. Well educated in the humanities, Felix Manz was proficient in Hebrew, Latin and Greek. His next two years would be spent evangelizing or in Zurich's prison. He would eventually be put to death by drowning as a mockery of his "rebaptism". Said the church-state, "If it's water they want, we'll give it to them."

Also in the group was Conrad Grebel, whose father was a distinguished member of Zurich's City Council which had voted to banish Anabaptists. Educated at the universities of Basel, Paris and Vienna, Conrad had also been a staunch supporter of Zwingli. Now there were fundamental differences.

A year before this memorable meeting in the Manz home, Grebel had written to a friend,

> In reading the New Testament we have found another view of the church than that which Zwingli has given us. In Zurich as in the rest of the Christian world, every newborn child is baptized and is henceforth considered as a church member; as a result, church and people are identical, the church is everybody's church. But in the New Testament the church is a fellowship, not of

the many, but of the few who truly believe
and who live aright (See Matthew 7:14).

A third member was George Blaurock, a former priest in
whom the fires of the Reformation had long been burning.
He had met with Zwingli several times but came away
dissatisfied with the latter's halfway reforms. On fire for a
purer church, Blaurock found in Manz and Grebel a more
meaningful fellowship which agreed on a church free of state
interference and politics.

As the group met on that cold January night, they reviewed
recent events and the mind of Zurich's state-church. They
read from the New Testament, reflected and prayed for
God's guidance. From their knees they arose to agreement.
They believed in the Spirit who empowered the Anabaptist
church to be Jesus' witnesses of nonviolent love. Moreover,
from that night in 1525 to the present, this belief
demonstrates to a warring world that, in Christ, sin's war is
over. In the cross-resurrection-ascension-rule-indwelling
Holy Spirit, the victory over sin's violence and death has
been won, and the church is called to live nonviolently.

In a spontaneous act of the Holy Spirit, George Blaurock
confessed his sin, and in repentance arose and asked Conrad
Grebel to baptize him in the New Testament church of Jesus
(Acts 2:38). Then the others in repentance and faith said
they, too, were ready to be baptized in the eternal life of the
Holy Spirit (John 14:6).

That amazing night was all about a voluntary church
composed of believers who had repented of their former way
of life, deciding by the grace of God to commit their lives to
the whole gospel, believing that in Jesus Christ the first-fruit
of God's Eternity had come on earth as it is in heaven (1
Corinthians 15:20, 23). From that meeting, they went forth to
affirm that to be a Christian was to be a citizen of God's
here-and-now kingdom in which disciples do not resist evil

with swords made with human hands (John 18:36), but in the power of the Holy Spirit (2 Peter 1:3-4).

The gospel confronts a fallen world with a decision, a choice between sin's world of law enforced by coercive violence, and God's voluntary nonviolent kingdom of the Spirit whose fruit is described by the New Testament as "love, joy, peace, patience, gentleness, faithfulness, and self-control" (Galatians 5:22).

This brings to the author's mind the words we used at our 20th century church camp when we sat around the closing camp fire; in an act of dedication to Jesus and God's kingdom, each camper lit his or her candle from the burning fire, a symbol of Jesus' Holy Spirit:

> To every one there openeth
> A way, and ways, and a way,
> And the high soul takes the high way,
> And the low soul gropes the low.
> And in between on the misty flats
> The rest drift to and fro.

Anabaptism Means "Nachfolge Christi"

The two most important words Anabaptists heard Jesus speak were "Follow me." They had been attracted to Zwingli when they heard him say, "To be a Christian is not to talk about Christ, but to walk as he walked."

German was the language spoken where the Anabaptist movement originated. The two German words they used to sum up the Christian life were "nachfolge Christi" which means "to follow Christ". Not sitting in a building called "church" listening to sermons about Jesus; not reciting creeds about the Holy Trinity; not singing about God, but "nachfolge Christi"—following Christ moment by moment in every aspect of one's life. As one Anabaptist put it, "No one can

173

truly know Christ except he follow him in life." He was right. The Lord Jesus has come to give a fallen world a new life to enflesh, not a new ritual to recite (Matthew 7:21-27).

Early in this century, Charles Sheldon wrote a book entitled, *In His Steps*. It depicts what life would be like if Christians followed Jesus' example in every area of their life. Each thought, attitude, word and action is examined by asking the question: "What would Jesus do?" Would Jesus use violence to protect himself? Would Jesus drop bombs on those the state calls enemies? *In His Steps* answers, "No", and points to the Garden of Gethsemane where Peter used his clumsy hand with a sword to save Jesus. The Lord rebuked Peter and healed the wound Peter's sword had inflicted, saying a few hours later to Pilate, "My servants do not fight" (John 18:36).

Through the centuries, theologians like Reinhold Niebuhr have convinced many in the church that, in an imperfect world, it is impossible to "be perfect as your heavenly Father is perfect" (Matthew 5:48) and resist enemies with love instead of guns.

Niebuhr included Anabaptists when he wrote,

> The Christian utopians think they can dispense with all structures and rules of justice simply by fulfilling the law of love. They do not realize that the law of love stands on the edge of history and not in history, that it represents an ultimate and not an immediate possibility.

Said Niebuhr,

> The perfect disinterestedness of the divine love can have a counterpart in history only on a life which ends tragically, because it refuses to participate in the claims and counterclaims

of historical existence. It portrays a love "which seeketh not its own." But a love which seeketh not its own is not able to maintain itself in historical society. Not only may it fall victim to excessive forms of the self-assertion of others; but even the most perfectly balanced system of justice in history is a balance of competing wills and interests, and must therefore worst anyone who does not participate in the balance.

Spoken in 1939, Niebuhr's teaching encouraged Christians to take up arms and resist Hitler. In an imperfect world in which evil rises up to seek its own national interests at the expense of other nations, Niebuhr advocated choosing a lesser evil—the Allied forces—to wage war against a greater evil embodied in Hitler.

I agree with Niebuhr that "the perfect disinterestedness of divine love" is not the practical way to succeed as the world measures success, in terms of power, possessions, prestige, privilege, and the like.

Inevitably, the Way of God's cross brings conflict with fallen Babylon and leads to suffering at the hands of a self-centered society that seeks its own welfare and safety. But Jesus did say, "If anyone would follow me, let him take up his cross" (Matthew 16:24) . . . not his bankbook, or titles of property, or insurance policy.

In following the way of the cross as a fallen world's only salvation, the New Testament makes it clear that "the word of the cross is foolishness to those who are perishing, but to those who are being saved it is the power of God" (1 Corinthians 1:18). The "perfect disinterestedness" of the cross that "seeketh not its own", will, in one way or another, be victim to the world's selfishness. But the gospel does not end with victims on a cross. It goes on to Jesus' glorious resurrection, ascension, rule at the "right hand" of God, and indwelling Holy Spirit who assures us that when we abide in Jesus, we are part of His deathless kingdom.

Paul asked,

> Who shall separate us from the love of Christ? Shall tribulation, or distress, or persecution, or famine, or nakedness, or peril, or sword?
> - Romans 8:35

This is the gospel's confident and joyous answer: "No, nothing, nothing, nothing can separate us. We are one for eternity! As we are called to suffer with Jesus, we have an inheritance in the risen Christ that is imperishable, undefiled, and unfading." (1 Peter 1:3-9)

If our brief pilgrimage in the flesh is all there is, then the way of the cross that seeketh not its own welfare is foolishness. But what if our sojourn in the flesh is a testing ground where our future is being determined?

As I recall, Jesus said that those whose ambition is to advance their life will end up losing their life, and those who are willing to give their life away will find real life. (Luke 17:33)

The gospel calls this counsel "the word of God that abides forever":

> Do not love the world or the things in the world. If any one loves the world, love for the Father is not in him. The world passes away, and the lust of it; but he who does the will of God abides forever.
> - 1 John 2:15-17

Jesus' "perfect disinterestedness of the cross" allowed Him about thirty short years on planet-Earth, but after two millennia, His life continues to determine the way we divide calendar time and inspires the best selling book of the ages which says,

> He who says he abides in Him ought to walk
> in the same way in which he walked.
> - 1 John 2:6

If the church cannot walk in the steps of Jesus, then Jesus is an imposter and the church should lock all doors. Her message is bogus.

The Risen Indwelling Christ Makes It Possible

The Apostles did not believe "nachfolge Christi" is impossible for the church that abides in God's Holy Spirit. Rejoicing, they followed Jesus to the death.

Zwingli criticized Anabaptists, saying, "They talk as though the Messiah were here." He IS here! This is the good news— the heart of the gospel: "Christ in you" (Colossians 1:27, 3:11) and "with you always!" (Matthew 28:20). Mainline "just war" churches act and talk as though the Messiah has not come to deliver a fallen world from its violence and death, thereby denying the good news of the gospel (Colossians 1:13). Did "nachfolge Christi" Anabaptists actually give evidence of a more perfect life than the quality of life in mainline churches?

In 1531, Sebastion Franck, an opponent of the Anabaptists, described them with these words,

> The Anabaptists . . . soon gained a large
> following . . . drawing many sincere souls
> who had a zeal for God, for they taught

nothing but love, faith, and the cross. They showed themselves humble, patient under much suffering. They break bread with one another as an evidence of unity and love. They helped each other faithfully and called each other brothers . . . They died as martyrs, patiently and humbly, enduring all persecution.

It's hard to understand how Catholic and Protestant leaders could heap such praise on Anabaptists one minute and the next, hound them like dogs and burn them at the stake as heretics. What charge was brought against them? The same charge that was leveled against Jesus: Treason! A threat to the established order by refusing to defend it. The Constantinian church that blends in with the state hates nothing more than people who refuse to fight for their country. Both Catholic and Protestant churches continue to teach that the highest duty of the Christian is to serve in political office and in the armed forces.

In his *Institutes of the Christian Religion*, John Calvin, wrote,

Civil magistry is a calling, not only holy and legitimate, but by far the most sacred and honorable in human life.

I grew up in a typical mainline church in which I was baptized as a baby and had my first picture taken in a soldier's uniform. With my mother's milk I imbibed the glory of war, taught that it was my sacred duty to vote and help elect candidates running for political office, that there is no higher vocation than that of serving in public office. The assumption of my baptism was that I am a citizen of a Christian nation; therefore, it is my duty to become involved in its "Christian" activities.

A New Baptism, A New Life, A New Church

Conrad Grebel, Felix Manz, George Blaurock, and the others who met in Zurich on that winter's night on January 22, 1525, experienced a different baptism. The next day, a Sunday morning, Hans Oggenfuss, a tailor from Stadelhofen, near Zurich, hurried to deliver a new suit to Wilhelm Roubli, a priest who was being forced to leave the region because he, too, had come to reject infant baptism. A heretic! On his way to deliver the suit, Hans heard two men talking at the village well. One was Fridli Schumacher whose name corresponded to his trade. The other was Hans Brotli, a former Catholic priest. With his wife and child, persecuted pastor Brotli had lived in Zollikon for six months without a parish assignment. The Schumachers had welcomed the Brotli family into their home. Pastor Brotli was one of the group that had been baptized the night before by the former priest, George Blaurock, in the Manz home. With great joy and excitement he had returned to Zollikon to share that meeting with his dear friends. Seeking God's guidance, Brotli and Schumacher, along with other farmers in Zollikon, had been meeting for weeks in Bible study and prayer to discern their risen Lord's will for their life and that of the church in Europe. Convinced that the group's decision the night before was consistent with what they had been reading in the New Testament, now Schumacher asked to be baptized.

The tailor could hardly believe what he was seeing and hearing. The amazed Hans Oggenfuss saw Brotli draw water from the well and sprinkle it on the head of Fridli Schumacher, who had been baptized as an infant in the state-church. Now of his own volition, Fridli asked to be baptized into a very different church that is neither Catholic, Protestant, nor Anabaptist—a church in sharp contrast to the reformed church of Luther and Zwingli which was perpetuating the medieval concept of a church whose membership consists of everyone in the territory who were baptized as babies.

During that next momentous week, before the coercive power of church and state moved in to stamp out the fire of the Holy Spirit, there was a meeting in Zollikon on Wednesday night, January 25, 1525, in the home of Ruidi Thomann. This event helps us understand what was stirring in the hearts and minds of many earnest Christians; not only in Zollikon, but throughout Europe.

Ruidi, an elderly farmer of a well-known Zollikon family, invited Brotli, Blaurock, and Roubli—the three banished clergyman—to join him and some others for supper. Forbidden to assemble and teach, the three priests had been given eight days to leave the region. Ruidi wanted to be with his friends for one last agape-meal before they left to face a hostile world.

By the time they were ready for Bible study, others had come: Marx Bosshard, Ruidi's son-in-law; Heinrich Thomann, the brother of Ruidi; Jacob Hottinger, a well known elderly gentleman from the village; Hans Bruggbach from a neighboring village; and Felix Manz, in whose home the movement was born less than a week before.

After they had read from the Scriptures and reflected on the claims of God's gospel on their life, Hans Bruggbach began to weep and confess his sinful condition. After the group prayed for Hans, he asked to be baptized.

Felix Manz quoted Acts 10:47: "Can anyone forbid water for baptizing?" George Blaurock answered, "No one!" Then, using a metal dipper from the kitchen, Manz poured water over the head of Hans Bruggbach, with the words, "I baptize you in the name of God the Father, God the Son, and God the Holy Spirit."

Then Jacob Hottinger who had spent many hours with Felix Manz and Conrad Grebel in prayer and Bible study during the previous weeks, made the same confession and request for believer's baptism, which was administered in the same simplicity of the early church.

After making their confession of faith, they sat at the kitchen table, and with bread and wine from the pantry, they listened to George Blaurock explain the meaning of the Bread and the Cup and give the invitation: "He who believes that God has redeemed him through His death and rose-colored blood, let him come and eat with me of the bread and drink with me of the wine."

This incident recalls to my mind a Service of Holy Communion we had when a fire in our church building led us to meet in the homes of members on the following Sunday. The Lord's Table set in the homes of church members helped me understand as never before Jesus' words:

> Wherever two or three are gathered in my
> name, there am I in the midst of them.
> - Matthew 18:20

How long was it before Zwingli's church-state police in Zurich put an end to this revolutionary New Testament house-church in Zollikon? Not long. On January 30th, Zurich's police moved in and arrested those whose radical discipleship had turned Zollikon upside down. A few months later after their release from prison, a reborn church, cradled in Zollikon, moved out to take root in Moravia, Germany, and the Netherlands and become the only Reformation church that completely broke away from the state and its systems of violence and centuries-old "just war" doctrine.

A Historic Meeting to Remember

Few Christians know about the meeting of Anabaptist leaders who met in Schleitheim on the borders of Switzerland to define what made the radical discipleship of

181

this re-formed church so unique.

On February 24th, 1527, at Schleitheim, Michael Sattler, a former Benedictine monk, and about a dozen others gathered secretly, close to the border of Switzerland, to define what they found Anabaptists believed. Scattered and without any one leader, Anabaptists were being given all kinds of false labels. Those gathered at Schleitheim wanted their church to be judged, not by gossip and misrepresentation, but by the basic New Testament teachings which united them and set them apart from the Constantinian church

At the secret meeting presided over by Michael Sattler, the group agreed on Seven Articles:

1. Baptism: Only those should be baptized "who have been taught repentance and the amendment of life and who believe truly that their sins are taken away through Christ, and desire to walk in the resurrection of Jesus Christ and be buried with him in death so that they may rise with him. Infant baptism is excluded."

2. Church Discipline: Sheep who stray will be disciplined based on Matthew 18:15-20 which could be paraphrased:

If your brother sins, go to him alone . . .
If he listens, you have won your brother . . .
If he refuses to listen to you, take with
you two or three . . .
If he refuses to listen to them, tell the congregation.
If he refuses to repent, be separate until he does.

3. The Lord's Supper: "Concerning the eating of bread, we have become one and agree that all those who desire to break the one bread in remembrance of the broken body of Christ and all those who wish to drink in remembrance of the shed blood of Christ must beforehand be united in the one body of Christ. Whoever does not share the calling of the one God to one faith, to one baptism, to one Spirit, to one body, together with all the children of God, may not be made one loaf together with them, as must be true if one wishes truly to break bread according to the command of Christ."

4. Separation from the World: Schleitheim agreed that the kingdom of God Jesus inaugurated stands against a fallen world's violence, lust, greed, confusion and misplaced trust in political and human (as opposed to Biblical) solutions to problems.

5. Selecting a Shepherd for the Local Church: "The shepherd in the church shall be a person according to the rule of Paul" (1 Timothy 3:1-10). Emphasis was on the candidate's spiritual stature and vision, not on his personality and ability to preach interesting sermons. Schleitheim put an end to recruiting pastors from outside the congregation based on educational credentials and social connections rather than their spiritual stature.

6. War and Serving in Political Office: "The sword is the ordering of God outside the perfection of Christ." The state is outside the "perfection of Christ" and is used by God "to punish and kill the wicked, and guard and protect the good. Within the perfection of Christ the sword is not allowed."

> When the people wanted to make Christ king, he fled. We should follow him and do likewise. Christ suffered, not ruled, and has left us an example to follow.

7. The Swearing of Oaths: "Do not swear at all, either by heaven, for it is the throne of God, or by the earth . . . for it is his footstool, or by Jerusalem, for it is the city of the great King. And do not swear by your head, for you cannot make one hair black or white. Let what you say be simply 'Yes' or 'No'; anything more than this comes from evil." (Matthew 5:33-37)

Anabaptists believed the Articles of the Apostles' Creed. Schleitheim's affirmation had only to do with daily discipleship.

After the secret meeting, Michael Sattler mounted his horse to go back home. When he arrived late that night there was a candle in the window to greet him. With a light heart, Michael quickly locked his horse in the barn and ran to greet his wife who was waiting at the door.

"Quick. Come inside and close the door," she whispered.

"What is it? What's the matter?" asked Michael.

When she told Michael that spies had discovered the Anabaptists in Rottenburg, he realized why his wife was so troubled. For two years the state-church had been hounding Anabaptists in that part of Europe. Soldiers would soon be breaking down their door.

Several days later, soldiers rushed into their house, grabbed Michael, and discovered the papers of Schleitheim. Michael and his wife were pushed out the door and taken to the prison in Horb. Later, fourteen horses were saddled and Michael, his wife, and their partners in the gospel, were taken to the prison in Binsdorf, where they were held for three months until their trial.

The trial opened in Rottenburg on May 17, 1527. Twelve men and women accused of attempting to overthrow the Roman Catholic Church and the civil order were given the opportunity to hire a defense attorney. They declined on the ground that this was not a civil case but rather a defense of their faith. As Christians, they were ready to give reason for what they believed.

The judges asked Michael if it were true that he refused to

fight for the state. Michael replied that as a Christian, he could not use weapons to kill, but if he could he would rather fight on the side of the Turks than on the side of Christians. At least the Turks were honest in their fighting. Their sacred duty to kill enemies is clearly stated in the Koran. But when Christians fight and kill, they deny their Lord who said, "Love your enemies" (Matthew 5:44) . . . "my kingdom is not of this world. If it were my disciples would fight" (John 18:36).

Chosen to represent the group, Michael addressed the judges with these words:

> Ye ministers of God, if you have neither heard nor read the Word of God, we would suggest that you send for the most learned men and for the Book of the Divine Scriptures, and that they, with us, weigh these things in the light of God's Word. If they show us from Scripture that we err and are in the wrong, we shall be gladly taught and recant.

The officer representing the state, replied angrily, "The only one you will have discussion with is your executioner."

The judges retired for an hour and thirty minutes and then returned to read their verdict:

> Michael Sattler shall be delivered to the executioner who shall, firstly, cut out his tongue, and then throw him upon a cart, and with red hot tongs tear pieces out of his body twice, and on the way to the place of his execution, make use of the tongs five more times in like manner. Thereupon he shall burn his body to ashes as an arch heretic.

On the morning of his torture and execution, Michael prayed for his judges and persecutors in the Spirit of God's reconciling love. He admonished them to repent and receive God's New Creation of the Spirit. Then Michael's sentence was carried out. When the flames burned through the cords that fastened him, Michael lifted up two fingers as a sign of his victory and joy in sharing his Lord's sufferings with the Resurrection-faith that nothing can separate believers from God when they abide in his perfect will (Romans 8:35-39).

A few days later Michael's wife was suffocated to death by drowning.

Today Anabaptists are best known as Hutterites, Mennonites, and Amish. How did they become divided?

Anabaptists Called Hutterites
An Example of Complete Communal Life in Christ

Persecuted by both Catholic and Protestant territorial-churches, some Anabaptists in 1525 found refuge in Moravia where their skill in farming was welcomed by the feudal lords of large estates. Thousands of refugees fleeing from Upper Austria and the Tyrol settled in Nikolsburg and formed several church communities.

In 1528 when a disagreement over the use of the sword and the payment of war taxes divided them, those who rejected the sword and unconditional allegiance to the state were told to pack up and leave.

A Communal Hutterite Church is Born

About 200 adults left with their families. After a day's travel, to share and meet the needs of everyone, they spread out a cloak. As each laid his or her few possessions on it with a willing heart, a commitment was made to share whatever they had for the sake of equality (2 Corinthians 8:14). Then they appointed some to use the group's earthly wealth for the common good as the newborn church did on Pentecost:

> All who believed were together and had all things in common; and they all sold their possessions and goods and distributed them to all, as any had need.
> - Acts 2:44-45; 4:34-35

This event in the vacated village of Bogenitz where the refugees had camped for the night gave birth to the Hutterite church. Living without private property has been the distinguishing mark of the Hutterite church, or Bruderhof, from that day to this.

After a three-week journey on foot that carried the sick, the aged, and the little children in wagons, the Bruderhof (the word means "house of brothers"), arrived in the Moravian territory of Austerlitz where they were welcomed and shown great kindness by the townspeople, including the nobles who needed their skills in farming. Living at first in tents and a burned out vacant farmhouse, they were given wood to build houses and freed from paying rent and taxes.

Persecuted exiles continued to pour into Austerlitz, especially from the Tyrol mountains. One of them was Jakob Hutter. He had been organizing groups of hounded Anabaptists and leading them on secret and dangerous journeys to Moravia.

Dissatisfied with the quality of communal life in Austerlitz, the Tyroleans left and founded another Bruderhof thirty miles away at Auspitz where Jakob Hutter was recognized as their leader. During his short ministry of less than three years, communal life became so orderly and viable that it defined Hutterite life for over 450 years, to the present day.

A Tragedy in the City of Munster

In 1534, during Hutter's ministry at Auspitz, a tragedy happened in the Netherlands city of Munster. The pacifist Anabaptists had not yet become clearly distinguished from a revolutionary spiritualist movement with an emphasis on the imminent Second Coming of Christ.

One of their leaders was Jan Mathys, a baker of Haarlem who would not wait for the power of God to bring in the new age. He decided he would inaugurate it by force. Popular democratic support gave him the opportunity to persuade the revolutionists that God had chosen the city of Munster as the place where the New Jerusalem would be established. Radicals flocked to Munster in large numbers and gained control of the city by force.

After Mathys was killed in fighting, the troops of the bishop of Munster laid siege to the city while John of Leyden was proclaimed Munster's new king. Polygamy was established, community of goods was enforced, opponents were slaughtered. Though they carried on their struggle heroically for several months, eventually everyone inside the city was slaughtered, either in battle, or after, being taken as captives and tortured by military forces aided by Catholics and Lutherans.

Because of their radical views, those in Munster were mistakenly linked to the Anabaptists. The result was a wave of increased persecution which struck the Hutterites in Moravia.

When the persecution reached Auspitz in 1535, Jakob Hutter wrote a long letter of protest to the government in Moravia, explaining what they believed and how they were very different from those who wildly had taken over the city of Munster. Hutter wrote,

Here we lie upon the barren heath, as God wills, without harm to anyone. We do not wish, nor desire, to do harm or evil to any man, yea not to our worst enemies. And all our life and deeds, words, and work, are open to all. Yea, before we would knowingly wrong a man to the value of penny we would rather lose a hundred pounds, and before we would strike our greatest enemy with the hand, to say nothing of a gun, sword, or halberd, as the world does, we would rather die and let our own lives be taken. We have no material weapons, neither spear nor gun, as every one can see. Altogether our preaching and testimony, life and walk, is that men should, according to the truth and righteousness of God, live peacefully and in unity as the true followers of Christ.

The Martyrdom of Jakob Hutter

In spite of Jakob Hutter's letter, the persecution continued with fury for almost a year. Bruderhofs were broken up and forced to scatter in small groups. Jakob Hutter managed to get back to the Tyrol mountains where he continued his witness. During the night of November 29, 1535, he was betrayed and captured. Two months later he was condemned to death and burned at the stake.

From the time of Hutter's martyrdom, those in the Bruderhof were known as "Hutterites". Even in the face of terrible persecution, Brother Jakob openly and joyfully shared his vision of the church as a reconciled house-hold of God, all of whose members suffer when one suffers, and all rejoice in the joy of one (See 1 Corinthians 12:26).

Hutter left the Hutterites so well organized economically that they were able to maintain their communal life until 1622 in

Moravia, until 1685 in Hungary, and from 1770 until 1874 in the Ukraine. Between 1874 and 1877, groups of Hutterites migrated from Russian to North America where about 420,000 members now live communally in almost 400 communities in western United States and Canada.

The Hutterian Church Today

If you were to visit a Hutterite community today, you would find a people of simple dress, depending on agriculture or ranching for their livelihood, operating their own schools, rejecting the military and all violence. Bruderhofs average about 130 members who live on communal property ranging from 15,000-acre ranches to 3,000-acre farms. When a Hutterite community grows to about 130, half of the families move to a new location purchased by the members and start another communal church.

Visitors are welcomed warmly by a people in homemade garb who live a simple life and speak a German dialect. Baptism takes place about the age of eighteen for those who choose to remain in the community. The decision not to be baptized in the Hutterite church is to decide to leave one's family and friends in the Christian community and live in the "world". After baptism, Hutterites usually choose a mate in marriage from their own church. Like baptism, marriage is for life.

According to their ability, each one helps with the community's work: cooking, canning, cleaning, sewing, teaching, nursing, parenting, farming, ranching, constructing facilities, or whatever needs to be done. Hutterites do not go to church in a special building for a few hours a week. Abiding in Christ, their church is their common life. Their place of worship is their community—Jesus' enfleshment of peace on earth. The colony is a spiritual ark which provides security in the midst of life's storms and floods. Within the communal church the need of one is the concern of all. The wealth of one is the wealth of all.

Such voluntary communal life is the result of the Holy Spirit's agape, not the coercive communism of the state. The Hutterites are a living answer to our risen Lord's petition: "Father, that they may be one, even as we are one" (John 17:11), and to the Apostles' teaching, "Be not conformed to this world" (Romans 12:2).

Have Hutterites been able to withstand the pressure of North America's culture of violence and to reject all war?

Four Hutterites Who Kept the Peace of Jesus

That they have was evident in 1918 when four Hutterites arrived at a U.S. military camp and, as Christians, declared their absolute objection to all killing. David, Michael, and Joseph Hofer, and Jacob Wipf refused to swear an oath that they would obey all military commands. They were treated as Jakob Hutter was treated in 1536. At Alcatraz their clothes were taken from them and ordered to put on military uniforms. Refusing, they were taken to a deep, dark, and damp dungeon below sea level with water oozing through the walls. Wearing only light underwear, they were thrown into a dungeon. Military uniforms were thrown in after them with the warning, "If you don't give in, you'll stay here until you die."

During the first four and a half days in separate cells, they received only a half glass of water every 24 hours. At night they slept on cold, wet concrete floors with no blankets. The last day and a half they had to stand with their hands tied above their heads. At the end of five days they were taken to a courtyard with other prisoners who were shocked to see all four covered with a rash, bitten by insects, their arms so swollen they could not get their jackets on. For the next 4 months at Alcatraz, the four were locked in their cells with nothing to eat until evening. Only on Sunday were they allowed to walk in the courtyard for an hour under heavy guard.

In November, chained together and guarded by six men, they were transferred to the prison at Fort Leavenworth in Kansas. Arriving there at 11 o'clock at night after a four-day journey, they were hurriedly driven up the street at the point of bayonets. Covered with sweat when they reached the gate, the four were told to take off their clothes and put on the prison garb that would be brought to them. By the time it arrived, they were chilled to the bone. Joseph and Michael Hofer were in such pain they had to be taken to the hospital. Jacob Wipf and Michael Hofer were put in solitary confinement. Once more they refused to obey military orders. For two weeks, nine hours a day, they stood with their hands stretched through prison bars and chained together, getting only bread and water.

When Joseph and Michael Hofer became critically ill, their brother Jacob sent a telegram to their wives who immediately left their children and took a train to Leavenworth. When they arrived they found their husbands close to death, hardly able to speak. The next morning Joseph was dead and his body in a coffin. Marie was told she could not see her husband. In spite of guards, she was able to get to the commanding officer and pleaded to see her husband once more. Told where her husband's body was, she found Joseph in a coffin dressed in death in the military uniform he had refused to wear in life.

His brother Michael died a few days later in the presence of his wife, father, and his brother David who had been released from his cell for a short time. Just before he died, with arms outstretched, his family heard their beloved Michael say, "Come, Lord Jesus! Into Thy hands I commend my spirit."

In the name and Spirit of Jesus these four disciples engaged the world's evil Powers and Principalities and won the battle with weapons the world knows nothing about. Prison guards crucified their body of flesh and blood that came from their mother' womb. Their real self had been baptized in the eternal Spirit and came from the womb of God no enemy can destroy (John 11:25-6). They lived, and moved, and had their new being in God's here and now peaceable kingdom which is beyond tragedy (1 John 5:4-5, 20-21).

The reason why Hutterites reject war and all violence is the same reason for their remarkable communal society which has continued for almost five hundred years in spite of fire, dungeon, and sword. Their communal church is not a social experiment, not a Utopia. It is the fruit of the Holy Spirit given to the church on Pentecost, a testimony to Jesus' victorious resurrection (Acts 4:31-37).

Hutterite economics is determined by the same Holy Spirit of God in whom Jesus lived communally with the Twelve, not a man-made system based on the ideology of a Marx or Lenin.

Some say that such community of goods ignores the part of human nature which is bent on self-will and acquiring personal possessions and private wealth. Hutterites by no means ignore this human instinct. They like to quote this jingle from their *Great Article Book* written about thirty years after their first community started in Moravia,

> Communal living would not be hard
> If there were not such self-regard.

The idolatry of self-regard is controlled by Spirit-regard.

Thank God for the Hutterites and their vision of the New Testament church as the beginning of a New Society under the reign of the Eternal's self-giving Spirit. It is this Spirit who creates spiritual structures for work and education, for care of the sick and elderly. In other words, it is a way of life that the world of the flesh does not understand.

We turn now to the Anabaptists known as Mennonites.

Anabaptists Called Mennonites
Another Model of Jesus' Peace Church

All Anabaptists had been stirred by Luther and Zwingli who claimed the freedom to approach God solely by faith based on the merits of Jesus' death on the cross; without the mediation of priests or saints; without good works such as purchasing indulges to escape purgatory; without accepting the infallible authority of the Pope.

A Priest Named Menno Simons

In 1528, when a priest named Luther was teaching that the sole authority of the Christian is God's Word in Scripture, Menno Simons, another priest in southern Europe was reading the New Testament for the first time. For the next seven years, Menno struggled with questions such as infant baptism, a Catholic territorial church tied to the state and its systems of coercive power, and salvation synonymous with observing the Sacraments as prescribed by the one true church. Several key events led Menno Simons to become an Anabaptist.

On March 20, 1531, something happened in a nearby city that shook the pillar of infant baptism in the temple of Simons' heart and mind. A tailor by the name of Sicke Freerks Snijder was put to death by the state-church on the charge that he had been baptized a second time. Simons wondered why this Christian, an unpretentious God-fearing man, was willing to die for the sake of his "second baptism". In his martyrdom, the tailor probably did more in a moment of time to spread the gospel than all the preaching he could have done during a long life on earth. Tertullian was right: "The blood of the martyrs is the seed of the church."

Influenced by Anabaptists such as Obbe and Dirk Philips, well-educated sons of another Netherlands priest, Simons' gradual inner turning was almost complete by 1535. One morning while sitting at his desk, he heard a knock at his door. It was a woman of his parish so distraught she could hardly speak.

"Father", she gasped, "My son . . . my son Hendrick . . . he joined the Anabaptists . . . Remember when Jan van Geelen was here. Jan told us we would not get anywhere with our new faith if we just sit back and allow ourselves to be killed. He told us to arm ourselves and fight to conquer the whole province of Friesland. Then we would be free to spread the good news that Jesus was coming again, right here in our midst. Hendrick believed him."

"Now my son is dead." She sobbed as she told her pastor what had just taken place at the Old Cloister, a nearby monastery. Like those in the city of Munster, three hundred sincere souls saw themselves as God's elect called to do battle with the wicked and help hasten the Second Coming of Jesus.

The sobbing woman's story of the massacre of three hundred at the Old Cloister, including her son Hendrick and Simons' brother, Peter, was a continuation of violence the priest knew in his heart was a contradiction to Jesus' life and gospel. Moreover, it was a contradiction to the Anabaptist movement that had renounced all violence and was now persecuted by the church that had ordained him to be a priest.

When the member of his parish finished her tragic story and left, Simons sank down in his chair and reached for the Bible that had become the new authority for his life. He knew the truth, but what had he actually done to help Hendrick, his brother Peter, and the people of his parish, to know the truth? Many of his flock had been caught up in the violence. The thought of these "poor, misguided sheep", as Simons called them, would not leave him. Hendrick and Peter had given their lives for something false which he was afraid to oppose.

In his heart, Simons knew what was right, but he had been afraid of what would happen to him if he made a complete break and openly identified himself with Anabaptists like Obbe and Dirk and the Way of Jesus' nonviolent cross. It meant persecution and suffering, the end of a secure and respected ministry in the powerful established church, and an unknown future.

It's one thing to know what is right, and another to have the courage to do what is right.

Simons' Affirmative Action

As Menno Simons looked out the window at a beautiful and peaceful summer day, he was no longer afraid. Although he remained in his assigned parish, he began to speak freely about the New Creation of the Spirit that comes through repentance and simple trust in the God Jesus enfleshed. No longer did Simons baptize babies. He simplified the Mass. He spoke out against violence.

One night, about nine months later, after making a public statement declaring his conversion and unconditional commitment to a church separated from the state, Simons quietly slipped away. Now he was ready to "nachfolge Christi" wherever the Counselor would lead, come what may.

How should he begin his new ministry? Simons was not sure. Like Saint Paul, he needed to retreat from the world and prayerfully reflect on the mission to which God was calling him. He invited some of his most trusted Anabaptist brothers and sisters to join him in a secret yearlong "Arabian retreat" during which he was baptized by Obbe Philips.

Gradually, Simons decided what his mission would be. Because of their widespread persecution, Anabaptists had scattered throughout Europe's lowlands and were like sheep without a shepherd. He would move among them, help them form local congregations and be a shepherd to these dispirited flocks.

For twelve years, Menno Simons had been a priest in the Catholic Church that had been firmly established in the world for twelve hundred years. Now he had joined a new movement the world did not want, and the world was putting to death anyone who was part of it.

Luther had the powerful protection of the German princes. Zwingli never moved without the support of the civil government of Zurich. Simons began his new ministry with only the power and protection of God's Holy Spirit.

Unlike Hutterite Anabaptists in Moravia, those in the Netherlands and Northern Germany retained private property. Believing that God is the Owner, they practiced mutual aid and assisted each other in times of need.

Simons' View of the Church

Simons' Anabaptist vision led him to a "congregational" view of the church: a voluntary gathering of the converted, born of the Spirit in their own unique society in which the life and teaching of Jesus would become the foundation for their community's culture—a church separated from the world and its politics of self-interest; a church of free, uncompelled people who, unlike Augustine, would not use force to compel anyone to do anything.

During his twenty-five years of preaching and organizing churches, Menno Simons was unswerving in teaching God's nonviolent way of the cross. As a result, Mennonites throughout the world have come to be known as a "peace church" that rejects war, and loves friend and foe alike. It has ministered to the sick, the hungry, the prisoners of war, on both sides of a conflict. Like the Quakers, they are known for waging peace instead of war.

A church based on such a radical life-style of nonviolence—going against the grain of the world—does not continue from one generation to the next by baptizing babies and assuming they will grow up and practice a life of nonviolent love as citizens of God's peaceable kingdom. Jesus said only a few choose this life (See Matthew 7:14). The rejection of all violence must be a spiritually discerned truth to which the Christian commits his or her life at the time of baptism if one is to withstand the pressures of the military culture of every nation-state.

Menno Simons had not tacked Christian nonviolence to a new kind of gospel he discovered. His spirit discerned the truth about the very meaning of salvation: the Lamb of God has delivered His church from a fallen world's evil and its sin. *Nachfolge Christi* means loving as Jesus loves through the power of the indwelling Christ. And loving as Jesus loves means the willingness to share in Jesus' redemptive suffering on the cross rather than make suffer those the world calls "enemies" in order to preserve one's life in the flesh a little while longer. Jesus made His twenty-nine or so years in the flesh spell E-T-E-R-N-I-T-Y. He has come to empower every soul to do the same.

How did Menno Simons and his family manage to escape arrest and execution during his twenty-five years of preaching, shepherding and writing? By moving from one place to another, by secret night-time meetings in the homes of those who loved Menno and, at the risk of their own life, offered him refuge from the storms of prejudice and hate. In the Netherlands province of West Friesland where Menno spent the first five years of his new ministry, Tjard Reynders was arrested and broken on the torturer's rack because he shared his home with Menno for a short time.

So effective was Simons' ministry in the region that, after trying unsuccessfully for several years to wipe out what his enemies called "the accursed sect", the governing authorities decided the only way they could stop the movement was to get rid of their leader. To accomplish this, they sent a letter to Queen Mary, the Catholic ruler of the Netherlands, saying,

> This sect would doubtless be and remain extirpated were it not that a former priest, Menno Simons who is one of the principal leaders of the aforesaid sect and three or four years ago became a fugitive, has roved about once or twice a year in these parts misleading many simple and innocent people. To seize and apprehend this man we have offered large sums of money, but until now with no success. Therefore we have entertained the thought of offering and promising pardon and mercy to a few who have been misled if they would bring about the imprisonment of the said Menno Simons.

A year later, Emperor Charles V put a price of 100 gold gilders on Simons' head, decreeing death to anyone assisting him in any way, or found reading his books. Forced to leave the Netherlands because of persecution, Simons fled with his sick wife and small children to an area along the Baltic seacoast where many Anabaptists had come from Holland to escape the Emperor's wrath, and where a more tolerant king of Denmark ruled.

Typical Mennonite Peace-Making

A story based on the *Mennonite Encyclopedia* and material from Mennonite historian, John Horsch, tells about an incident from this period which illustrates the peace of Jesus practiced by the Mennonite church for almost five hundred years.

Children in the Mueller home in Wismar on the north shore of Germany were excited. Tomorrow would be Christmas. They were looking out the window at the falling snow when one of the children shouted, "Look, there's a ship in the harbor."

Everyone in the Mueller family, including their guest, Menno Simons, ran to the window to see what ship it could be. "It seems to be stuck in the ice," said Mr. Mueller.

"Why would a ship venture out there at this time of winter?", Simons asked. Mr. Mueller decided to find out. By afternoon he found that the cargo of the ship were refugees, Dutch people of the Reformed church who were fleeing from persecution in England because of their refusal to follow the commands of the Catholic regime then in power.

"They must be cold and hungry," said little Hans. "Why don't they walk ashore? The ice is thick. We skated there yesterday."

"The city council won't permit them to come ashore. The ruling authorities are followers of Luther and the people on the boat believe in the teaching of John Calvin," their father replied.

"Then we must do what Menno Simons teaches and help them", said Mrs. Mueller.

Simons smiled and said, "Let's do what Jesus teaches and help them. Our Lord said, 'Blessed are the merciful for they shall obtain mercy'. What can we do? How shall we begin?"

"Let's begin by seeing what food and blankets we can share," said Mr. Mueller. "I will go to Anabaptists in the neighborhood and ask them to do the same thing."

"I will go with you and speak to those I know," said Simons.

Before long, many Wismar followers of Menno Simons were pulling loads of food and blankets on sleds to their brothers and sisters in Christ, cold and hungry on their boat stranded in the ice.

The next morning, some of the refugees walked ashore and visited in the homes of their new friends. In the Mueller home, refugees heard Menno Simons read the Christmas story from Luke. When he read the words, "there was no place for them in the inn", one of the refugees said, "Thank you for making room for us refugees. This is the true Spirit of the Christ we worship this Christmas day."

It was a time of great joy as those to be called Mennonites refused to obey the ruling authorities that banned the refugees from their city. When the ship broke loose from the ice, its sails were lifted in the mysterious breezes of the Holy Spirit. It is the same Spirit, the fruit of which is the love they experienced from Menno Simons' peace-church. This church has been known for almost five hundred years for befriending all of God's children, no matter how the state labels them.

During the twenty-five years of his ministry among Anabaptists, Brother Menno wrote twenty-five books, many pamphlets and countless letters of comfort and challenge to the congregations he organized. Also two hymns, one with these lines:

> My God, where shall I wend my flight?
> Ah, help me upon my way;
> The foe surrounds both day and night
> And fain my soul would rend and slay.
> Lord God, Thy Spirit give to me,

Then on Thy ways I'll constant be,
And in Life's Book, eternally!

Menno Simons' View of War

A volume entitled *The Complete Works of Menno Simons*, contains his teaching about the Christian and war:

> Our weapons are not weapons with which cities and countries may be destroyed and human bloodshed in torrents like water. But they are weapons with which the spiritual kingdom of the devil is destroyed and the wicked principle in man's soul broken down, flinty hearts broken, hearts that have never been sprinkled with the dew of the Holy Word. We have and know no other weapons beside this, the Lord knows, even if we should be torn into a thousand pieces, and if as many false witnesses rose up against us as there are spears of grass in the fields and grains of sand upon the seashore.

> Christ is our fortress; patience our weapon of defense; the Word of God our sword; and our victory a courageous, firm, and unfeigned faith in Jesus Christ. Iron and metal spears and swords we leave to those who, alas, regard human blood and swine's blood alike.

Simons may not have been a great writer or a great orator, but he demonstrated a great character, a faithful Spirit, a pure mind, and a serene soul, which was exactly what Anabaptists needed; a shepherd to help them "constant be" in the face of the foe. Today, almost half a millennium after Menno Simon's death in 1561, this church is called by Menno's name and still known for their witness to God's here-and-now peaceable kingdom.

In the new Mennonite Minister's Manual is an old set of baptismal questions from the 1700's. The second question asks the novice desiring membership in the church:

> Do you promise, by God's grace, to follow Jesus, the Lamb, all the days of your life, ready to love your enemies, and suffer wrong nonresistantly?

When all would be disciples of Jesus are asked that question at their baptism and answer with an emphatic "Yes!", the church will once again turn the world upside down by daring to love as Jesus loves, enfleshing God's Holy Spirit of peace in every aspect of their life, every day of their new life.

Evangelism and Its Dangers

Unlike Hutterites and Amish, the Mennonite church actively reaches out to evangelize a fallen world and baptize all nations in the name of the Father, Son, and Holy Spirit. Mennonites now number about 900,000 members in 60 countries on all continents of our planet.

In reaching out to bring others to Christ and His church, especially in heavily populated urban areas, Mennonites face the constant temptation to compromise with the world's culture of war and violence. In such metropolitan areas, many Mennonite churches are tending to become more and more like mainline "just war" churches. Aware of this, many Mennonites are praying for a recovery of the Anabaptist vision of the church, the vision given to the church on Pentecost:

> Only Jesus! There is no other name under heaven given among men by which we must be saved.
> - Acts 4:12

Not Menno Simons, not Martin Luther, not John Calvin, not Jakob Hutter. Not the Pope. Not Billy Graham. Only the crucified, risen, ascended, ruling, indwelling Christ can break down the dividing walls that separate us as nations and races and save a fallen world from perishing in sin's violence. Simons would have been grieved to hear that the Peace Church he loved so dearly had been given the name "Mennonite". Knowing how such names mislead and confuse, Menno wrote,

> We must rid ourselves of the name "Anabaptists". It is a hateful title we must never choose. Hereafter we call ourselves "the Brethren".

As the church of Jesus enters the Third Millennium, may Menno Simons' vision of God's peaceable kingdom be recovered and enfleshed, not only by all Mennonites, but by all Christians of every church and every denomination. Abiding in the living God is this world's only ethnic, racial, and nationalistic cleansing . . . and peace.

Anabaptists Called Amish
A Third Model of the Church Living in Community

Today's 81,000 Amish were originally Swiss Mennonites. In the late 1600s, hoping to find a friendlier atmosphere, many moved northward into the lower Rhine River region along the border of France known as Alsace-Lorraine, where my great-grandparents were born.

In their new homeland and fed up with religious intolerance, the Mennonites wanted to be friends with their new neighbors, even if they belonged to the church which had labeled them "heretics" and hounded them as criminals. Happily, they found some Catholics and Protestants ready for mutual friendship, even willing to assist them when they were in need. Some even agreed with the Anabaptists but to avoid trouble, they had remained in their traditional church.

Neighbors friendly to Mennonites came to be known as "The True-Hearted". As many Mennonites mingled with these True-Hearted Catholics and Protestants, more conservative Mennonites believed such inter-mingling was going too far. For them God's word forbids children of light having fellowship with those groping their way in the darkness of a lost world.

The Conservative Jakob Ammann

One who questioned such close friendship was Jakob Ammann, a young Mennonite Elder who believed true Anabaptists should shun members of other churches, not socialize with them. It was his conviction that to become close friends with those of very different beliefs was to compromise one's faith.

Ammann was also disturbed to find young Mennonites taking their turn as town watchmen who had to use force, if necessary, in dealing with troublemakers. Even though true disciples rejected war, some had even joined the town's militia. As an Elder in the Mennonite church, Ammann wrote a letter of protest to the ruling civil authorities stating emphatically that Anabaptists "were not in a position to have one single member serve as a public watchman or in the militia as some had previously done." Acting boldly, if not always gently and lovingly, Jakob Ammann was attempting to stop what he saw as a drift toward compromise with the world. He wanted to preserve a pure church.

Because Ammann was convinced that a pure church was a disciplined church, he started observing Holy Communion twice a year instead of once, as was the Mennonite custom. Why did Ammann think observing Holy Communion twice a year would lead to a more disciplined church? Remember, those at Schleitheim agreed that before coming to the Lord's Table, each congregation was to examine their life to see if all members were in unity and peace with one another. If there was quarreling and disagreement among them, the congregation should not partake of the Bread until there was "one loaf" (1 Corinthians 10:17). Ammann connected more frequent Communion with more frequent self-examination and repentance for sin. He believed this would help keep the church in spiritual health.

Ammann Returns to Switzerland to Ask Questions

Having spent most of his life in Switzerland, Ammann saw signs that his brothers and sisters in his homeland were also becoming lax. So, in 1693, Ammann and three other like-minded ministers visited Swiss Mennonite communities to question Elders about their teaching and stress the need for a holy life in separation from those who lived as friends of the world. These visits sparked debates which focused on two strong leaders with opposing views: Jakob Ammann and Hans Reist, a senior Swiss Elder. The result of their bitter disagreement would end in a separate and more conservative church known as the Amish.

Swiss Elder, Hans Reist, rejected Ammann's call for shunning on the grounds that the Lord ate with sinners and associated with those looked upon as impure. Swiss Mennonites did exclude wayward members from Communion, but did not shun them socially. Since the purpose of the Lord's Supper is to express God's reconciling love, not sin's separation, the controversy between Ammann and Reist was sad.

To settle the issue Reist and his group were invited to meet with Ammann's party at Niklaus Moser's barn, but Reist failed to show up. Hoping for reconciliation, an even larger group was invited to a second meeting. In-between meetings the debate continued. Elder Reist wrote a letter telling the churches "not to pay any attention to younger men", referring especially to Jakob Ammann.

At the second meeting Hans Reist again was absent, along with a number of Swiss Mennonites who also opposed social shunning and changing the once-a-year Holy Communion tradition. When one of the sisters went out to tell brother Hans they were waiting for him, Hans sent word back that he and his friends were too busy harvesting their crops to be bothered.

Brother Jakob's reaction only added fuel to the fire. In a moment of anger, Ammann excommunicated Hans Reist and the other like-minded Elders. Those at the meeting were shocked at Ammann's impulsive action and called for a "cooling off" period. But Ammann was adamant. His angry action was matched by the stubbornness of Elder Reist. Those in attendance were in a daze. Ammann's associate, Peter Zimmerman, spoke the last words, "There you have it". With those words the meeting broke up. Both sides walked out without a handshake or kiss of peace.

The Amish Church is Born

So it was that in 1693, a more conservative branch of the Mennonite church in Alsace-Lorraine came to be known as the Amish.

There is room in the church for differences such as the frequency for observing the Sacrament of Holy Communion, how to discipline those who go astray, and such matters, but there is no excuse for refusing to come together as brothers and sisters to pray and listen to one another when there is a grievance and to forgive as God forgives.

Weeks later, realizing that he had been too quick to excommunicate, Ammann did ask for forgiveness and for a reconciliation of the two groups, but Elder Reist and his group said it was too late. They were content to let the matter stand where the meeting in the barn had left it.

Nothing is more violent than Christians refusing to sit together at the Lord's Communion Table as God's reconciled family. As we eat of the Bread and drink from the Cup, the miracle of our soul's renewal that takes place there is beyond our human understanding. All branches of the church come to the Table of Holy Communion to partake of a Holy Mystery, not to agree on a precise explanation of the Bread and Wine and precise rules on how the Sacrament is to be administered. More important than our explanations of the holy mystery is our love for one another to show that we belong to the One whose cross, resurrection, and indwelling have made the Sacrament possible.

Both Jakob Ammann and Hans Reist wanted to preserve a church true to Jesus' life and teaching. Reist honestly believed Ammann was too legalistic, that the letter of the law kills, only the Holy Spirit gives life (2 Corinthians 3:6). Ammann honestly believed Hans was too tolerant, that a pure New Testament church must be disciplined according to God's word (Romans 16:17; 1 Corinthians 5:9-12; 2 Thessalonians.3:6,14).

Ammann believed using hook-and-eyes, instead of buttons to fasten clothing was essential in combating self-pride. Many Mennonites did not think buttons were little idols and, therefore, refused to conform to Ammann's dress code- a reminder of an elderly Quaker couple driving for miles in their horse-drawn buggy in complete silence. Dressed in a black suit now covered with dust, continuing to look straight ahead, Hans broke the long silence by observing in a stern voice, "Mary, I think the whole world is queer, except thee and me." Then, after another long pause, added, "And, Mary, sometimes I think thee art a bit queer."

The Amish Migrate to America

During the next fifty years in Europe, war and social upheaval beyond the control of Ammann and Reist scattered both Mennonites and Amish half way around the globe. After an eighty-three day voyage during which one child was born and seventeen persons died, the "Charming Nancy", the first boat carrying a large group of Amish to another continent, docked in Philadelphia on September 18, 1737.

The first Amish to land in North America found refuge in Penn's Woods and were part of William Penn's Holy Experiment to form a Christian state which would not use coercive force. Penn believed the peace-loving Quakers could demonstrate a new kind of Christian government in the New World which would be a model for all nations to follow. But by the end of the century, the Quakers had withdrawn from the Pennsylvania legislature because it had established a military force typical of every state.

Penn's Holy Experiment failed. Because of his open-door policy, Pennsylvania was flooded with immigrants from all parts of Europe. They brought with them a variety of views, almost all very different from those of George Fox and the Quakers. The Scotch-Irish argued that Penn's friendship with the Indians was unrealistic coddling. The Holy Experiment failed because most of the people who came were on a different spiritual wavelength from the Quakers. Trusting only in God's sword of the Spirit to reconcile the new tribes of Israel with the tribes of Indians—not in the world's sword of metal—was foreign to the immigrants who landed on American soil. They were looking for lots of land, not lots of new friends with strange customs. Among them were Penn's own two sons who deceived the Indians in land-grabbing schemes.

Now living in twenty states and in Canada's Province of Ontario, the Holy Experiment of the Amish has worked for more than three centuries because they have been bonded by a common commitment. Approximately 70 percent of the Amish live in the three states of Indiana, Ohio, and Pennsylvania. Half of the Pennsylvania Amish are concentrated in Lancaster county known worldwide for its plain people with their traditional dress and horse and buggy transportation.

Amish Lifestyle

Even though the Amish retain private property, acknowledging God as Owner, they use their material possessions as good stewards and share with each other as God shares with them. None in the Amish community are on public welfare. None of their parents are placed in Homes for the Elderly. They take care of one another within a warm and loving family relationship which starts at birth and continues to the grave. The only nursery school Amish children know is their familiar home with an ever-present mother and a father never far way. Their homestead is a farm in which the entire family is busily involved and where grandparents find security in their old age.

The Amish think today's children are spoiled by being driven by parents from swimming pools to games and from one program to another, hoping they will become "well-rounded", happy adults. In contrast, the daily routine of Amish children includes washing dishes by hand, feeding the animals, pulling weeds, and helping with the many family chores they are trained to do by parents they learn to respect and obey.

For a young married couple, family planning means plans for a large family, averaging seven children who walk to one-room Amish schools for eight years, often having the same Amish teacher with whom the family has a close relationship. Amish schools are controlled by parents who elect a school-board that hires and fires and determines a simple curriculum based on the three R's, geography, health, and the practical skills needed in everyday life without the trappings of athletics, clubs, dances, cafeterias, bands, guidance counselors, and the like.

The Amish school and the Amish community and culture are one. The school is drug- and violence-free because Amish culture adamantly opposes both. Each morning in their one-room school, the class begins with reading from the Bible, songs, and the Lord's Prayer. Religion is not taught as a separate subject, just as sex is not a separate subject. The Amish believe religious and sex education are the responsibility of family and church. These subjects are instilled by their Christian culture, not taught by separate institutions.

Teaching children to respect teachers, not to cheat on examinations, to tell the truth in every spoken word, to play fairly, to keep one's body clean and healthy, and to earn an honest living from the soil, Amish religion permeates the Amish school. Laws of nature are learned first hand from the world of nature in which Amish participate every day of their life. In the Amish school, sacred and secular, private and public, are not mixed à la Augustine. They have never been separated. Amish schools did not just happen. They were fought for with nonviolent weapons of the Spirit.

I remember the Amish struggle with the state when a law was passed in 1925 extending compulsory school attendance from fourteen to fifteen years of age. Since Amish schools go only to the 8th grade, this meant that, at least for one year, their children would have to be bused from their own familiar school to a strange high-school with strange teachers, teaching a strange curriculum based on a strange nationalistic culture which takes the military and its wars for granted. The long struggle with the state finally ended in 1956 by allowing the Amish church to have a one-year vocational course taught in their own community by their own teachers. For three hours a day, a dozen or so fourteen year olds met in Amish homes for "vocational training".

I remember, too, that just as this skirmish with the state was settled, another much more serious demand by the state's Department of Education threatened their culture. Small neighborhood elementary schools, in walking distance for Amish children, were being replaced by large consolidated schools to which required busing.

Once again, saying they must obey God rather than men, the Amish refused to obey a law which would turn the training of their children over to the state.

At first, a few Amish accepted the argument that it would be good for their sons and daughters to be exposed to children of other religious and social cultures, that the nation's pluralism of the consolidated school would broaden Amish appreciation for the "real" world. That argument collapsed when parents saw the consolidated public school exposing their children to sex-education with an emphasis on safe sex rather than sacred sex, on swearing allegiance to a nation-state that prostitutes its resources on a military system trained to kill, and on encouraging the mindset of competition to make America Number One in every human endeavor.

When discussions with the state failed, the Amish built their own one-room elementary schools in defiance of the law and continued to educate their children with their own teachers who used a curriculum harmonious with their biblical faith.

One Amish leader explained their opposition to public school's so-called "progressive education" saying, "With us, our religion is inseparable from a day's work, a night's rest, a meal, or any other practice; our education can much less be separated from our religious practices."

The struggle with the state went on for 25 years. Hundreds of

Amish fathers were arrested, voluntarily choosing to go to jail rather than have their children go to schools which would instill values in their children contrary to Amish deepest religious convictions.

Finally, in 1972 the Supreme Court ruled in their favor, stating,

> Amish objection to formal education beyond the 8th grade is firmly grounded in central religious concepts. They object to high school and college education primarily because the values it teaches are in marked variance with Amish values and the Amish way of life. "Higher education" tends to emphasize intellectual and scientific accomplishments, self-determination, competitiveness, worldly success, and social life with other students. Amish society emphasizes learning-through-doing, a life of "goodness" rather than a life of intellect, wisdom rather than technical knowledge, community welfare rather than competition, and separation rather than integration with contemporary worldly society.

The Amish Way of Responding to Violence

Entitled "Witness", Hollywood made a movie about the Amish. Although enlightening in some ways, the movie reflects that Hollywood still does not understand the Amish church and its culture of nonviolence. As a gang ridicules and attacks a group of Amish young people because of their quaint dress and customs, a macho Hollywood hero rescues them with his fists, the kind of "operation rescue" the Amish church does not appreciate.

On a summer evening of 1957, two young men just released from prison decided to celebrate their new freedom by robbing a young Amish couple in Ohio. In the course of the $19 robbery, the husband, Paul Coblentz, was killed and his wife, Dora, raped. The released prisoners fled in a stolen car. Before they were captured, a deputy sheriff was shot to death. Michael Dumoulin, age 20, was sentenced to a long term in prison, and 19-year-old Eugene Peters was sentenced to death by electrocution.

Condemning capital punishment, the Amish community, including the raped Dora Coblentz, fleshed out their faith by writing hundreds of friendly letters to Eugene in prison and pleading with the governor of Ohio to spare the killer's life. Amish families invited the murderer's parents to their homes, and Amish leaders visited Eugene in prison. Seven hours before the scheduled execution, the governor commuted Eugene's sentence. Many testimonies tell how that witness of merciful agape enriched the spiritual life of the Amish community and helped Hollywood and the world understand what it means to be a disciple of God's nonviolent Messiah.

The Meaning of "Gelassenheit"

Amish culture is embedded in the German word "Gelassenheit". It means submission, self-surrender, yielding humbly to the sovereignty of God and trusting in the Holy One's power to deliver His children from evil and death. It does not recognize the power of a fallen world's systems of domination. Gelassenheit stands in sharp contrast to sin's culture of ruthless competition and aggressive confrontation expressed in divorce, lawsuits, domestic violence, war, and the like. Gelassenheit is inherent in this school verse:

> I must be a Christian child,
> Gentle, patient, meek, and mild:
> Must be honest, simple, true

In my words and actions too.
I must cheerfully obey,
Giving up my will and way.

The Amish meet for worship every other Sunday, not in a special building, but in each other's homes. These homes are built with movable partitions to accommodate the congregation which may consist of 125 adults and as many children. Benches and song books are transported from home to home for the service which consists primarily of singing and two sermons by ministers chosen from the congregation by lot (Acts 1:26). Lasting from 7:30 to noon, the long church service certainly teaches Gelassenheit as the children wait patiently and submissively for eating and relaxed fellowship after the service.

Mainline churches try to grow as big as possible. When an Amish congregation grows to a certain size—about twenty families—they divide and start another house-church under the same bishop.

The Amish church follows what they call "Ordnung" which could be translated "ordinance" or "discipline". For the Amish, the Ordnung which determines their daily life is neither written nor memorized; as they say, "We just know it, that's all."

Just as children come to understand rules of grammar and then use them without thinking, so the Amish come to an understanding of community customs and live accordingly. Some are explicit and determine the way the Amish dress and which modern gadgets and machinery they can or cannot use.

Since electric power is forbidden by the Old Order Amish, hardly any modern appliances and machines can be used. Public phones are used in an emergency, but are not allowed in homes for idle conversation. We might see a mechanical forklift in an Amish carpenter shop, but it cannot be used as a machine for transportation. Taxis are used when necessary, but cars cannot be purchased and used for travel as an end in itself. Most people find such Ordnung hard to understand.

The Amish Way of Controlling Technology

If what we prize most is individual freedom, we cannot justify such customs. If what we treasure most is a well-ordered life of peace in community, and not making idols of things, we are willing to submit to the Ordnung to be a part of the beloved community. To be free for a quiet and contented life *in community*, the Amish have decided to be free from an unbridled pursuit of self-gratification and the desire to own the latest models of the things technology can produce.

Freedom has two sides: freedom for and freedom from. Amish are not free to buy every electric appliance or car we see advertised a hundred times a day, but they are free from consumerism and its worrisome debt, and the "I must have that" mindset that is never satisfied. Amish are not free to buy the latest fashions, but they are free from the anxiety of what to wear and the need to shop for unnecessary items, adding to the stockpile already in jammed drawers and closets. Amish are not free to accept Social Security checks, but they are free from the fear of old age and how they will be cared for. Amish are not free to experiment with the world's "alternative life-styles". However, they are free to mature as persons who know they are infinitely loved and valued by an Infinite God and a family-oriented community. Their Ordnung does not countenance drugs, killing, or suicide as a way out of a messed up life. Amish are not free to kill in war, but they are free to live in a peace this world can neither give nor take away.

When Amish youth are baptized about the age of eighteen, they promise to follow the Ordnung of their church, believing the way of their community is in harmony with God's life Jesus enfleshed. Although a world of glitter and glamour surrounds Amish children on every side, four out of five Amish youth decide to be baptized and spend the rest of their life in the Amish church community.

The Amish do not skim the daily paper to find a "brave new world" by means of some new gadget. The Amish have set a limit to their material hankerings and let their life lived in response to Christ's love be the index of their wants. These "quaint" folks have so much to teach mechanized Christendom which makes our life fit the machine.

The Amish Way vs. Augustine's Way

For more than 300 years, the Amish way has been tried and not found wanting by those who have stayed the course. It is not Augustine's way of mixing with sin's world. Instead, it is the Spirit's separation from a world which is enamored with itself, trapped by the idolatry of gadgets, gimmicks, guns and glitter.

Recently, I saw an Amish wood carving which tells the true story of an Indian raid in which Jacob Hochstettler refused to let his sons use their rifles to kill attacking enemies. The carving shows Jacob stopping his sons from shooting at hostile Indians who have surrounded the family's cabin.

When one of the boys heard the farm dog barking and opened the door, he was shot in the leg by one of the Indians stalking the house. He and his two brothers ran to get their hunting guns to defend the family, but their father would not allow them to shoot.

Jacob hid his family in the cellar. When the Indians set fire to the house and the family tried to escape through a window, the attackers killed Jacob, Jr., his mother and his sisters. The father and two sons were taken captive. Months later when the Indians allowed Jacob to go hunting by himself, he was able to escape by canoe on the Susquehanna River where I fished and canoed as a lad. Eventually, the father was reunited with his two sons.

A fallen world asks, "What was accomplished by that Amish family's willingness to suffer and be killed rather than kill their attackers? Their Christian love didn't prevent the Indians from destroying their home and most of their family." True, those in that Amish family were not free from a fallen world's violence and death, but they were free for their new and eternal life in the kingdom of God Jesus inaugurated. This Amish family didn't allow a temporal world's violence to separate them from the Eternal's kingdom no attacker can destroy with fire or firearms. The Hochstettlers were dwelling in a house not made with hands the Indians could not, and did not, destroy. They knew their real home is with the Father whose Spirit is love (1John 4:16) and whose purpose for each of us is eternal life.

The real frontier of the Hochstettler family was not Berks County in Pennsylvania. Jacob's family longed for a frontier without geographical borders. Abba had prepared for them a better frontier that will not disappoint them (See Hebrew 11:13-16).

To those who say, "But if we trust Christ for peace instead of war planes and "smart bombs", we might die," we answer, "True, we might die," but it would be a clean death, our love responding to Christ's love in obedience to His New Commandment (John 13:34). We have only a few years to live in the flesh and then we hear a shout that school is out, and lessons done, and we homeward run to a heaven without guns and without the politics of nation-states and their parading armies. The question is, will we be prepared for such an environment? Will we then be at Home with the Eternal, or total strangers to a life-style we never knew and we hear Jesus say, "I never knew you, depart from me you evildoers" (Matthew 7:23)?

Which Model for the Church?

From the Anabaptist vision of the kingdom of God, we have viewed three different models of Jesus' nonviolent church: Hutterite, Mennonite, and Amish. Each nonviolent; each a little different. Which of these three models with their nonviolent lifestyle should we see as the most authentic pattern for the church to follow in the Twenty-First Century?

Answer: The church should not try to copy any of them.

The model for the church to follow is not Amish, Hutterite or Mennonite, just as it is not Roman Catholic, Eastern Orthodox or Protestant. The only blueprint for the church is the living, creating, loving, holy Spirit of God in the risen, triumphant Christ. In our wickedness, ignorance and mortality, only abiding in Christ and His word can save us. He is the Christian's model in every age.

Abiding in the Holy Spirit and living nonviolently day by day, we don't have to wait until we find the perfect church model. Only God is perfect. In the crucified-risen-ascended-ruling-indwelling Christ, God is with us to enable us to love as Jesus loved. Jesus is our model and our empowerment.

In Dostoevsky's novel, *The Brothers Karamazov*, two brothers stand in stark contrast to each other. With a brilliant mind, Ivan is a questioning agnostic, always pointing out the failures of the various political systems but never living as a positive solution to the problem of evil. His brother, Alyosha, has no intellectual answer to the critical questions Ivan asks. Significantly however, he says to Ivan, "I do not know the answer to the problem of evil, but I do know love."

While we remain in sin's world of the flesh, unanswered

questions in an imperfect church are not fatal. What is fatal is not to know the self-giving Holy Spirit of God's love and peace Jesus Christ offers to sin's self-centered, perishing world. It is not for us to wait, therefore, until we find a flawless peace-church in which to follow the Lord's New Commandment to love as He loves and live day by day as a citizen of the Holy One's nonviolent community. Where we are right now, whatever our circumstances, it is our responsibility to be servants of Jesus, growing in His likeness day by day (2 Corinthians 3:18):

> until we all attain to the unity of the faith and of the knowledge of the Son of God, to mature persons, to the measure of the stature of the fullness of Christ, so that we may no longer be tossed to and fro and carried about with every wind of doctrine, by the cunning of men, by their craftiness and deceitful wiles. Rather, speaking the truth in love, we are to grow up in every way into him who is the head, into Christ, from whom the whole body is joined and knit together.
> - Ephesians 4:13-16

This is the secret of living creatively, peacefully, and eternally.

Chapter 7

Repent, Believe the Gospel and Be Jesus' Peace Church

> I was not disobedient to the heavenly vision, but declared first to those at Damascus, then at Jerusalem and throughout all the country of Judea, and also to the Gentiles, that they should repent and turn to God and perform deeds worthy of their repentance.
> - Acts 26:19-20

So spoke Paul when he stood before Festus, the Roman procurator of Judea and his visitor, King Agrippa. They asked to hear what Paul had to say. After all, the well-known evangelist was being held prisoner right there in Caesarea, waiting to be removed to Rome where he would stand trial. Hoping the hearing would help him specify the charges he would bring against Paul, the procurator consented to let Paul speak.

When on trial for one's life, one usually does not emphasize secondary matters. He or she comes directly to what is primary. Agrippa and Festus heard Paul testify to three crucial points: his persecution of Christians prior to his Damascus Road conversion; his vision of the crucified and risen Jesus who had transformed his life from sin's violence to his new self, reconciled to the God of peace and to both Jew and Gentile; and the need for everyone to turn to God, repent, and live by deeds worthy of repentance.

At one point, Festus interrupted the hearing and shouted, "You are out of your mind, Paul. Your great learning is driving you insane."

Paul replied,

> I am not mad. The king knows about these things. I am persuaded that none of these things has escaped his notice, for this was not done in a corner.
> - Acts 26:25-26

Like Paul, all who are not disobedient to the heavenly vision of Abba's peaceable kingdom realized in Jesus, are shouted down as mentally imbalanced. Jesus himself was considered mad by many, including His own family (Mark 3:21). For the last sixteen centuries those declaring Jesus Christ to be God's nonviolent Messiah, like Paul, are considered a bit queer and are ignored, not only by an unbelieving world, but by the major segment of the church. This same church conforms to the likeness of a warring world, not to the image of the Prince of Peace who said,

> My kingdom is not of this world. If it were my servants would fight to prevent my arrest.
> - John 18:36

Jesus was describing His action to a political enemy, a ruling authority of government, not to his next-door neighbor. This conversation with Pilate had to do with international relations, not mere private and personal relationships between two persons. Churches are wrong that teach a dual Christian ethic; one for person-to-person relations and another very different political ethic. There is one Spirit who is above all and through all and in all (See Ephesians 4:4).

How many mainline Catholic, Orthodox, Protestant, and Pentecostal churches are engaged in a serious discussion of Jesus' teaching of nonviolence, which includes a Christian's relation to his/her enemies of state? Based on half a century of first-hand observation, I would say almost zero. I would welcome hard evidence to the contrary.

The Meaning of Christian Nonviolence

By Christian nonviolence, I do not mean a favorable attitude toward peace between nations. For example, one Elder in a church responded to my suggestion that there be a group to study the biblical meaning of Christian nonviolence by saying, "Howard, why do you want to discuss such a subject? Everybody is in favor of peace. No one wants war." Nor am I referring to nonviolence as defined in the dictionary: "The policy or practice of seeking one's ends without resort to violence." The Bible has nothing to say about nonviolent agape as a political policy to protect national interests defined by the State Department. Nor am I thinking of Peace Movements separated from the person of Jesus, which spend time, energy and money to lobby against a particular weapon's program; or to favor one political peace process; or one kind of military action rather than another; nor the 57 varieties of pacifism and the refusal to fight in a particular war such as Vietnam. Only God knows how many so-called pacifists have refused to go to war because they did not want to suffer and be killed. This is just plain cowardice, not Christian nonviolence. Disciples of the nonviolent Messiah do not have the privilege of selecting the mass-murdering war favorable to their mood at the moment.

I am certainly not limiting nonviolence with saying "yes" to a ban on nuclear weapons. A hand grenade, a rifle, or a bayonet can be as much an agent of Satan as an atomic bomb. All war is hell, not just nuclear combat.

Violence is inherent in every nation-state and its coercive systems (1 Samuel 8:10-13) and in every human who rejects the rule of the Holy Spirit Jesus inaugurated. Jesus even linked violence with a way of thinking that leads to violent action and made it synonymous with the act (Matthew 5:21-48).

Violence is not limited to war. Tobacco treats the user's body violently. Drug and alcohol addiction abuse their victims in a violent way. Those whose "god is the belly" sooner or later experience violent pain. Those who drive recklessly are violent killers. To fight in court over money and property is to act violently. Gossip is a form of violence in that it damages the reputation of those to whom it is directed. Perhaps nothing is more violent than divorce. In abortion, the fetus is the enemy that must be destroyed. There is no more deliberated violence than the planned killing of those on Death Row. Even meetings on the subject of nonviolence can become violent as we have seen in Northern Ireland and the misnamed "Peace-Process" in the Middle East between Israel and the Palestinians.

At the beginning of a new millennium, our nation continues to ponder the question: "What caused two teen-age boys to walk into Columbine High School in Colorado with guns and shoot to kill twenty-five of their classmates and a teacher, and plant enough bombs to blow up the school?" Psychologists, teachers, ministers, political leaders, parents and students have many different explanations. All agree there is not merely one cause, but living in a violent culture, as we do, is certainly part of the explanation.

One of the dictionary definitions of the word culture is: "training of the mental or moral powers, or the result of such training." The culture in which we humans live trains us to be violent.

Christian Nonviolence and The Military

At the heart of our culture of violence is the military teaching of violence and the war system built into the life of every nation-state on the face of the earth. Military training takes for granted that we must make enemies suffer and kill them when they threaten our national life and welfare. The whole structure of military training and military life is the preparation of people to take part in mass maiming and/or slaughter. Military planners do not sit with the Bible in their hands asking what Jesus would do.

Dr. Gordon Zahn, author, professor and National Director of the Pax Christi USA Center on Conscience and War, points out that "individual soldiers are trained to operate on the basis of unquestioning obedience to their military superiors. The military-training program is designed to subject the individual trainee to a process of depersonalization in the interest of increased military efficiency." Military training, therefore, is the process of handing over one's moral and spiritual life to another person so he or she will kill when the command "Kill!" is given. The soldier in battle does not ask questions. The soldier obeys.

From the moment you step off the bus at Marine boot camp, officers yell and scream at you in an atmosphere of fear. After you are there for two days, you may be up at 3 o'clock in the morning cleaning perfectly clean floors with a toothbrush; a completely irrational act. Why do you do it? Because you are commanded to do it. From now on, you will do anything you are commanded to do. People do such irrational things because they fear the consequences of not doing them. Once the military gets their pupils to wash clean floors at 3 o'clock in the morning with a toothbrush, they are only one step away from being totally controlled, which is the goal of military training. The military creates people who are afraid to function as authentic persons, afraid to stand up and say, "Don't yell at me, I'm a human being." Afraid to stand up and say, "Don't tell me to wash a clean floor with a toothbrush at 3 o'clock in the morning." Afraid to say, "Don't tell me to kill." Afraid to say, "No, I refuse to kill."

This is the military way of "building men", but what kind of men? Does this process of military training nurture the mind of Christ? If it does not, how can the church allow her children to learn the most efficient way to kill with a dagger, or deploy missiles with razor-blade precision to destroy entire communities? Is learning eight different ways to kick people in the groin the art Jesus teaches? Is learning how to pull out people's eyes and slit their throat part of instruction for church membership? In the military, this is precisely what you are trained to do. No questions asked. If this is what our country trains young people to do, why should we be so surprised that the nation's culture is violent? If this is what our nation spends hundreds of billions of dollars to be the best at doing, why don't we honestly admit that we train our young people to be violent in a war system the public school system honors and takes for granted?

> God is not mocked, for whatever a man *(or nation)* sows, that he will also reap.
> - Galatians 6:7

This is what concerned Russian Orthodox Christian Leo Tolstoy at the end of the 19th century when he wrote:

> As military slaves, young men are dressed up in costumes and subjected to intensified methods of stupefaction and brutalization accomplished by educating children in the savage superstitions of patriotism . . . removing them from all natural conditions of human life and locking them together in narrow barracks, and, under the influence of shouts, drums, and music, making them perform exercises invented to teach them

obedience. Thus, they become unthinking machines . . . obedient to the power of the agents of government. Now all express their readiness to dress up in fools' attire, to jump, to contort their bodies, to kill, provided only that they are commanded by a man who is clad in pretty red livery embroidered with gold. Let these young men be killed by the thousands, let them be torn to pieces, while the generals and politicians live in luxury.

The style and material of military uniforms change from century to century. The violent nature of the military remains the same. It has been the same hell since the Stone Age. Science and technology only add to its madness.

In the United States when the cold war military budget reached $300 billion, the Chairman of the Joint Chiefs of Staff, Colin Powell, gave as a reason for spending so much money on the art of killing, "I want to scare the hell out of the rest of the world," and then added, "I don't say that in a bellicose way." The word bellicose means "inclined to fight".

If spending $300 billion on military power to scare the hell out of the rest of the world does not mean being inclined to kill any who threaten our national interests, I don't know what in hell it does mean. As my professor, Harry Emerson Fosdick, told us, "There is one thing you don't do with bayonets, and that is to sit on them."

No matter how nice a guy the General or Chairman of the Joint Chiefs of Staff may appear to be, or what church he belongs to, the state's military system is designed to be used to kill, not to sit on.

$300 billion spent for mass killing is not friendly to the Holy One who said,

> A new commandment I give to you, that you
> love one another; even as I have loved you.
> By this will all men know that you are my
> disciples.
> - John 13:34-35

John, the Apostle who recorded these words of Jesus, followed with a letter to the churches which is consistent with the Master's new commandment:

> God is love, and he who abides in love
> *(agape)* abides in God, and God abides in
> him. In this, love is perfected with us, that we
> may have confidence for the day of judgment,
> because as he is, so are we in this world.
> - 1 John 4:16-17

To consent to spend $300 billion to operate a war machine to kill as expertly as possible those the state perceives to be enemies, is not to be in the world as Jesus was in the world.

The Military's "Friendly Fire" and "Smart" Bombs

Peg Mullen of Brownsville, Texas, whose son had been killed by "friendly fire" in Vietnam, organized a busload of mothers to protest in Washington, in spite of a warning that her house would be burned down if she persisted. This mother persisted because she knew from her own family experience that there is no such thing as "friendly fire" in war.

During Desert Storm, we heard about the accuracy of "smart bombs" which were supposed to hit only military targets of the enemy. My friend, Don Mosley, one of the founders of the Christian community, Jubilee Partners, burst the balloon of that lie after returning from a visit to Iraq while the rocket's red glare and bombs bursting in air lit up the night sky over Baghdad. Don told the pathetic story of his meeting with the husband whose wife and four daughters were among the many who were incinerated when two American "smart bombs" hit the "America shelter" in Baghdad where women and children and a few elderly men had gone for the night to escape U.S. "friendly fire".

The father, a Palestinian, Mohammad Ahmed Khadar, after he got his Master's Degree and married Adiba, moved to Iraq where they purchased a home in the "America" neighborhood. Mohammad became a professor at the University of Baghdad. When the bombing became more than they could bear, he sent his wife and four daughters to the "America shelter". He had made preparations to move his family on February 14th to Amman where he had relatives, but it was a day too late for Adiba and her four daughters. The "smart bombs" struck the shelter on February 13th.

After joining the grieving families at the shelter, and asking, "How can human beings do such things to each other?", Mohammad returned to his empty house and tried to burn himself to death as his family had been burned to a crisp a few hours before. As they had been together in life, he wanted to be together with his family in death. A neighbor intervened and prevented him.

Now, as Don told us, even though his wife and daughters had been dead for weeks, Ahmed Khadar could not help going to his front gate some afternoons, hoping to see his nine-year-old beautiful Ghana, the youngest, come skipping around the corner from school. But Ghana didn't appear. The "smart bombs" were not as smart as Colin Powell and President Bush claimed they would be. Bombs are never smart. Disciples of Jesus can have no part of them.

The director of a pediatric hospital in Baghdad told a New York Times reporter that the first night of the war the electricity was knocked out and "mothers grabbed their children out of incubators, took intravenous tubes out of their arms, removed babies from oxygen tents and ran to the basement where there was no heat. I lost more than 40 premature babies in the first twelve hours of the bombing."

Very often it is when the bombs stop falling that war's worst happens. The human consequences of Desert Storm became shockingly clear after the war was over. The not so "smart" bombs had caused starvation, disease, and the deaths of tens of thousands of children. The death toll of children continues because most means of modern life-support had either been destroyed or severely damaged. When will the United States stop killing children in Iraq?

When the youth of our nation are told on television to join the Marines and "be the best you can be", when our national anthem sings about "bombs bursting in air", wondering if our flag is still there, the glory of war and its unspeakable violence go together like bees and honey. It's all woven into the fabric of public education, a part of a violent culture into which every human is born. We imbibe its false patriotism with our mother's milk.

As I write, the media carries the story of a new inner-city public high school in Chicago's South Side armory where black recruits once drilled before marching off to kill fellow Christians in Europe during World War I. Today, in military-style, youngsters are being educated in public school classes in the Chicago Military Academy, the nation's first public school run by the Army's Junior Reserve Officer Training Corp. No questions asked by Congress. The school's commandant, said, "We are using military methodology to educate these students. The kids are motivated. It helps them develop self-confidence, self-esteem, and comradeship. It helps to develop character."

So it is. The "military" is at the heart of our national culture which sucks all of us into its orbit, as the Lord warned Israel would happen when they chose to have a king to be like the other nations of the world (1 Samuel 8:9-18).

Question: Did the Lord call Israel to be like the other nations of the world? Does Jesus call his church to be like the nations of the world? Is this God's will for a redeemed church?

The New Testament testifies that at the beginning of His public ministry, Jesus was given a glimpse of all the kingdoms of this world and the glory of them as Satan enticed Him, saying,

> All these I will give to you if you will fall
> down and worship me.
> - Matthew 4:9

Jesus rejected the temporal glory of the nations which live in fallen Babylon by the violent power of coercive law, choosing instead the eternal glory of God who rules by the nonviolent power of the Holy Spirit's agape He embodied:

> Have this mind among yourselves, which is
> yours in Christ Jesus, who, though he was in
> the form of God, did not count equality with
> God a thing to be grasped, but emptied
> himself, taking the form of servant, being
> born in the likeness of men. And being found
> in human form he humbled himself and
> became obedient unto death, even death on a
> cross. Therefore, God has highly exalted him
> and bestowed on him the name which is
> above every name, that at the name of Jesus
> every knee should bow, in heaven and on
> earth, and every tongue confess that Jesus
> Christ is Lord.
> - Philippians 2:5-11

God's sharing of His life in Jesus is the blessing Jehovah promised Abraham would come to all the families of the earth (Genesis 12:3). He would come as a Messiah born to a family of Israel. It was this Messianic hope proclaimed by all the Old Testament prophets that saved them from complete despair. This easily could have resulted from Israel's continued disobedience, causing Isaiah to cry out,

> We have become like those over whom thou
> hast never ruled, like those who art not called
> by thy name. There is no one that calls upon
> thy name.
> - Isaiah 63:19; 64:7

Just as Israel's knowledge of God's holiness made them aware of their sinful nature more than any other people, so their awareness of their separation from God produced the most contrite and repentant people on earth, crying out with the Isaiah,

> Woe is me! For I am lost; for I am a man of
> unclean lips, and I dwell in the midst of a
> people of unclean lips; for mine eyes have
> seen the King, the Lord of hosts.
> - Isaiah 6:1-5

In his repentance, Isaiah found cleansing, forgiveness, and the discernment of spirit to hear the Holy One's question: "Whom will I send, and who will go for us?" Isaiah's repentant soul responded, "Here am I, Lord, send me." It was through repentant Isaiah that we in fallen Babylon receive our clearest Messianic vision of Jesus, the world's nonviolent Suffering Servant (See Isaiah 53).

In the holiness of Christ on the cross, we have our clearest awareness of the nature of God and are led to repent and be restored to a new life in the presence of Holy God. Only as we repent and are cleansed and forgiven at the foot of the cross can we share in the reconciling ministry of Christ and receive power to love as God loves and demonstrate the miracle of God's peace on earth.

This is Jesus' call to a self-addicted world,

> The time is fulfilled, and the kingdom of God
> is at hand. Repent, and believe in the gospel.
> - Mark 1:15

The time is fulfilled. God's salvation in Christ is fulfilled. The blessing Jehovah promised through Abraham to all the families of the earth has come in the Prince of Peace. There is nothing more that God can do to bring us to our senses and to our only real peace.

Instead of mimicking the state and its systems of violence, the church is called to witness to Jesus' victory over the evil powers and principalities (See Colossians 2:13-15).

An old Georgia farmer confronted Clarence Jordan, founder of Koinonia Farm, with the words, "I hear you folks won't fight."

"Who told you that?" Clarence replied. "We sure will fight."

Surprised the farmer said, "Well, you won't go into the army, will you?"

"No, we don't fight that way," said Clarence. "Do you see that mule over there? Now, if that mule bit you, would you bite it back?"

"Nope," replied the farmer. "I'd whack that mule with a two-by-four and knock its head off."

"Exactly," said Jordan. "You wouldn't let the mule set the

level of your encounter with him. You would use a weapon the mule doesn't know how to handle, but you do. Well, that's what Christians are supposed to do—use weapons of the Spirit Jesus uses, not the weapons of the world the enemy uses."

For too long, the church has been using the same weapons that the world uses to combat evil.

The Pope's Call to Repentance

On November 14, 1994, anticipating the Third Millennium, Pope John Paul sent an historic Apostolic Letter to all Catholics. It was a plea to begin the new era by becoming more aware of the sinful violence of Mother Church in past centuries and to repent of such sin in order to live as a Christ-like church.

In his surprising pastoral Letter, the Pope asked his flock to recall "all those times in history when they departed from the spirit of Christ and his Gospel, and, instead of offering to the world the witness of a life inspired by the values of faith, indulged in ways of thinking and acting which were truly forms of counterwitness and scandal".

Referring to the Catholic Church, the Pope continued,

> She cannot cross the threshold of the new millennium without encouraging her children to purify themselves, through repentance of past errors and instances of infidelity, inconsistency, and slowness to act. Acknowledging the weaknesses of the past is an act of honesty and courage which helps to strengthen our faith, which alerts us to face today's temptations and challenges, and prepares us to meet them.

Another painful chapter of history to which the sons and daughters of the church must return with a spirit of repentance is that of the acquiescence given, especially in certain centuries, to intolerance and even the use of violence in the service of truth.

Praise God for Pope John Paul's courage to confess past infidelities of the church, asking Catholics to repent of their "counterwitness" of violence instead of witnessing to the nonviolence of the cross.

Godly Grief Leads to Works Worthy of True Repentance

It remains to be seen whether the Pope's plea for repentance for past violence by the church will produce genuine godly grief which leads to a rejection of all war, or merely worldly grief expressing only superficial momentary sorrow for past violence, still leaving a "just war" church unchanged in the new millennium. According to the Apostles,

> Godly grief produces a repentance that leads
> to salvation and brings no regret, but worldly
> grief produces death.
> -2 Corinthians 7:10

Both godly grief and worldly grief affirm the truth of the soul's freedom to reject violent patterns of behavior. Human behavior is not determined by forces over which we have no control. If our life is controlled by our environment and our environment within the state relies on military power for protection, then we will necessarily be programmed to act violently. If this were true, the Pope's plea to repent would be meaningless because to repent means to be able to change, to turn around and go in a different direction.

Godly grief that produces true repentance expresses two things: freedom to change and a faith that inspires and empowers us to change. Worldly grief that produces death is the expression of our freedom to change, but without faith to change our old life. Dietrich Bonhoeffer called it "cheap grace"—grace that wallows emotionally in the comfort of forgiveness without accepting the challenge to take up one's cross and follow Jesus to the death. This, Bonhoeffer did when he voluntarily returned to Nazi Germany in 1938 to challenge Hitler's violence. During the last days of the war, he was beheaded. Unfortunately, after rejecting violence, Bonhoeffer made the mistake of joining the group that planned to use violence to assassinate Adolph Hitler.

Godly repentance leaves no room for the blame-game which accuses either others or external circumstances, making them responsible for our violence. Repentance which leads to a new direction for our life accepts full responsibility for our actions because the basis for accountability is between the Christian's soul and God. Godly repentance which leads to radical change and discipleship is essentially a religious experience which presupposes an awareness of God as Redeemer and Judge. Without some personal awareness of God's holiness and love, remorse for sin will fade and leave the soul worse than before. Godly repentance is likely to be a never-to-be-forgotten crisis-experience at a particular moment when the soul becomes aware that violence begets violence and surrenders all to the Almighty.

Until Jesus becomes the ALL of our lives, He is not the Lord who empowers us to go against the grain of the world's violence and say No! to the state's systemic militaristic method of dealing with those the political authorities tag as our enemies. This is the beginning of the Christian life based on the soul's awareness of falling short of the mark set for us in Christ and the need to cry out over and over again with the publican,

> God be merciful to me, a sinner.
> - Luke 18:13

Only Christ Can Cast Out Sin's War System

The war system is sin and only the indwelling Christ can cast out its curse. The state will never legislate its end. It is up to the church to be the church and say No! to the sin of war. We can only hope and pray that the Pope's Pastoral Letter will inspire elders, pastors, bishops, cardinals, and patriarchs of all branches of the church to repent and express "godly grief" for the suffering and death we of the church have caused in the past and continue to cause in the present.

Now it is time for the church to renounce ALL war and its mass slaughter as contrary to Jesus and His Way of the nonviolent cross. When the visible Body of Christ on earth does repent and bears the fruit of godly grief, the word of the church on domestic violence, abortion, capital punishment, and all other forms of violence, will be taken more seriously. The church as a visible community of peace will take on a new meaning, not only to Christians, but to the secular world that recognizes the difference Jesus, Son of God, Savior, makes when He is followed and taken seriously.

At the beginning of Lent in the year 2000, the Pope visited the Holy Land for a week during which he again asked God to forgive the church for her past violence. He referred not only to the burning of heretics at the stake during the Inquisition and those slaughtered by Christians during the Crusades, but also to the Christian persecution of Jews through the centuries which reached a climax in the Holocaust.

In Jerusalem, Israeli Prime Minister Ehud Barak, whose grandparents perished in the Treblinka death camp in Nazi-occupied Poland, said to Pope John Paul II, "I think I can say, your Holiness, that your coming here today is a climax of this historic journey of healing."

The Christian's Individual Responsibility

If the Twenty-First Century is to be a journey that heals a violent world of its war-sickness, it will be because each of us as Christians accepts full responsibility for our own participation in a fallen world's war system and decisively submit to "Jesus Christ, Son of God, Savior" as our one and only standard of truth. If the church is to embody the peace of Jesus and reject the "just war" heresy of mass slaughter which mainstream Christianity has engaged in since the time of Constantine, Christians cannot wait for pope, patriarch, and pastors of churches to renounce totally all war. The people in the pews must go into all the world and make their confession of faith in Jesus, the nonviolent Messiah, by rejecting war's legalized murder. This means trusting in the risen Christ for our victory over every enemy, not the military might of the state.

As nation-states and their political parties continue to advocate the state's sword of steel which slaughters to protect material possessions and life in the flesh, let the church be the church of the risen, nonviolent Messiah. In doing so, it will repent sin's violence and, one by one, confess Jesus as the Lord who has toppled Satan (See Isaiah 31:8).

In our so-called Information Age, the height of folly and futility is expecting to discover the answer to our problems by listening to the political pundits as they respond to questions in between commercials on TV talk shows. Neither the problem nor the answer to the problem is political. It is theological; our alienation from God's Spirit and truth (John 4:23-14) who has "delivered us from the dominion of darkness and transferred us to the kingdom of his beloved Son" (Colossians 1:13).

As Jesus made crystal clear to Pilate, the kingdom of God and the political kingdom of nation-states are two very different realities (John 18:36). Jesus rejected the fallen world of Pilate and his counterparts in the world in every age (Matthew 4:8-10).

This can be understood only as we experience a new consciousness of the living God in Christ, who comes to the individual as All and in all, as abundant life, not as the destroyer of life.

The Church Must Break Away from The "Just War" Heresy

In the name of "Jesus Christ, Son of God, Savior", let the Pope of the Catholic Church, the Patriarchs of the Orthodox churches, the Bishops and Councils of Protestant churches, dare to break with human reason's "Just War" tradition, responsible for the violence of the Crusades, the Holocaust, and all the wars in between. Let them declare to a fallen world,

> As the representatives of Jesus Christ, the Prince of Peace, we renounce all war and solemnly call upon all Christians to show our godly grief for past violence by producing deeds worthy of repentance and, witnessing to the ruling and sovereign God of peace, our only Savior, we reject totally a fallen world's war system.

In the early 1900s, a writer for *The New Republic*, reviewing with approval in *The New York Times* a book about the influence of "dangerously unpatriotic elements" among American intellectuals, warned readers of "a permanent adversarial culture" in the United States. This is an accurate description of what the church of the crucified-risen-indwelling Christ should always be in a fallen world: a permanent adversarial culture which represents a unique standard of human behavior based on God's call to the church to be holy, even as He is holy (See Leviticus 11:44).

Corporal Jeff Patterson, a 22-year-old Marine stationed in Hawaii, sat down on the runway of the airfield, and refused to board a plane bound for battle. He asked to be discharged from the Marine Corps, saying:

> I have come to believe that there are no justified wars . . . I began to question why I was in the Marines when I began to read up on America's support for the murderous regimes of Guatemala, Iran under the Shah, and El Salvador . . . I object to the military use of force against any people, anywhere, anytime.

This is an expression of the "permanent adversarial culture" the church of Jesus should represent everywhere in every age. The only problem with Jeff is that he joined the Marines in the first place. His deed was late in coming, but better late than never.

What is the church waiting for?

In *The Jesus I Never Knew*, the readable story of his maturing spiritual life in Christ, Philip Yancey refers to a stirring sermon delivered by Tony Campolo. Entitled, "It's Friday, but Sunday's Comin", it was based on a sermon an elderly black pastor had preached in Tony's church.

The title of the sermon tells the story: "Friday's Dark World of Violence and Death Has Been Vanquished by Sunday's Resurrection and the Dawn of a New Easter Era". Yancey makes the point that in between Friday's worst and Sunday's best, is Saturday where all of us live out our days waiting for the completion of our life in Eternity's heaven.

Yancey concludes his book,

> I know a woman whose grandmother lies
> buried under 150-year-old live oak trees in the
> cemetery of an Episcopal church in rural
> Louisiana. In accordance with the
> grandmother's instruction, only one word is
> carved on the tombstone: "Waiting".

The question we must ask is, What is that grandmother
waiting for, and what are we Christians of the church waiting
for? In his struggle to find the answer to loving enemies as
Jesus teaches us to do, and not killing them as the world
teaches, Philip Yancey came to the wrong conclusion: that
the church must wait for the Second Coming of Jesus to
consummate His kingdom before the church can reject war
and love enemies as Jesus' Sermon on the Mount teaches.
Only when Jesus comes again and universal peace prevails
on that climactic Sunday can Christians love as Jesus loves,
Yancey reasoned. On Saturday, where we live out our
remaining days, the church must continue to fight and kill as
the world does.

Jesus' conquest of the Powers and Principalities does not
apply to Saturday. Christians must wait for Sunday to
celebrate Jesus' victory over the violence and death of sin's
fallen world. Then the love of Jesus and the peace of God
will prevail. Only at the End-Time will God's right replace
the sinner's might. Only then can the sword become a
plowshare. In the meantime, the church must wait to
renounce war and its violence.

In his popular book Philip Yancey echoes the way "just war'
churches explain their acceptance of the "just war" church
and the reason their members continue to slaughter each
other at the command of the state. They do it by calling war
evil, but then refuse to reject war's evil because they say the
kingdom of God has not yet fully come in a world of sin

which is <u>not yet</u> ready to love as Jesus loved.

Yancey writes,

> The only possible explanation lies in Jesus'
> teaching that the kingdom of God comes in
> stages. It is "Now" and also "Not Yet,"
> present and also future. Sometimes Jesus
> stressed the present aspect, as when he said
> the kingdom is "at hand" or "within you." At
> other times he suggested the kingdom lay in
> the future as when he taught his disciples to
> pray, "Your kingdom come, your will be
> done, on earth as it is in heaven."

To say that the kingdom of God is both "Now and "Not yet",
present and future, is indeed in accord with the New
Testament. Abiding in Christ, the Christian's citizenship in
the kingdom of God, begins in the Now, awaiting
consummation when voices of the church triumphant shall
shout,

> The kingdom of the world has become the
> kingdom of our Lord and of his Christ, and he
> shall reign for ever and ever.
> - Revelation 11:15

The big question is: What is the <u>nature of Christ</u> in whom the
church NOW abides, awaiting the NOT YET? If the nature
of Jesus is the Eternal's self-giving agape-love the New
Testament proclaims from Matthew to Revelation, and if
Jesus expects the church here and now to abide in His Holy
Spirit of agape-love and be the visible light of His Spirit in a
sin-darkened world, then the church cannot wiggle out of the
demands of the gospel by saying "NOT YET". Because the
whole world is not yet redeemed and wars and rumors of war
continue, does that mean disciples of Jesus are to join in and
kill as the unredeemed world kills? Rape, because there is so

much rape in a lustful world? Steal, because prisons are filled with thieves? Is the church to join the world as nation rises against nation and respond to evil as an unredeemed world responds in sin's spirit of vengeance? NO! This is the good news:

> I have said this to you, that in me you may have peace. In this world you have tribulation; but be of good cheer, I have overcome the world.
> - John 16:33

> God disarmed the principalities and powers and made a public example of them, triumphing over them in Christ.
> - Colossians 2:15

Because of Jesus' <u>FIRST Coming</u>, the gospel proclaims a victory of peace here and now for a fallen world of violence and death. The victory has been won! We are more than conquerors in Christ who loves us and died for us that we may NOW begin to live in the kingdom of God's peace so when we soon put off the flesh we will feel at home in the NOT YET.

This is not to expect a perfect church, only a <u>faithful</u> church, a church <u>obedient</u> to the clear teaching of Jesus and His gospel (See His last conversation with the Twelve in John 13-17). For the church to wait for Jesus' Second Coming to obey His Sermon on the Mount, rejecting war and its slaughter, rape, and unleashing of the beast in humans, is to deny the redeeming power of Jesus and His cross-resurrection-indwelling Holy Spirit. It is to say, "Jesus first coming was not enough to save us from evil. We must wait for Jesus' second coming to be delivered from evil by the Lamb of God. This is a lie and makes Jesus out to be an imposter.

At age 88 with bags packed (very lightly), Marge and I are also waiting. Waiting for the time when we put off the burden of the flesh with all of its change and decay, and our Spirit-person enters the Home our Lord has prepared for us (John 14:1-2). But if we are not at Home with Jesus NOW as we abide in His Holy Spirit whose fruit is love, joy, and peace (Galatians 5:22), if we live now as though we had never heard of Jesus whose gospel is all about eternal life in the God of peace, if we live as though we have not been reconciled in Christ to the Father and to all in His Family, is our waiting on Saturday going to square with our perfect peace with the Lord on that last Easter-Sunday? Is going ALL OUT for political and military victories for our particular nation preparing us for heaven where there will be no nation-states and political parties? Waiting to love our enemies until Resurrection Sunday is a misplaced love and makes Jesus irrelevant in the NOW.

The first disciples of Jesus were not ridiculed, persecuted, and put to death on Saturday because they were merely "waiting" for Jesus' Second Coming on Sunday when all that is wrong shall be put right. The early church was persecuted unto death because the church had a radically different lifestyle on Saturday that went against the grain of Rome. Their nonviolent lifestyle which rejected war collided head-on with Rome's domination-power. Jesus' Resurrection on Sunday was a living reality for the Christians on Saturday. Risen from the dead and indwelling His disciples, Jesus had struck evil a death blow. The victory was won!

Celsus, Rome's historian, accused Christians of refusing to fight for the good of the Empire. Evidently the early church was not waiting for Jesus' Second Coming to love their enemies as Jesus taught in His first coming (Matthew 5,6,7). They were not waiting for Jesus' agape-kingdom to come to live in peace with all people. Abiding in Christ, the God of peace was with them to give them the victory over sin, violence and death. They rejected the state's system of the sword to deal with enemies. Jesus was their Ruler and Spirit-Giver, not Caesar.

Receiving a letter from a reader critical of the worldly lifestyle of the visible church, the novelist Flannery O'Connor replied,

> The Church is founded on Peter who denied Christ three times and who couldn't walk on water by himself. You are expecting his successors to walk on the water. All human nature vigorously resists grace because grace changes us and the change is painful. To have the Church be what you want it to be would require the continuous miraculous meddling of God in human affairs.

True enough, God's grace does change us and change is painful in many ways. But we should expect the church to be very different from the world because God IS MEDDLING IN HUMAN AFFAIRS every moment of every day in the crucified-risen-ascended-ruling-indwelling Messiah, who has broken down all the walls of hostility which separate us from God and from one another (See Ephesians 2:14-16). The church is to be IN the world, but not OF the world (John 17:14-19). What is it, Flannery O'Connor, that you are waiting for? Haven't you heard? "It is finished!"(John 19:30)—not Jesus' life in the flesh, but the Father's work to transform this fallen Babylon into which we are all born. Jesus put the finishing touch on God's Peace-Plan (See Ephesians 1:3-10).

The church is founded on the God-Person whose name is Jesus, not on the man called Peter (Ephesians 2:20). The Lord does not expect any of us to walk on water or to complete the perfect kingdom of God on earth here and now. But based on Jesus' clear teaching, He does expect His church, at least, to have enough of the Holy Spirit's agape in our hearts to say to sin's warring world, "Enough is enough. We refuse to obey the state's command to kill those to whom we have been reconciled by our crucified and risen Lord (2 Corinthians 5:18-21).

Here and now we must obey the command of our Ruler to love our enemies as He did, rather than the command of political rulers to kill the bastards as the state wants us to do. Yes, our human nature does resist change which is painful, but God's grace is greater than our resistance. What we are now is more important to God in Christ than what we shall be after we put off the flesh. Why? Because if we do not choose now to become alive in Christ while given the opportunity, there is no reason to think it will automatically happen after we put off the flesh. Our salvation is a matter of the heart's intention while we are still in the flesh.

As the American poet, James Russell Lowell, wrote a century ago,

> Once to every man and nation
> Comes the moment to decide,
> In the strife of truth with falsehood,
> For the good or evil side;
> Some great cause, God's new Messiah,
> Offering each the bloom or blight,
> And the choice goes by forever
> Twixt that darkness and that light.

God must be tired of a "waiting church" that continues to fight "just wars" to overcome evil in this world while waiting for the Second Coming of Jesus to end war. Jesus needed to come only once to provide the Way of peace and offer us the precious privilege of abiding in Abba's Spirit of peace. God's grace in Christ is sufficient. We must not continue to "dis-grace" God by idolizing the state and the kind of power Jesus rejects (See Matthew 20:25-28).

It is not enough to repent of past violence. The church must bring forth good fruit worthy of repentance by rejecting in the present time the world's systems of violence.

Christians Must Stop Pretending Some War is Good

Because of the new electronic Information Age, the Holy One of Israel is enabling the human race to see in a new way the horrors of violence and war the moment they happen anywhere and everywhere in the world. We can no longer hide from our brothers and sisters when hundreds of thousands are driven from their homes in the Balkans, or a million murdered in Rwanda.

> I saw you on the front page of the paper.
> You were in tears.
> Now I am in tears.
> So across the miles, in time suspended, we cry together.
> Keep holding the child in your arms.
> I will hold each of you in my heart.

In a new age of nuclear, biological, and chemical weapons with the potential of destroying the planet-Earth which a good God created for abundant life, the church of Jesus can no longer pretend it is God's will to engage in "just wars". Bishop Augustine's rules are as obsolete as Bishop Usher's chronology of the age of the earth.

War is sin from which the Lamb of God <u>has delivered</u> a war-sick world (John 1:29; 1 John 3:8-9). The role of Christians is not to spend our time analyzing current events, predicting when, what, and where something will, or will not, happen if . . . This is the game the Apostles wanted to play when the church was about to be born on Pentecost, asking, "Lord, is this the time you will restore the kingdom to Israel?" Jesus answered,

247

It is not for you to know the time or circumstances of these events which God alone controls. It is for you to have faith to receive the Holy Spirit who will give you power to be my witnesses everywhere in the world.
- Acts 1:6-8

The task of Spirit-filled Christians is to be a continuing witness to the Answer, not an endless analysis of the Problem. Christ is the Answer. We are the Problem. The church is God's new creation in His Holy Spirit. The fruit is agape and peace in a NOW KINGDOM, not a continuing Inquirer's Class endlessly discussing interesting subjects, hoping peace will soon come in the Middle East, along with cheaper gasoline.

A Church That Kills Does Not Look Redeemed

In 1933, Martin Buber, a Jew, was asked by a New Testament scholar why, in the light of Jesus' life and work, Jews continue to wait for a Messiah? Buber replied that Jews cannot believe Jesus is the Redeemer because after 2000 years, the world is not redeemed. "We sense its unredeemedness", said this devout biblical scholar. Buber said this when Hitler came to power. Soon he was to be adulated by millions of Germans, both Catholic and Protestants, leaving a scorched earth in their track of Nazi tanks and bombers. How did Christians in Europe and the United States respond? By mimicking Hitler and leaving a scorched Germany in the tracks of their military power.

When Martin Buber said of Christianity, "We sense its unredeemedness", he was thinking of the visible Catholic-Protestant-Orthodox-Pentecostal churches yet to break away from the chains of the world's war system to provide a world of violence with a visible sign that in Jesus Christ the first-fruit of God's kingdom of peace has come on earth as it is in heaven.

Almost twenty centuries have come and gone since the church was born on Pentecost in a redeemed people of God. These people inherited the role of Israel as God's people chosen to show a fallen world the Eternal Spirit of Paradise, lost because of Man/Woman's desire to be free from God, instead of free in God.

The Twelve called to carry out the mission Jesus had entrusted to them were ordinary men like you and me. One betrayed Him; one denied that he ever knew Him; all deserted Him in the hour of His arrest. God's gift of His Holy Spirit changed their doubts and denials to affirmative action. The Twelve and their companions went forth in the likeness of their nonviolent Messiah. Tired and world-weary Romans saw in the church a new breed of people, a swordless and loving way of living together, radically different from their fallen world called Rome.

Some say, and I am one of them, that the church lost its claim to be a unique society when Christianity became the official state religion in the fourth century. At that time, it started to become enmeshed in the political structures of sin's world addicted to arranging its own destiny and relying on the kind of power Jesus rejected (Matthew 25:20-28).

During these twenty centuries since Pentecost, two basic forces have been at work within the church: one, the power of the Holy Spirit who would shape the true church, the New Israel, in the likeness of Jesus (2 Corinthians 3:18); the other, the pressure of the "flesh"(Romans 8:6) to lower the standard of the church so that it will be more acceptable to more people, content with something less than God intends it to be.

The organized and visible church may continue for another twenty centuries, or twenty millennia. For all we know, the church may still be in its infancy, awaiting forms never before experienced or envisioned.

As each of us lives out his or her allotted span of years within the organized church, two things are constant and will never change: one, the norm for the form of the church will always be Jesus Christ; and two, we will always be given the strength and courage to be faithful to the true form of the Body of Christ if we abide in Christ, one day at a time, and confidently leave tomorrow and the future in the hands of an omnipotent, omnipresent, omniscient God. We can be sure of this: God always equips us for the mission he calls us to carry out. In Christ we are able to witness to His here and now peaceable kingdom which has no place for sin's violence and war.

You and I cannot determine the visible, institutional form of the church, but we can control the form the church takes in our own life. As individual Christians we are responsible for the way we live as members of the Body of Christ. You don't have to wait to hear the Pope, or the Patriarch, or the official body of the visible church to which you belong say, "It is the sacred duty of all members of the Body of Christ, the Prince of Peace, never to participate in sin's wars and slaughter our brothers and sisters to whom we have been reconciled". You have heard Jesus say it. You have seen Jesus enflesh it. Now, as Jesus' representative, do it!

Each of us will be held accountable for the form of the church we embody. With a vision of a New Covenant, the prophet Jeremiah made clear to his disciples their individual responsibility to let God be God on his terms:

> In those days they shall no longer say, "The fathers have eaten sour grapes, and the children's teeth are on edge." But every man shall die for his own sin; each man who eats sour grapes his teeth shall be set on edge.
> - Jeremiah 31:25,29-30

You and I will be judged by our own deeds, not by those of our father. The question will not be, What was your family denomination? What did your branch of the church believe? No, it will be very personal: Did you, as a person, reach out in the holy Spirit of agape to the poor and oppressed; and by the way you responded to enemies, did you give a fallen world a clear, visible sign that you have been redeemed by a nonviolent Messiah? It is the same Messiah who said the best proof that the Father has sent Him to redeem the world of sin's violence and death is our oneness in His Spirit of love and peace and our oneness with each other (See John 17:21).

A Disciple Who Did Not Follow The Crowd

I am thinking now of a simple Austrian peasant who took personal accountability very seriously. One by one, the countries of Europe were being occupied by Hitler's Armed Forces many of whom were members of Protestant and Catholic churches and wore belts inscribed with the words: Gott mitt uns—God is with us. Along with their families back home, they clicked their heels and said, "Heil Hitler!"

Austria was no different. Franz Jägerstätter was different. He dared to say, "Phooey Hitler!" A student of the Bible and a devout Christian, Jägerstätter knew in his heart and mind that what Hitler was doing was evil. When he refused to be conscripted to kill, his friends and neighbors considered him queer. When he was tried for treason, his lawyer and his priest tried to persuade him to change his mind for the sake of his wife and two children.

"Your first responsibility is to your family", they insisted. Jägerstätter knew that Jesus would never have gone to the cross if he had followed such advice. This "uneducated" peasant understood what every serious reader of the New Testament knows: the Christian's first allegiance is to Christ,

251

the Lord. Each soul is responsible for accepting or rejecting their first loyalty to their Maker.

Franz Jägerstätter accepted his Christian responsibility. In the Brandenburg Prison in Berlin, he was beheaded at 4 p.m. on August 9, 1943, totally alone and almost totally unknown so far as the organized church in Austria was concerned. We can be very sure of this: his soul was not alone when he left sin's fallen world in the flesh (See Romans 8:35-39). Before the execution of this One Solitary Witness to Jesus and his nonviolent Way of the cross, Jägerstätter wrote,

> Today one can hear it said repeatedly that there is nothing any more that an individual can do. If someone were to speak out, it would mean only imprisonment and death. True, there is not much that can be done any more to change the course of world events. I believe that should have been done a hundred or even more years ago. But as long as we live in this world, I believe it is never too late to save ourselves and perhaps some other soul for Christ. One really has no reason to be astonished that there are those who can no longer find their way in the great confusion of our day. People we think we can trust who ought to be leading the way and setting a good example are running with the crowd.

Franz Jägerstätter did not run with the crowd. Neither did another Solitary Figure who said, "Take up your cross and follow me. I am the way, the truth, and the life" (Matthew 10:38; John 14:6).

Franz Jägerstätter exemplifies what the Bible makes crystal clear: no matter what the organized form and official teaching of the church to which we belong, as Christians each of us is responsible to take on the form of Jesus Christ and be obedient to His word, no matter what happens. We may not belong to a peace church, but every authentic Christian belongs to Jesus, the Prince of Peace and nonviolent Messiah, who says to his church in every age,

> You did not choose me, but I chose you and appointed you that you should go and bear fruit and that your fruit should abide.
> - John 5:16

And the fruit of Jesus' holy Spirit is peace (Galatians 5:22). Peace that abides, peace that comes from our new life of reconciliation with God and with God's people of every race and nation (2 Corinthians 5:17-20). On the cross Jesus Christ triumphed over the power of sin which separates us from God and from one another and always results in violence of one form or another. When He becomes the Lord of our life and we abide in Him as the branch abides in the vine, we are empowered by His indwelling Presence to walk and work in peace even as He did when He lived in the flesh. To be a Christian is to be:

> changed into his likeness from one degree of glory to another; for this comes from the Lord who is the Spirit.
> -2 Corinthians 3:18

When we take the whole Christ as our crucified, risen, ascended, ruling, and indwelling Lord and Savior, for our whole life that includes all human relationships, we have eternal security in the midst of every possible circumstance Satan would use to destroy us. In Christ we are victors, not victims.

Dr. William Neil, former head of Biblical Studies at the University of Aberdeen, presently teaching in the Department of Biblical Studies in the University of

Nottingham, has written with prophetic insight,

> It may well be that the organized church in its
> present form will have to go much further
> downhill before it recovers. Machinery that
> gets rusty has to be overhauled or scrapped.
> While it is certain that Jesus founded the
> church, it is far from certain that he intended
> it to take the outward shape of any one of its
> present branches. Yet amid much that is
> irrelevant in the church's present activities, it
> is still the custodian of God's revelation and
> that is imperishable. It is still the channel of
> supernatural power and whatever changes in
> the structure are made, men and women will
> always find, in its worship, in its sacraments
> and in its scriptures, the renewal of their own
> lives and strength and incentives to move
> society so far as they can to conform more
> and more to the mind and Spirit of Christ.

To repent is to change from walking in the world of the
flesh, controlled by the Powers and Principalities, to
walking in the Spirit, controlled by Jesus Christ and being
conformed to His likeness. So let it be with the church of
responsible and faithful disciples as we move into the Third
Millennium: a time to celebrate new beginnings in our
nonviolent Messiah who is in our very midst, saying,

> Behold, I make all things new.
> - Revelation 21:5

Now do it!

An incident in the life of David has a message for the church
in this hour. David had been anointed by the Lord to replace
Saul as king, but only the tribe of Judah in the south
accepted his rule. The northern tribes of Israel continued to

give their allegiance to Ishbosheth, Saul's son.

Abner, Saul's chief captain, resolved to lead the reluctant tribes in the north to submit to David that there might be one kingdom and one God-anointed ruler. Abner confronted the elders of Israel with these words:

> For some time you have wanted to make David your king. Now do it! For the Lord promised, "By my servant David I will rescue my people from the hand of the Philistines and from the hand of their enemies."
> - 2 Samuel 3:17-18 NIV

And they did it! All the tribes came to David at Hebron and said,

> Behold, we are your bone and flesh. In times past when Saul was king over us, it was you that led Israel out and brought Israel in; and the Lord said to you, "You shall be shepherd of my people Israel and you shall be prince over Israel."
> - 2 Samuel 5:1-2

The covenant which united the twelve tribes of Israel under the kingship of David was the old covenant of law, a covenant now obsolete which only promised that the new would come in a nonviolent Messiah who would

> abolish the bow, the sword, and war from the land, and I will make you lie down in safety. And I will betroth me to you forever; I will betroth you to me in righteousness and justice, in steadfast love, and in mercy. I will betroth you to me in faithfulness, and you shall know the Lord
> - Hosea 2:18-20

We have the Messiah and the power of His resurrection and indwelling. The Messiah and God's peace on earth have come!

In December 1990, a group of eighteen U.S. church leaders went to the Middle East to help bring peace to that war-torn region. They represented the highest level U.S. church leadership ever assembled in such a peace effort. When they returned, they issued a statement which included these words: "Our Christmas pilgrimage to the Middle East has utterly convinced us that war is not the answer. We believe the resort to massive violence to resolve the Gulf crisis would be politically and morally indefensible." They concluded, "At this moment the resolution of the Gulf crisis will take a miracle. But in this season we are reminded that the Middle East is the cradle of miracles. That miracle must be acted and prayed into being."

Dear readers, peace, the miracle of miracles, has already happened. The crucified-risen-ascended-ruling-indwelling-Christ has fulfilled the peace-mission God gave to Jesus. Now the Lord waits for His church to manifest to the world the meaning and power of his peace-miracle.

Let us as individual Christians, and as the Body of Christ, here and now, repent of our sinful violence, and from this day on demonstrate Jesus' gift of peace to a warring world. Let us not run with the crowd. Let us so live peaceably with all of our brothers and sisters that the world will know that we have been redeemed, that the nonviolent Messiah has come to abide in us as we join in singing this Song of Victory:

> Faith of our fathers! We will strive to win all nations unto thee;
> And through the truth that comes from God, Mankind shall then be truly free.

Faith of our fathers, holy faith! We will be true to thee till death.

Faith of our fathers! We will love both friend and foe in all our strife,
And preach thee, too, as love knows how, by kindly deeds and virtuous life.
Faith of our fathers, holy faith! We will be true to thee till death.

Amen. So let it be!

Chapter 8

Rethinking Schools For Our Children

> Jesus then said to the Jews who had believed in him, "If you continue in my word, you are truly my disciples, and you will know the truth and the truth will make you free."
>
> I am the way, the truth and the life; no one comes to the Father but by me.
> - John 8:31-32; 14:6

A publication, *Rethinking Schools*, represents a nation-wide group of teachers dissatisfied with extreme nationalistic interpretations of history at the expense of telling the truth about the dark side of a nation's history. It was written in connection with the 500th Anniversary of the "discovery" of America by Christopher Columbus, in reaction to a 100-page book called *Rethinking Columbus*. A critical review of the usual children's books about the glorious achievements of the explorer, the book featured articles by Native Americans and others.

Within a few months, 200,000 copies of the book were sold, telling the truthful story of how Columbus enslaved Arawak Indians of the Caribbean to mine gold, a people he had described as "so naive and so free with their possessions that no one who has not witnessed them would believe it. When you ask for anything they have, they never say no. To the contrary they offer to share with anyone." Asking for more help from their Majesties who sponsored his voyage, Columbus promised to bring back "as much gold as they need . . . and as many slaves as they ask." His report was couched in such pious talk as "Thus the eternal God, our Lord, gives victory to those who follow His way over apparent impossibilities."

The book, *Rethinking Columbus*, told the story children in public schools had never heard. From his base on Haiti, Columbus sent out expeditions in search of gold he thought was on that island. Finding no gold, they returned to Spain with a different cargo: Arawak slaves. They picked the best five hundred from those enslaved, two hundred of which died on the voyage, which packed them together like animals in their own filth and stench.

Worked to death to mine the little gold in the Caribbean, when the Arawak tried to escape and were captured, those taken prisoners were usually hanged or burned to death. Because of disease, mass suicides, and their suffering, in two years, half of the 250,000 Indians on Haiti were dead. Genocide!

Because of this book on Columbus, published by *Rethinking Schools*, students began to see the 500th Anniversary of the Discovery of America in a new light. One student named Rebecca wrote, "The thought that I have been lied to all my life about this, and who knows what else, really makes me angry."

The National Council of Churches called on Christians to refrain from celebrating the Anniversary, saying, "What represented newness of freedom, hope, and opportunity for some, was the occasion for oppression, degradation, and genocide for others."

Are our children really learning who Jesus is?

The time has come for all churches to rethink schools to assure that the children entrusted to their care learn the truth about Jesus who claimed to overcome the world of violence and death and to have the authority to send His church into all the world to make disciples of all people (See John 16:33, Matthew 28:18-20).

A young teenager seeking enrollment in a church school when asked how much he knew about Jesus, replied, "Wasn't he one of the saints?" Another lad, asked the same question, said he had never heard of Jesus. Both were better than average students in public schools. Our children are not learning about Jesus in public schools. Education for job-skills, yes; education for life, no.

From a Christian perspective, the problem of public schools is not the lack of teachers and inadequate salaries, not class-size and obsolete buildings, not more accountability to make sure students are learning the 3 R's. The problem is a system of education geared to a fallen world's culture of godless nationalism, synonymous with the use of violent and coercive military power in problem solving. Without exception, all public schools extol the nation and the duty of citizens to defend the nation from the "tyranny" of our British brothers, as George Washington and the other founding fathers did.

To see how wrong we were in fighting that "just war" to be free, we need only look at the way Canada has developed in a continuing relationship with England without bloody war. Instead of being "enslaved" by the British, Canada, in fact, is as free as the United States. Today, we have no greater ally than England. This same country in 1775 was demonized as Satan. Members of mainline churches in America declared England had to be defeated in a holy military crusade.

Public Schools and The War System

This is the war system public schools take for granted and perpetuate. Public schools do not offer our children a choice between a violent and a nonviolent way of defending one's nation. The military system and the public school system are one and the same. ROTC and the art of war is as much a part of the curriculum as the art of reading, writing, and arithmetic. Military heroes are glorified and praised. The vocation of the soldier is honored. History is taught within the context of victories won or lost on the battlefield.

Requiring an oath to defend the Constitution from every enemy, both foreign and domestic, nationalism is woven into the fabric of every public school. Jesus is a non-entity in public schools which had their origin in the godly zeal of the nation's Pilgrim and Puritan founders. Yale, the first university, began in Connecticut's village of Branford when ten preachers each set a few books on a table, saying, "I give these books for the founding of a College in this Colony."

Today's public schools represent secular education. The word "secular" means, "pertaining to this world, temporal, earthly, not religious".

There are many reasons why public schools have become godless and earthbound. One is the nation's tradition of keeping church and state separate. This means the state shall not favor an established church or religion and the church shall not try establish control over the state. Good!

In a pluralistic society, public schools do not, and cannot, make Jesus and His Way of the cross the model to follow. Public schools do not, and cannot, encourage children to seek first Jesus' kingdom of God and His righteousness. This demands the assurance that a good God who created a good universe will supply all our needs when we learn to share life on the planet as our Creator shares life with all in the Human Family.

Another reason for our secularized system of public education is the growing divisions of religions in America: Catholic, Protestant, Orthodox, Jewish, Muslim, etc., and the fear of religious indoctrination. The fear is not unfounded, but fear of religious indoctrination has led to a worse fear: indoctrinating children to believe that God does not exist, or does not matter. What matters "within earth and time" are cash and comfort, flashiness, fame, real and practical life in the flesh.

The result of secularized public schools is a secularized public mind and culture. With no emphasis on a holy and sovereign God, there can be no emphasis on a holy and disciplined life that stands under the judgment of God or has a sense of dependency upon God. Life has its separate departments, each requiring only specialized skills, along with the right pills, to be put to use.

After a university lecture during which the speaker referred to "sin" several times, two women undergraduates were heard discussing his views. "What did he mean by sin?", asked one. Her friend answered quite casually, "Oh, that has something to do with Adam and Eve."

According to the Bible, sin has to do with being out of God's purpose and plan and the resulting violence that afflicts every godless person, family, corporation, and state in a fallen world. The soul needs a Redeemer and the encouragement to focus on the new life that is redeemed of sin's violence and death—something public schools do not, and cannot, accomplish.

Alternative Christ-Centered Education

This is not a plea to change the public school system, but rather a plea for parents within the Body of Christ to provide their children with alternative schooling consistent with the life and teaching of Jesus, not education hostile to the gospel of God's peace.

After a dozen years of molding their mind in public schools, the state has the absolute loyalty of the nation's youth when it comes to waging war. Graduating, youngsters may have a few questions, but they often enlist in the military with the comment, "What else is there to do?" The state and mainline churches offer no clear alternative. Parents and teachers have thought as little about the Christian Way of Jesus' nonviolent Spirit as those graduating from public high schools.

For two thousand years, the only nonviolent churches which have been able to enflesh Jesus' Way of agape and withstand the pressure to conform to a warring world and its coercive power have been those that have had the courage to stand up for their conviction. They hold the conviction that the crucified-risen-ascended-ruling-indwelling Christ is our only peace, and they have established their own church related schools. In the schools, the teaching during the week is consistent with their teaching on Sunday.

These churches did not evade their responsibility by saying, "as parents we want our children to go to public schools and grow up and make their own decisions. We don't want to force what we believe on our children. We want them to come to their own conclusions. We want them to be their own person." Such thinking is a "red herring". Our children do not choose to be free. They are free! Freedom of choice is the God-given characteristic of every human. But choices are never made in a vacuum. Freedom is not an end in itself that stands by itself. The nationalistic culture of public schools determines the way the mind of those in the classroom develops. Secular public schools and the war system are synonymous.

In his book, *Christ and Man's Dilemma*, my seminary teacher, George Buttrick, tells us that when the poet Shelley died, his widow asked a friend where she should send their surviving young son to school. The friend answered with confidence, "Send him where he will learn to think for himself." Recalling her husband's way of thinking, Mrs. Shelley replied, "No, I will send him where he will think like other people."

In the book's chapter on "Christ and Education", Dr. Buttrick responded,

> They were both wrong. In our America, in our cult of business, we have taught people to think for themselves—very much for themselves! Totalitarian lands teach people to think exactly like other people. In neither extreme is there hope, nor in any neutral belt between extremes. The only hope is above our extremes and our neutralities- in a better wisdom than man's wisdom. We must learn to think according to the mind of Christ. Secular education is bane rather than blessing, despite all its fine bestowals on our common life, to the extent it remains merely secular. Its basic assumptions, usually made unawares, will not stand scrutiny, as its issues and our deepest nature well prove. The word and power of Christ remain: "Take my yoke upon you and learn of me (Matthew 11:29). He is truth for life and death and eternity. Therefore He is truth for education.

The United States glories in her freedom. No one is truly free who is not in the discipline of God in the Person of Christ, whose indwelling Spirit makes us free to love as God loves. Discussing the reality of human bondage to sin, Jesus said,

> Every one who commits sin is a slave to sin. If you continue in my word, you are truly my

disciples, and you will know the truth, and the truth will make you free.
- John 8:31-32

At the beginning of the 21st century, everyone agrees that public schools in the United States are in trouble, but from a Christian view of life, not one of the suggested solutions deals with the pivotal problem: the absence of Jesus from the school and its teaching.

Putting more and better paid and trained teachers in safer school buildings to assure smaller classes so children will graduate from public schools more skilled in the same secular subjects, does not change the moral and spiritual environment of the system. Indeed, such "progress" may only serve to make children more competitive with an idolatrous materialistic goal to be "a success" measured in terms of better jobs to make more money to have all the things corporate business pressures the world to consume, and then to have a military second to none to protect what has been gained.

The more property and wealth we accumulate, the more we feel the need of a powerful military force to protect our prosperous life from enemies who might take it away. The more goods we stockpile, the more military weapons we feel we need to protect our accumulated wealth. The two stockpiles are inter-related. There is a close relationship between being the wealthiest nation in the world and being the mightiest nation in the world.

That one-politics, one-party is less militaristic and violent than another is an illusion. When it comes to giving absolute allegiance to the State and its Constitution, swearing an oath to defend the nation with military power and advocating a military budget to equip the nation's Armed Forces to fight and win any possible war, there is no difference among the country's major and minor political parties. Old established parties and new reformed parties are alike in calling for a military budget to train military forces to fight and kill. Political parties may differ on the wars the nation should be involved in. All parties, however, subscribe to the need of armed forces to kill when they think the war has a noble goal.

Ruling authorities would not send their daughters and sons off to have promiscuous sex if it would benefit our country, but they are willing to send them off to kill.

The public school system of every nation in the world inculcates national hubris and sovereignty which inevitably leads to nations fighting nations. The state is geared to public education which is geared to nationalism and the war system. The Gospels of Matthew, Mark, Luke and John teach disciples of Jesus to reject this system, and their pupils in the Early Church rejected it for more than two centuries.

The answer is not parents taking their children to Sunday Schools of mainline churches which support the state in the need for a fighting military force to wage "just wars". Until a united church has her own schools that put first the peaceable kingdom of God, the answer is seven-day-a-week homeschools with parents sharing and living their faith in Jesus as God's nonviolent Messiah, even though it means going against the grain of the world. Only when it comes in conflict with the world does Christian character mature.

A Nobel Peace Prize Mother Speaks on Her Son's Behalf

When violence was raging in northern Ireland, Mairead McGuire who was later to be awarded the Nobel Peace Prize, wrote a letter to her son, Luke; a letter in which a mother asks what she can do to help her toddler grow up in a violent world to know God's peace in Christ. Mairead's letter began:

> Today you picked a little yellow rosebud from
> the garden and carried it into the house to give

it to me. Your little baby-face beamed at me as you gave me the rose bud. What joy that moment held for me—joy knowing how deeply I love you, and then when I went to put the rose in water, I realized it had no stem, and that without water it could not grow from a rosebud into a beautiful full rose, but that soon, all too soon, it would die.

I felt sad for a moment at this thought and as I watched you toddle across the room I wondered how I might help you, my little rosebud, grow and "blossom" into manhood. What can I teach you that will help you grow up in this "thorny" world and yet know peace, joy, and happiness?

Mairead's letter tells little Luke about the need to have courage to refuse to hate and kill another human being; to stand tall, armed only with the weapon of love, and not to let the world plant in his heart the false seed of pride in any country's flag. It is this seed that produces the flower of nationalism which grows wildly, trampling and killing all life around it. She tells her son that people are more precious than national structures.

In closing, Mairead tells her son she will not be able to protect him from suffering in the harsh winters of life, but to remember that "summer will return, the sun will shine again, and the road will be covered in beautiful, oh so very, very, beautiful, yellow roses of love."

This is not sentimental hogwash. This is the gospel's theology of Jesus' nonviolent kingdom of the Spirit—the good news of God's Victory already won. At the end of the tunnel is the light of the cross-resurrection of Jesus, who said,

Because I live, you too shall live. Whoever
lives and believes in me shall never die. Do not
fear those who kill the body, but cannot kill the
soul, but rather fear him who can destroy both
soul and body in hell.
- John 14:19; Matthew 10:28

Though rejected by a sin-darkened world, the light of God's
Spirit of agape enfleshed in Jesus will never be extinguished.
The Holy Spirit's self-giving love and peace is the
quintessence of life. Parents committed to the Way of Jesus'
nonviolent cross must provide their children with an education
that teaches Jesus' Way of the nonviolent love Mairead
McGuire wants her son to follow, but will not unless nurtured
to do so.

What can we do?

What are the alternatives to public schools and their "just war'
military culture?

Peace-parents can scour their community to try to find a
private school more in tune with their faith. In almost every
community, there are "Christian" schools operated by
churches of various denominations. However, there is no
guarantee that such schools reject the world's system of war in
resolving conflict. Most likely, these are schools operated by
mainline churches which still cling to the nationalist "just
war" tradition: kill or be killed.

"Christian" schools differ in their theology. A school of the
United Methodist Church will probably be closer to the
theology of peace-parents than a school operated by a
Southern Baptist church. Parents will have to visit "Christian"
schools in their community and, after making known what
they are looking for, have in-depth interviews with principals
and teachers. Then they can determine whether they want to
commit the training of their children to one of them.

269

Every community has at least one Catholic elementary and high school. Even though the Catholic church doggedly clings to her "just war" doctrine, it may be that one of the community's Catholic schools comes closest to the peace-education in Christ which Protestant parents want for their children. I have come to know Jesuit priests whose teaching of Jesus' nonviolence comes through in their refusal to perpetuate the Catholic "just war" heresy.

For parents who choose a private school in their community for their children, it is essential that there be at least one extended family meeting each week where mothers and fathers intentionally share their theology of Christian nonviolence with their children; using carefully selected books of stories from the Bible and other sources about heroes of peace who flesh out Jesus' Way of God's reconciling love and peace in dealing with conflict. These are the heroes whose courage, convictions, and conduct surpass that of the combatant soldier. Making use of prime time in the daily life of their young daughters and sons, the home should be the primary school for teaching God's primary place in all of life. This is why homeschooling for some or all of the twelve years of grade school should be seriously considered. At first, this may seem to parents to be a responsibility greater than they can handle. But homeschooling has become a rapidly growing national movement with all fifty states recognizing its legitimacy.

In Florida, for example, the State's Department of Education has found it necessary to provide a separate office and staff to work with parents who want to become involved in the homeschooling of their children.

Although standards for homeschools vary from state to state, the following are a few facts which generally apply:

1. Special college training and credentials are not required of

parents to be homeschool teachers.

2. Homeschools are not required to follow a particular time schedule or a prescribed curriculum. To determine the progress of the children, once each year the learning of the children must either be evaluated by a registered teacher, or children must take tests given by the Department of Education.

3. Parents select their own teaching materials and their methods of teaching. The source for selections can be as inclusive as the whole world. Local libraries and the Internet are widely used. Homeschooling provides the opportunity for the nonviolent kingdom of the God of peace to be the model for the child's education.

4. To signify completion, a GED, rather than a public school certificate is given, but a high school diploma is not necessary to enter college. SAT scores are sufficient.

5. Within urban communities, there are usually Associations of Homeschools which bring together parents involved in the program for sharing and mutual support. There are opportunities for parents from several families to cooperate in the teaching of one homeschool.
6. There is a National Center for Homeschools to assist those seeking help with their program.

Homeschooling is an ideal opportunity for a faith-based approach to the education of children. Christian homeschooling should highlight this teaching of Jesus:

> These things I have spoken to you, while I am still with you. But the Counselor, the Holy Spirit, whom the Father will send in my name, he will teach you all things, and bring to your remembrance all that I have said to you. Peace I leave with you, my peace I give to you; not as

the world gives, do I give to you. Let not your
hearts be troubled.
- John 14:25-27

Christian nonviolence is the fruit of the Spirit (Galatians
5:22). The curriculum of Christian homeschooling will be
molded by the Counselor, the Holy Spirit Jesus enfleshed. The
teaching of the gospel of God in Christ depends upon the
indwelling Spirit, not the parent's brilliant mind. The gospel is
communicated through the language of the Spirit whose fruit
is agape, joy, peace, gentleness, and the like (Galatians 5:22).

The ultimate goal of our life on planet-Earth and the highest
education any school can help us attain has been given to us in
the crucified-risen-ascended-ruling-indwelling Lord of Life
(Colossians 1:15-20). If Jesus *is* who He claims to be and the
Bible proclaims He is, if He supremely matters, then secular
education is tragically blind and our trivializing of His life and
teaching is plunging a fallen world into chaos and self-
destruction.

The high purpose of mothers and fathers entrusted with babies
is to help their children build the foundation of their entire life
on God's gospel of the Holy Spirit in Christ. This is the goal
of Christian parents who are given opportunities every day to
help their children mature in the Way of God's peace on earth
as it is in heaven.

An Example of Homeschooling

Former editor of the *Jesus Journal*, Dale Recinella asked his
twelve-year-old son, Chris if he might like to write to Ken
Cofield, an inmate in a prison near Tallahassee. When Chris
hesitated, his dad said, "Think about it and pray about it and
let me know in a few days what you decide." In his twelve-
year-old mind, the first thoughts of Chris were, "What if Ken
doesn't want me to write to him? What if this and what if
that?" That night he asked his dad for more information about

Ken. Dale replied: "Well, he's been in prison for a long time. He's in for first-degree murder. He missed the chair by one jury vote. He used to be a really tough guy, but a few years back was converted and became a new person. He stopped fighting and now he's trying to live by Jesus' Sermon on the Mount. He's really a great man and a powerful Christian."

Wow! What a story. Chris started to write and has come to know Ken as a person: his personality, his hobbies. They even exchange jokes. For Chris, this man is not just a person behind bars; not just a crime statistic. He is now a friend, a brother in Christ, as the lad remembers something Jesus said,

> Do not judge, or you too will be judged, for in the same way you judge others, you will be judged, and with the measure you use, it will be measured to you.
> - Matthew 7:1-2

Chris says,

> Writing to Ken has changed my view of life and judgment. It has shown me that prisoners are not monsters or animals. They are God's children, my brothers in Christ. Consequently, they deserve to be treated like human beings.

> Ken and I have been writing for only about three years. Despite this I feel we have known each other for many years. I am glad that we write to each other. It has been a great experience that I will never forget. I hope it has meant as much to him as it has to me.

Dale Recinella took a moment at home to ask his son if he would like to write to a murderer in prison who had become a new person in Christ. Chris and Ken have been sharing life together through letter writing. Perhaps more than a year of schooling, this experience has helped Chris mature in Christ because his dad took a few minutes at home to talk to his son about doing a teaching of Jesus: being a friend to those in prison (Matthew 25:36).

This is Christian homeschooling that transforms life, schooling as fluid and flexible as the Spirit of the living God. Not set in a fixed and rigid system, homeschooling is set in Jesus, the indwelling nonviolent Christ who said,

> Let the children come to me, do not hinder them; for to such belongs the kingdom of God. And he took them in his arms, and blessed them, laying his hands on them.
> - Mark 10:14-16

Teaching Jesus' Way of nonviolence should begin at home within the family circle, more difficult than demonstrating outside on the streets. It is easier to join a March on Washington and call on Congress to act as the world's peace-maker than it is to teach Jesus' Way of God's reconciling Spirit of peace, day in and day out, within the walls of our own home.

If a father cannot control his temper when his child spills or breaks something which causes damage to household furnishings, or inconveniences a mother's busy schedule, occasional words about loving as Jesus loves will hardly inspire children to take up their cross and follow a nonviolent Messiah. Lashing out at another driver who runs a stop sign and smashes Dad's new car will not make him a credible teacher of Christian nonviolence in the eyes of his children.

It is time for Christian parents to rethink the education of their children. America's children can explain what is on TV Channels 5, 6, and 7, but how many can explain what's in Matthew 5, 6, and 7?

These are written, that you may believe
that Jesus is the Christ, the Son of God;
and that believing
you may have LIFE in his name.

- John 20:31

May the PEACE OF GOD
which passes all understanding,
keep your hearts and your minds
in Christ Jesus, now and forever more.
Amen.

- Philippians 4:7

About the Author

Before knowing where an author is taking them, readers should know where the writer is coming from.

Following our family's Reformed Church tradition, I was baptized as a baby and confirmed at the age of 12. With my family I attended the Worship Service on Sunday, joined in singing familiar hymns, recited the Apostles' Creed and the Lord's Prayer, listened to the sermon, mingled with relatives and friends at the close of the Service, and then went back into the world.

The church was one part of the world I lived in, but for me not the most important part. My real teenage world conformed to the shape of three balls: football in the fall, basketball in the winter, and baseball in the spring and summer.

When I started high school, my ambition was to make the varsity in all three sports. As a freshman, I practiced with the varsity football squad and played in one game. As the basketball season got under way, the coach had me playing with the first team. My dream was coming true.

One Saturday morning while living in the kingdom of sports, I was playing basketball in the church gym when I discovered tiny spots all over my body. Chicken pox, the doctor told me. No problem. In a couple of weeks I would be back again with my high school team ready for our opening game.

Not to be. Instead, while waiting to get back to school, I found myself overwhelmed by the thought and fear of death, which suddenly had become real to me for the first time. My struggle with death was so real that I stayed out of school for the rest of the school semester. Struggling with the power of death, I went to my brother's Pocono mountain retreat where I worked in his tree nursery, camped in the woods and spent time hiking and fishing. I had time to reflect, read, and be open to the inner world of the Spirit who was becoming more real than the world of sports and claiming my attention in a new way.

On a spring evening in 1928, en route to my favorite trout stream, my mind focused on catching the big one I knew was at the bottom of a familiar swirling waterfall, while sitting in the back of the farm's pickup truck with my cousin, Bill. As we turned out on the highway, the heavens opened and I beheld a great company of people praising God. This was their heavenly message: "Be not afraid! He is risen!"

In that moment in time I entered the strange new world of the Bible; a joy not known before or since filled my whole being. I experienced the new birth Jesus spoke to Nicodemus about (See John 3:1-15), the new world of the Spirit Paul experienced on the Damascus Road (See 2 Corinthians 5:17).

Arriving at our destination a few minutes later, instead of walking along the wooded banks of the Tobyhanna River, I danced my way. I had been given a vision of Jesus, not simply as one who lived in a place called Galilee two millennia ago, but as a Cosmic Presence within my person. It was the experience that taught me to say with the evangelist Paul,

> It is no longer I who live, but Christ who lives
> in me. For to me to live is Christ.
> - Galatians 2:20; Philippians 1:21

That was the beginning of my discernment of the church as the People of God called to enflesh God's kingdom of purity and peace Jesus enfleshed.

A sentence from Jeremiah sums up my certainty of Jesus:

> The Lord made it known to me and I knew.
> - Jeremiah 11:1

With my new birth in God's Spirit came the desire to be ordained as a minister of Jesus to witness to God's reconciling love in Christ.

After graduating from Methodist' Wyoming Seminary Prep School and Presbyterian Lafayette College, the time came for graduate school. I chose Union Theological Seminary in New York City because of its ecumenical vision of the church. Union's faculty and students came from all over the world and many different denominations. Union did not prepare me for a comfortable denominational ministry in a tradition-bound local church, but her inclusive seminary helped keep alive and enlarge my vision of the here and now kingdom of God that includes and transcends churches of every denomination, race, and nation.

My wife, Marge, was with me at Union for these three years during which she audited classes, and together we were blessed by Union's inclusive student body and faculty.

Our First Church

Graduating from seminary in 1939, we accepted a call to serve St. John's Reformed Church in Reading, Pennsylvania. In the 1940's, the walls of racial segregation in the nation were shaking, but not in the institutional church where the walls should never have been built in the first place.

Convinced that we all partake of the one Spirit and one loaf (1 Corinthians 10:17), I started to visit some of the city's black pastors. I found a warm welcome from colleagues in the black Methodist, Baptist and Presbyterian churches. Convinced of the sin of segregation and experiencing our unique fellowship in Christ, before long we pastors were discussing what our congregations might do together to witness to our God-given unity in Christ.

Our first ecumenical ministry was a Lenten School of Religion which brought together three black and three white congregations as the reconciled family of our one Lord. On six Wednesday evenings of Lent, after attending one of a half-dozen classes taught by the six pastors, an ecumenical company sang and prayed together, inspired by a combined choir of sixty voices and by some of the most powerful and prophetic preachers in the United States such as Mordecai Johnson, President of Howard University in the nation's capital, and Benjamin Mays, President of Morehouse College. I can still hear the words that opened each Worship Service:

> Behold how good and pleasant it is for
> brethren to dwell together in unity.
> - Psalm 133:1

Our next major mission was a summer camp in Pennsylvania's Pocono Mountains where Jesus had cast out my fear of death. Obtaining a hundred acres of property unused because of World War II, we were able to meet as a communal church for rich experiences of worship, Bible study, and a fellowship of fun in the mountains.

In the 1940's, our agape fellowship in Christ produced another fruit of the Spirit known as "Reading Fellowship House". To get us started, a member of one of our churches, a black doctor and family physician for many of us, offered a house he had purchased as an investment.

As the name implied, Fellowship House invited people of all colors, classes, and conditions to meet for fellowship and study, hopefully to overcome racial and religious prejudice that we liked to define as "being down on what you are not up on."

When we began our ministry at St. John's, Hitler's blitzkrieg was just beginning. On a day Roosevelt called a "day of infamy," Japanese planes bombed Pearl Harbor. The world was at war. Soon, young men from St. John's were being drafted to serve in the Armed Forces. Before long, flags with a gold star appeared in windows of St. John's homes indicating that someone in that family had been killed in battle.

Confronted with a world at war, I veered from the perfection of Christ. I confess I lacked the courage to say to my flock, "As followers of the Prince of Peace we, as the Body of Christ, cannot participate in this carnage."

Although I did not wave the American flag and identify Allied military power with the power and purpose of Almighty God, neither did I say in simple and clear words, "If we are in Christ, we cannot slaughter each other in war."

Why not? As a new and young pastor, I would have been asked to resign. I wanted to remain in the ministry and didn't know what else to do. Also, I did not want to totally disrupt the life of a congregation we had come to love, ignoring Jesus' hard words I had often read in Matthew 10:34-39. I accepted Reinhold Niebuhr's "just war" position that although war is evil, in this case going to war against Hitler was the lesser of two evils.

I was wrong. Jesus Christ did not die on a cross to save us from the lesser of two evils. He came to deliver us from evil (Colossians 1:13). Period. His victory over evil is complete. Finished (John 19:30).

This is the lesson I learned: the time for a church to reject war is not when war has been declared by the state and nationalism is in the air. Then it's too late for dispassionate thinking. Christian nonviolence is a moment by moment, day in and day out lifestyle that permeates our whole life in Christ. If it is, when war comes, instead of a subject for debate, the slaughter of war will be rejected because it does not fit our new life in Christ in the peaceable kingdom of God.

A Call to Serve The Ecumenical Church

We remained at St. John's until 1951 when I received an invitation to go back to my hometown of Wilkes-Barre and serve as the Executive Secretary of the Wyoming Valley Council of Churches.

Following the Second World War, the Ecumenical Movement had come alive in Christendom. In 1948 in Amsterdam, 145 denominations from 44 countries joined hands and hearts to form the World Council of Churches.

In 1950 in the United States, the older Federal Council of Churches of thirty American denominations merged with groups like the YMCA and YWCA to form a new National Council of Churches of Christ in the U.S.A.

The ecumenical network also expressed itself in the United States in the formation of Councils of Churches at both the state and city levels. The Ecumenical Movement was alive and bursting with enthusiasm and energy around the world.

"Ecumenical" combines two Greek words which mean "the whole family". It applies only to the universal church of our Lord. The purpose of the Ecumenical Movement is not to unify the church. Christ, the Head of the church, has already accomplished that. Our purpose was to witness to the unity we already have in Christ.

Because there is not a denominational bone in my body, I could easily have remained in this ecumenical ministry for the rest of my life. But I heard another call.

To South Philadelphia to Integrate an All White Church

It was an invitation from the United Church of Christ to join my denomination's new Philadelphia Cooperative Ministry. Its goal was the racial integration of six churches, once large and flourishing congregations, most of whose members had fled to the suburbs to escape black and Hispanic newcomers in the neighborhood.

It is in the local congregation where the church is truly tested on the issue of race. In the local church, the rank and file members must choose either to be inclusive in Christ or exclusive in the world.

In this cooperative venture, my particular ministry was at St. Andrew's in South Philadelphia, where German Protestants had been moving out of their brownstone row housing because one of Philadelphia's largest public housing projects had just been built a few blocks away. Old and new neighborhoods clashed.

Our first task was to visit with these newcomers in the place they called "home". Since almost all of the newcomers were black, I believed St. Andrew's needed a black minister on our staff to convince our new neighbors our invitation was genuine.

About a year after we arrived, the opportunity came. Our National Board of Missions provided the money to select a student pastor to come and serve as my assistant. I went to Crozier, a Baptist seminary where I met an older black student who liked the idea of becoming a part of our team.

I told my Board of Elders and Deacons that I had found a

married student whose name was Frank Upthegrove. What I didn't tell them was that Frank and his family were black.

Mr. and Mrs. Upthegrove and their three sons appeared for the first time during our weekend Fall Planning Retreat for church leaders. To say those present were shocked would be an understatement. At our next Board meeting, the first question one of the Elder's asked was, "Pastor, why didn't you tell us Frank was black?"

I said I didn't think race and the color of one's skin made any difference in the church where we professed to have one Father whose son, Jesus, had made us one reconciled family (Ephesians 1:9-10; 2:14-18; 4:9). When I asked them if they thought it did make a difference, all they could say was, "We don't think St. Andrew's is ready to have a black assistant pastor."

I had decided not to make Frank's skin color an issue to be debated. As far as I was concerned the debate had ended at the foot of the cross where:

> There is neither Jew nor Greek, slave nor free, male nor female; you are all one in Christ Jesus.
> - Galatians 3:28

Some pastors just as sincere would have handled it differently. I wanted St. Andrew's to experience the shock of realizing that the Holy Spirit is color blind and that "being ready" is a matter of the heart, not the calendar.

I believe Frank and his beautiful family made the difference. In the next six or seven years, St. Andrews became a completely integrated congregation. My greatest joy was to join in laying hands of ordination on the head of Frank Upthegrove, the first black man to be ordained in the

Reformed branch of the merged United Church of Christ from which I had come.

The reason we give for our separation is that both black and white Christians feel more comfortable when we are with people of our own culture and habits. Of course we are more comfortable. That's the problem. God is with us in Christ to make us uncomfortable in our sin, not to sooth us in our economic, racial and national boxes.

Before being disturbed by racism in the secular world where we should expect sin's separation in a fallen world, we should first be disturbed by our racism in the church whose Head has destroyed racial bigotry.

I'm sorry to say that a number of years after we left South Philadelphia, I was told that the denomination's National Board of Missions sold the church property to a black congregation. St. Andrews went from an all white to an all black church, one as anti-Christ as the other. Although an integrated church was not preserved, I believe we were faithful in our witness (Galatians 3:28). We can control what we do in the present. We cannot guarantee what will happen in the future.

To the Ironbound as "Minister of Community Relations"

The Lord had one more mission for us within the denominational structures of the church. In the 1960's, the larger Protestant denominations were placing urban ministers in many inner cities where "black power" was beginning to respond to "white power" and fight violently for equal justice under law in contrast to the nonviolent strategy of Martin Luther King.

The United Church of Christ and the Reformed Church of America each had a dwindling congregation in the Ironbound section of Newark, New Jersey where blacks and

285

Hispanics were moving in. (Here we go again!) Not satisfied just to continue a conventional ministry to help their particular church survive in a changing community, their young pastors prevailed upon their denomination's national urban department to allocate funds for a new type of ministry to help relate their congregations, as well as sister churches in suburbia, with Newark's inner city people and their problems.

Their vision called for a minister whose focus would not be on serving a particular congregation, but on the whole community and its needs. I was invited to be their Minister of Community Relations. When I accepted the call in 1962, walls of racial hostility in cities like Newark were at their highest. Soon, Newark's inner city would go up in flames. Police were being trained to combat rioting mobs.

This new kind of urban ministry had no tried and tested guidelines to follow, only the gospel of Jesus whose out-reaching Spirit has no boundaries

One thing was clear. If I were to involve our churches in the inner city, I, myself, had to become involved. So for the first few months of my Newark ministry I walked the streets, meeting with people in their homes, schools, agencies, storefronts, and prison. I found myself in the middle of a world of drug addicts, prostitutes, unemployed, and very lonely people with real faces and names.

Located just across the river from New York, the city of Newark was the catch-all for those who bought and sold drugs and those who became their victims. There was no place in the entire metropolitan area where heroin addicts could go any hour of the day for help. Drug addiction was clearly Newark's greatest unmet need. Although we knew nothing about heroin addicts and their rehabilitation, we decided to make this the main thrust of our ministry.

To become involved we opened a storefront in the Ironbound, which we called the "Well", named after Jacob's well where Jesus stopped to talk to the Samaritan outcasts of his day (See John 4:4-6). Drug addicts were the outcasts, the untouchables of our day. At the Well, those perceived as Newark's worst enemies could come day and night to talk with friends who would not turn them over to the police.

As drug addicts started to come, I spent almost all of my time at the Well, along with the two young pastors and a few volunteers who mustered up the courage to have contact with the most feared people in Newark. Our ministry was one of listening, praying, and letting addicts know that God loves them, that we were there to share with them His loving concern for them as persons.

As the addicts came and went, there was little evidence that the Well was instrumental in getting the monkey of heroin off of their backs. Hopefully, seeds of God's healing Spirit were planted which led to the fruit of their recovery, which we did not see. Like alcoholism, heroin addiction is a disease that keeps recurring unless the addict has a new birth in the Spirit who has defeated the enemy. The Well in the Ironbound was removed by miles from Newark's inner-city ghetto where the great throng of addicts spent their time. At the Well, we had contact with only a few.

After about a year in our storefront, the opportunity came to launch a rent-free ministry in the basement of a large downtown office building that stood at the edge of Newark's drug-infested inner city. Such a location would enable the churches to minister to drug addicts in their own habitat.

I was excited. Here was an opportunity to have a facility in the heart of Newark and mobilize the resources of the city to meet the needs of the vast population of addicts. The interdenominational committee to which I was accountable was cool to the proposal saying, "If we move to central

Newark, the Well will lose its identity with our two Ironbound churches whose pastors initiated the ministry of community relations".

By this time, it was evident that the people of the two congregations in the Ironbound had no real interest in the Well and its ministry to heroin addicts. They wanted to keep their distance from the "lepers", not reach out to them.

Believing that if the physician is to heal, the best place to be is where the sick are, I kept the proposal on the agenda of our monthly meetings. Reluctantly, the committee finally agreed to accept the offer of the rent-free basement of the downtown office building with one condition: the Ironbound storefront also had to continue.

That was the beginning of great joy and grief even greater. Some of the grief had to do with the closing of the Well in the Ironbound a few months later because I had very little time to be there; grief, because at the new location in the very bowels of Newark, the number of volunteers dropped to zero. If the Well in the Ironbound frightened them, the Well in Newark's inner city was completely a "no-man's land".

As addicts came to the Well in large numbers, we were able to carry on only because of full-time volunteers who came from a national volunteer program of the United Church of Christ and because two "ex-addicts", one black and one white, heard about the Well and volunteered to work with us. They had been on drugs but were far enough along in their recovery that addicts could identify with them and say, "If they can do it, I can too". As a matter of fact, to keep going, the so-called "ex-addicts" needed to lose their life in ministry as much as those who came to the Well needed their ministry to get going.

One or two black doctors volunteered to treat addicts with methadone, a drug that satisfies the craving for heroin until the victim is stabilized sufficiently to hold a job and return to his or her family. Newark also responded with job opportunities and counseling from social workers and other professionals who wanted to learn more about the mysterious world of drugs and its victims.

Still, the "success stories" at the Well continued to be few. There was little evidence that the use of methadone, counseling, jobs, and friends at the Well, were producing the results we hoped for. Whatever real success we had, appeared to be the result of the presence and example of the two ex-addicts.

After almost three years of ministering to Newark's inner city street people in the region's first full-time ministry to heroin addicts and their families, I resigned, leaving the Well to the two recovering addicts who continued with their own ministries from two new locations, and to a third young man who had come to the Well to learn about drug addiction and was now ready to start a residential program which he had put together with a federal grant.

Needed: A Time for Renewal

Living at the heart of Newark's concentration of drug addicts left me completely frustrated, disillusioned, and drained physically, mentally and spiritually.

Frustrated because of my inability to deal with the enormity and complexity of the drug addiction problem; disillusioned because of the reluctance of the organized churches to risk getting involved with the inner city and its street people; worn out because I had placed too great an emphasis on community organization and mobilizing human resources to cast out the demon of drug addiction, and too little emphasis on the ever-renewing Christ and his Holy Spirit who makes all things new.

Gradually, I found renewal in body, mind and spirit in repentance and centering my life again in the perfection of Christ. I knew whatever time I had left in the flesh for Christian ministry would henceforth be outside the structures of the denominational church which I had questioned since my teenage conversion. I did not leap out of the denominational church. I just faded away.

Bible scholar John L. McKenzie had so many differences with the official teaching of his Catholic church, he was asked why he didn't up and leave. He replied, "It's the only game in town."

When I left I was aware of other games in town, but I had no desire to sign up. Just as I knew I had to leave a denominationally organized ministry, I knew I would continue to minister in Jesus' church that is neither Roman Catholic, Eastern Orthodox, Methodist, Mennonite, Presbyterian nor Pentecostal.

Quiet Retirement Turns into Active Redirection

After teaching in one of Newark's inner city black high schools for two years, my wife and I moved to central Florida. On the edge of Sebring's beautiful Lake Jackson, I designed and helped build our Dream House. While Marge continued her work with the Girl Scouts, I did my best to enjoy a "retired" life of writing, fishing, boating, swimming, and occasional visits to nearby Disney World when our five daughters and their families came to visit.

I soon discovered the ideal time for retirement: about two weeks, certainly not more than two months. The Hound of Heaven stayed on my tracks and rescued me from Adam and Eve's fantasy land of freedom to do as one pleases.

A Florida-based self-help housing program, sponsored by the Quakers to assist migrant farm workers own a decent house, invited me to join their staff. For five years, I served as one of their community organizers, helping rural towns form non-profit corporations and become eligible to receive a grant from Farmers Home Administration to hire and train a staff to implement the federal government's self-help housing program at the grass roots level.

After six or seven years in our Dream House in little Sebring, we decided to move northward to Florida's larger capital city of Tallahassee with its two universities.

Discovering Haiti and Haitians

It was the time hundreds of flimsy boats overloaded with a great company of Haitian refugees were landing in Miami and being detained at Krome camp. Representing our newly formed "Friends of Haiti", I visited refugees in Miami and extended our invitation: "Come to Tallahassee and join a multitude of people who are ready to help you get off to a new start. In the name of Jesus we welcome you to our Refugee House."

Today, some fifteen years later, there are more than a dozen hard-working Haitian families who now own homes in middle-class sections of Tallahassee. Relatives and friends often come to live with them for a few months until they earn enough money to rent a little apartment of their own and join our growing Haitian community that takes advantage of Tallahassee's excellent educational and economic opportunities. Marge and I think of ourselves as shepherds to our beloved Haitian flock, each of whom we love and call by name. For us, this is the church living in community.

Visiting Haiti several times during these years helped link needs of people and programs in Haiti with resources in Tallahassee we were able to tap through "Friends of Haiti". I discovered the best gift we can give to our friends in Haiti is friendship in Christ and encouragement to work out their own salvation. U.S. military occupation and economic aid has helped rob seven million people in Haiti of their self-dignity.

Joining With Other Forms of The Church

I had often read about the Christian community at Koinonia Farm in Georgia. In the 1940's, Koinonia was being machine-gunned by neighbors who didn't like the idea of blacks and whites living in such neighborly love. I wanted to take off my shoes and walk on its holy ground.

Unexpectedly, in 1983 I suddenly felt very close to Koinonia Partners when I found myself in the same prison cell with one of their members, Edwin Steiner. The Washington police had arrested a great company of us the day after Pentecost while praying under the heavenly dome of the Capitol's rotunda. As fifty of us spent the week in jail, Edwin and I shared a common cell and our common faith in Jesus' Resurrection Life as citizens of the here and now kingdom of God.

Ripples from Koinonia Farm have gone out to form the amazing world-wide self-help housing program we know as Habitat for Humanity, and the community known as Jubilee Partners where hundreds of war refugees from Central America and the Middle East have come to learn that agape and koinonia are not only common words in the New Testament, they are the Spirit of Christ alive in the Jubilee Community founded in the 1980's by Don Mosley and his wife when they went out from Koinonia Farm with a vision of God's kingdom on earth as it is in heaven.

We discovered Georgia is also blessed with a sister community of Christ, The Open Door, with a better approach to alcoholics and drug addicts than we had at the Well. Led by Ed Loring and his wife, Murphy Davis, Atlanta's street people find an open door to a dining room that serves bread for the body and, for their lonely souls, a loving fellowship with caring people who show them the respect they need to have self-respect and find their way into the Community of Christ.

In May 1984, Jesus tapped me on the shoulder while reading an article in Sojourners magazine entitled, "Eberhard Arnold on Christian Community, A Visit to the Bruderhof". It was about a communal church related to the Hutterites who have been living for 450 years as God's nonviolent kingdom on earth, which Jim Wallace and members of the Sojourner's community had just visited for several days.

I wrote to one of the Bruderhofs asking if Marge and I might visit for a couple of days. A week later, we received a friendly "Yes, please come and visit us here at New Meadow Run"- one of the six Bruderhofs in the eastern United States which originated in Germany in 1920, and in 1930 became one of the 350 Hutterite communal churches in the Midwest and Canada which date back to the 16th century.

Though I had grown up in the church of Jesus, had been to theological seminary, and for half a century was involved with a cross section of churches on the planet, our visit to the Bruderhof was an experience of a church I had never known. Those two days at the Bruderhof had about them enough of the atmosphere of the kingdom Jesus enfleshed to inspire me to spend the next year filling in what was a big blank in my education: the history and theology of the Anabaptists. In spite of the Catholic and Protestant violent attempt to wipe them off the face of the earth, I discovered they were alive and well—the church nobody knows.

In 1988, I spent a week at each of four Bruderhofs, participating in four weekend conferences that brought together a thousand participants to consider "A New Testament Church for the 21st Century". In addition to my living for a week in each of four Bruderhofs in the Eastern

United States and England, the dialogue between these communal churches and "outsiders" from many parts of the planet, made this one of the most memorable months of my long search for a great company of people committed as the church, by baptism to sharing all possessions and demonstrate, here and now, the private and public peace Jesus has made possible.

By no means perfect and called a "cult" by some, the Bruderhof is a disciplined church which enables parents and children, not just unmarried individuals as in Catholic monasticism, to live together in community as the reconciled family of God, sharing and caring for one another from the cradle to grave. Every seeker would do well to accept their invitation: "Come and see." The Bruderhof is a living demonstration of the church in the Book of Acts (2:44 and 4:32-35).

A New Ministry Focusing on Christian Nonviolence

Hoping to find a support group in Tallahassee, I went to the local diocesan offices of the Catholic Church with what must have seemed a strange question: "Can you direct me to any members of the Catholic Church who are seeking to follow Jesus' teaching of nonviolence?"

The diocesan director of social action smiled and asked me if I knew David Stewart. I did not. When I found David, he told me about a weekend retreat which had focused on Jesus' Sermon on the Mount. Not only did Jesus' gospel of agape get through to David for the first time, he realized he did not know anyone who gave evidence of following such teaching. Overwhelmed with Jesus' indwelling, David returned home with the desire to be such a person. Giving up his real estate business, David continued his spiritual pilgrimage by spending the next year reading the Scriptures and seeking the Lord's will for his life.

It was at this time in David's life that our paths crossed. As we prayerfully shared Jesus' gospel of nonviolent agape, it became clear that, although we had very different church backgrounds, we had been led to the same conclusion: the Messiah of the world is nonviolent and his Sermon on the Mount is to be followed as the Gospel of Matthew recorded it, not as "just war" theologians have reinvented it.

Out of our fellowship came many shared experiences such as "Good News Ministries", which included a "drop-in" at the core of Tallahassee's hangout of drug addicts, alcoholics and prostitutes who could come for a noonday meal, temporary shelter, clean clothes and a shower, counseling and job opportunities.

I'm sure the Lord led me that day to a diocesan office of the Catholic Church. It completed the ecumenical circle in which I had been moving throughout my ministry.

One day I was struck by an advertisement in a national Catholic newspaper, asking, "Are you ready?" At first glance I thought the headline was asking if I was ready for the imminent end of the world—a question I knew was not uppermost in the minds of Catholic priests and bishops.

Instead, the ad was asking readers whether they were ready to believe that Jesus is the nonviolent Messiah of a nonviolent church. It was an invitation to participate in a weekend retreat on "The Theology of Christian Nonviolence" led by an Eastern Rite priest, Rev. Charles McCarthy, affectionately known as "Charlie", the most devoted apostle and teacher of Jesus' gospel of nonviolence I have ever met.

That weekend with McCarthy at a retreat-center outside of Boston helped me put together all the pieces of God's Peace-Plan in Christ within the wholeness of the gospel. Since then I have been with McCarthy in a half-dozen conferences from

Friday evening through Sunday morning. As they leave, the typical response of participants is something like, "I have a new understanding of what salvation means. My life can never be the same."

Since the Christian meaning of nonviolence is almost unknown in mainline churches, focusing on this most neglected theme of the gospel for an extended period of time without interruption is essential for clergy and laity alike to begin to comprehend the fallacy of the "just war" heresy and why disciples of Jesus do not fight to survive physically.

The Holy Spirit used McCarthy's workshops to nudge me to found and edit *The Jesus Journal*, a monthly magazine we published for a dozen years to teach Christian nonviolence, not as a separate Peace Movement, but as inseparable from

> . . .the mystery hidden for ages and generations, but now made manifest to his saints (Colossians 1:26). In Christ all the fullness of God was pleased to dwell, and through him to reconcile to himself all things, whether on earth or in heaven, making peace by the blood of his cross.
> - Colossians 1:19-20

At the same time came our formation of Agape House. Not a house in one geographical location, Agape House invited to our meetings, held in many different places, anyone interested in exploring what Christian nonviolence is all about.

One who came was David Headly. Graduating from Florida State University with a degree in nuclear physics, David realized that, as a disciple of the Life-Giver, he could not use his knowledge in producing nuclear weapons of death. Taking seriously Jesus' Sermon on the Mount, David turned away from a lucrative vocation connected with war and found meaning for his life in serving Tallahassee's poor and outcasts as a volunteer with Good News Ministries. Now a nonviolent Quaker, this apostle of Jesus is a very wealthy man—rich in God's Spirit and truth that is not at the mercy of sin's violence and death.

Liberation Theology

Speaking to Latin America's hunger and poverty, massive disease and infant mortality, illiteracy and profound inequalities of income and tensions between the social classes, the Latin American bishop's conference at Medellin in 1968 emphasized that theology that matters is theology that liberates the whole of life, both personal and social.

Interpreting the 1980's uprising of the peasant poor in Nicaragua and El Salvador within the framework of "liberation theology", I joined teams organized by Witness for Peace and spent a month in these countries to identify with those struggling to enjoy basic material needs and find fulfillment of their life as sons and daughters in the family of God.

As we lived among the poor, I was impressed by their coming together within the church to share their common burdens, helping each other build modest houses, and other everyday common tasks. Their Christ-centered theology was liberating their total life—spiritually, socially and economically. Not merely a building to enter to receive the Sacraments, the church was becoming their base community.

Tragically, "liberation theology" did not liberate Catholics in Nicaragua and El Salvador from killing each other. The obsolete "just war" theology of the Catholic Church prevailed. Oppressed and oppressors alike slaughtered each other. The theology of Jesus does not put the sword in the hands of the oppressed any more than it puts weapons of violence in the hands of the oppressor. Violence is not of

Christ and His church. The liberation of Christ frees all in sin's fallen world from violence and death.

A Book is Born

Out of all the above experiences, this book was born. It had to be written. Reading the manuscript, some have called it "a labor of love." It is more. It is a labor that grows out of my deepest convictions in Christ.

What I have written is not about so-called pacifism. Nonviolence and salvation in Christ are synonymous. God's salvation and our peace are one and the same. The new creation in Christ and butchering people in war are complete contradictions. This is why to be the authentic church, Christians must again be the enfleshment of God's peace in Christ and completely replace participation in a fallen world's systems of violence with an agape nonviolent lifestyle in the here and now kingdom of God this book highlights.

The great need of our media-packed world is hardly one more book. At age 88, I venture this one, knowing it may fail to find a publisher. But I know the prayer that sends it forth will not fail because it goes forth in the Name of Jesus in whom all the promises of God find their Yes (2 Corinthians 1:19-20).

The Big Question is whether God's promise of peace in Christ will find a Yes in you and me who have been given the freedom to choose. We will be held accountable.

Endnotes

1. Unless otherwise indicated, all Scripture is from the Revised Standard Version of the Bible. CEV signifies the Contemporary English Version and NIV the New International Version.

2. The title, Haunts of Violence in the Church, is based on Psalm 74:20 NIV.

3. The quotation from the writings of John Henry Newman for the book's fly leaf was selected because it expresses what should be the mind of every Christian, the faith that the Creator has a unique plan for every soul and is to submit to the leading of the Holy Spirit for the fulfillment of that plan.

Newman (1802-1890), the writer of the great hymn, "Lead Kindly Light", went through radical change during his journey within the church. He began as an evangelical, became a member of the Church of England, and ended in the Roman Catholic Church.

Newman is best known as a leader of Britain's Oxford Movement which protested radical reforms of government in the 1830's, not because they advanced the cause of democracy, but because they secularized the authority of the "one, holy, catholic, and apostolic Church."

The Oxford men felt that the Church of England needed to affirm that its authority did not rest on the authority of the state. It came from God. In the tracts they wrote to uphold the authority of the church, those like John Henry Newman looked to the first centuries of the church as the true expression of the Body of Christ when Christians were united, accepted apostolic teaching, and refused to idolize the state.

In its emphasis on public worship and the place of the sacraments and symbolic acts to show reverence before God, the Oxford Movement was a version of "High Church" Christianity.

Interestingly, within mainline "just war" churches, the clearest protest against violence by the church has come from "High Church" Christianity, notably within the Catholic Church in movements such as Pax Christi, The Catholic Worker, and the monastics.

In 1841 a storm of protest thundered against the Oxford Movement when Newman wrote a tract stating that the Thirty-Nine Articles which governed the Church of England, were not necessarily Protestant and could be interpreted in the spirit of the Catholic church. When the Church of England's Bishop of Oxford forbid Newman to publish any more tracts, Newman concluded that the only way he could be truly Catholic was to enter the Roman Catholic Church which he did in 1845 and was followed by hundreds of Anglican clergymen.

Great courage and a deep conviction that he was being led by the Holy Spirit were necessary for Newman to make the radical moves he did during the course of his Christian pilgrimage. What he went through in wrestling with his search for truth is expressed both in the statement on this book's flyleaf and in his hymn, "Lead Kindly Light", an immortal prayer for guidance.

Chapter 1 - Peace Has Come To A Fallen World

1. I am indebted to Walter Wink's excellent book, *Engaging the Powers*, 1992, Fortress Press, Minneapolis. The book not only reveals the biblical meaning of Christian nonviolence, it makes clear the essential nature of Jesus whose unique mission was to engage the Powers and Principalities and by his cross, resurrection, and indwelling Spirit, overcame their world of evil with its violence and death. Wink shows that nonviolence is not an option for Christians. It is the Good News of peace the church should be demonstrating every day of her life in a "fallen world" of war.

2. *Abide in Christ*, Andrew Murray, 1985; Barbour and Company, Inc., 164 Mill Street, Westwood, NJ. Thirty-One meditations on Jesus' words, "Abide in me"(John 15).

3. *Resurrection: Release from Oppression*, Morton Kelsey, 1985, Paulist Press, 997 MacArthur Blvd, Rahway NJ 07430. Retelling the events surrounding the resurrection of Christ, the author emphasizes that when the risen Christ becomes the central reality of our life, the fire of God's Spirit possesses us and enables the soul to love others, even at the cost of ourselves. The Resurrection and God's indwelling agape-love-Spirit makes Christian nonviolence possible.

4. *Training in Christianity*, Soren Kierkegaard, 1941, Princeton University Press, Princeton NJ.

5. *Illusion of Power*, Tony Campolo, 1991, Word Publishing, Dallas TX.
6. *Violence from a Christian Perspective*, Jacques Ellul; 1969, Seabury Press, New York

7. *Peace Be With You*, Cornelia Lehn, 1980, Faith and Life Press, Newton, Kansas 67114, provided the story of St. Patrick, and helped me personalize the life of Michael

Sattler. I highly recommend Lehn's book to parents looking for peace stories to share with their children.

8. *One Solitary Witness*, Gordon Zahn, 1964, Templegate Publishers, Springfield Ill 62705. This is the remarkable story of Franz Jägerstätter, researched and told by Zahn.

9. *The Glorious Koran.* Translation by Mohammed Marmaduke Pickthall, New American Library, New York, NY

Chapter 2 - When and How the Church Turned to Sin's Violence

1. Dating from Emperor Constantine's fourth century rule, the name "Constantinian church" refers to all churches that accept Augustine's "just war" doctrine and involvement in the political process to achieve the nation's "common good" and defend it in war.

Public and university libraries have many volumes which glorify Constantine, pictured as the great Christian emperor who led the church of Jesus into the age of the "Christianized" state. The linkage marks the politicizing of the gospel by mainline churches and their theologians who contend that "Some kind of government, however deformed and corrupt it may be, is still better and more beneficial than anarchy." (Calvin's Commentary on 1 Peter 2:14).

The error of this premise is making God's kingdom of unconditional love synonymous with anarchy. That the opposite is true is clearly evident in the law-abiding nonviolent societies of the early church, and later, the Mennonite, Amish, Hutterite, Brethren, Quaker, and other similar movements.

2. *Will the Real Heretics Please Stand Up*, David W. Bercot, 1989, Scroll Publishing Co., Tyler TX 75706. A collection of

early church writings which show mainline "just war" churches to be the real heretics.

3. *Church History in Plain Language*, Bruce L. Shelley, 1982, Word Publishing, Dallas TX.

4. *It Is Not Lawful For Me To Fight*, Jean-Michel Hornus, 1980, Herald Press, Scottdale PA 15683. Covering the first three centuries of the church, Hornus quotes the Church Fathers extensively to contradict the argument that only a tiny minority of Christians rejected war and only because serving in the army required giving to the Roman emperor the homage that belongs only to God.

5. *The Early Christian Attitude to War*, C. John Cadoux, 1982, Seabury Press, 815 Second Ave. New York NY 10017. The source of the story of Maximilian. In a scholarly and charitable manner Cadoux starts with the teachings of Jesus, setting them one by one over against arguments used to justify Christians engaging in war. Cadoux documents how strong and deep was early church revulsion of war which was identified with the sin of murder. The author believes the error of the Constantinian church must be corrected if mainline churches are to be true to the gospel of peace entrusted to them.

Chapter 3 - The Bogus "Just War" Theology of Mainline Churches

1. *Christian Attitudes Toward War and Peace, A Historical Survey and Critical Reevaluation*, Roland Bainton, 1983, Abingdon Press, Nashville TN. One of the world's foremost historians surveys and examines the entire "just war" tradition of the church from its classical origin among the Greeks to the dropping of atomic bombs on Nagasaki and Hiroshima in 1945.

2. *WAR, Four Christian Views*, Robert G. Clouse, Editor; 1981, InterVarsity Press, Downer's Grove IL 60515. Four contributors present the four historic positions of the church on the question, "Should Christians ever go to war?

3. *Catechism of the Catholic Church*, 1994, Liquori Publications, One Liquori Drive Liquori MO 63057-9999. The latest Catholic Catechism since Vatican 11.

4. *The Living God*, a two-volume catechism of the Orthodox Church, 1989, St. Vladimir's Seminary Press, Crestwood, New York.

5. *It Is Not Lawful For Me To Fight*, Juan-Michel Hornus, 1980, Herald Press, Scottdale PA 15683. A French Reformed historian and Theologian examines early Christian attitudes toward war, violence, and the state. Hornus examines the double standard of the Catholic Church that placed the clergy above military life and its violence, but made it the sacred obligation of the laity to participate in "just" wars. This assumes that only the chosen few, the ordained clergy, can attain to such holiness, ordinary lay people cannot. In this way the Catholic Church can lay claim to following the Sermon on the Mount while, at the same time, mix with the state in Christianizing the world by engaging in war. The Gospel of Jesus rightly proclaims a single pattern of holiness for the whole church. There are no first and second-class citizens in the kingdom of God. All receive the same Spirit who enables clergy and laity alike to live as Christ's ambassadors of reconciliation.

6. Mark Twain's War Prayer is from his book, *Europe and Elsewhere*, Harper Brothers, 1923.

Chapter 4 - How To Interpret Old Testament Violence

1. *War and Peace: from Genesis to Revelation*, Vernard Eller, 1980, Herald Press, Scottdale PA 15683. In a

fascinating way Eller leads his readers through the Old Testament to the end of the New to show how defenseless love gains the victory that overcomes the world and purges it of evil.

2. *The Prophets*, Abraham J. Heschel, 1962, Harper and Rowe Publishers, 10 East 53rd St. New York NY 10022. A good summary of the unique contributions of the Old Testament prophets to civilization.

Chapter 5 - The Misuse of the New Testament to Justify War

1. *War and the Gospel*, Jean Lousier, 1962, Herald Press, Scottdale PA 15683. Helpful in understanding Romans 13:1-6

2. *Jesus Before Christianity*, Albert Nolan, 1978. Orbis Books, Mary knoll, NY. In portraying Jesus as a practical and realistic man, Nolan states that the reason Jesus ruled out force to liberate Israel was because he knew that it would be suicidal to take on Rome's military power, not because he was a "pacifist" and objected to all violence as a universe principle. Nolan writes, "All we can be sure of is that Jesus decided that in his circumstances and in his time the use of force to seize power for himself (or for anyone else) would be harmful to man and therefore contrary to the will of God. The saying, 'Those who draw the sword will die by the sword', which Matthew found somewhere and inserted into the story of Jesus' arrest (Matthew 26:52) is not, and was surely never meant to be, a timeless truth."

If the church accepts this "just war" premise that it is God's will to destroy and engage in mass killing when the time and circumstance are right, then the church takes unto herself a right the New Testament states belongs only to God (See Romans 12: 17-21).

Killing for a cause humans decide is "just", is not the gospel proclaimed by the New Testament. Rather is it the same old attempt of a fallen world to solve its problems on the basis of what is best for me and my family, my party, my race, my nation, pretending that the thinking which makes the decision is impartial and is in harmony with "the mind of the Spirit" (See Romans 8:5-11).

Chapter 6 - The Church that Continues to Live Nonviolently

(Monasticism)

1. I am indebted to Roland Bainton's classic two volume work: *Christendom, a Short History of Christianity and Its Impact on Western Civilization*, 1966, Harper and Rowe.

2. The story of Polycarp's martyrdom is found in the Letter from the Church of Smyrna of which he was overseer at the time of his martyrdom.

3. The story of Francis of Assisi is based primarily on the text of a pictorial presentation for children, *Francis, Brother of the Universe*, published to popularize the life of the most famous monk of the Middle Ages. Produced in 1980 in connection with the 800th anniversary of St. Francis' birth in 1182, it is available from the Paulist Press, 545 Island Road, Ramsey NJ 07446.

4. *The Monastic Journey*, Thomas Merton, 1978, Image Books, Garden City NY

(Anabaptists)

1. *The Recovery of the Anabaptist Vision*, edited by Guy Hershberger, 1957, Herald Press. Articles by recognized contemporary Anabaptist leaders on the rise and theology of the movement.

2. *War, Peace, and Nonresistance*, Guy F. Hershberger, 1969, Herald Press Scottdale PA 15683. A classic explanation of the Anabaptist's rejection of war and their nonviolent lifestyle.

3. *Anabaptist: Neither Catholic nor Protestant*, by Walter Klaassen, 1973, Conrad Press, Waterloo Ontario. Klaassen helps Protestants and Catholics alike to look beyond their traditional "just war" teaching to discover a tradition of peace as old as the Sermon on the Mount.

4. Anabaptists, A Social History, Claus-Peter Clare, Cornell University Press, 1972.

5. *A People of Two Kingdoms*, James C. Junk, 1975, Faith and Life Press, 718B Main Street, Newton Kansas 67114.

6. Details on the first Anabaptist congregation in Zollikon can be found in Fritz Blanke's book, *Brothers in Christ*, 1955, Zurich.

7. The seven articles of faith agreed on at Schleitheim and summarized in chapter 5, remain the tradition of nonviolence of Hutterian, Amish, and Mennonite Peace churches. For the entire statement, see The Schleitheim Confession, John Howard Yonder, Translator, 1973, Herald Press, Scottdale PA.

8. *The Nature and Destiny of Man*, 2 volumes, Reinhold Niebuhr, 1941; 1942 Charles Scribner & Sons Edition. The author disagrees with his teacher that Christians must at times participate in war as the lesser of two evils, but has learned much from Niebuhr's profound understanding of the nature of evil and its penetration into all facets of our person and our culture.

(Hutterites)

1. *The Chronicle of the Hutterian Brethren*, 800 pages, the original German text of 1565, translated into English by the Hutterian Brethren and made available in 1987 by Plough Publishing House. The first hand account of the moving of God's Spirit between 1517 and 1565, awakening many souls in Europe to the New Testament church who dared to live according to the Apostolic tradition of nonviolence. The volume concludes with an account of Hutterite history from 1565 to the present.

2. *Confession of Faith*, written in prison in 1545 by martyred Peter Rideman, is a classic statement of Anabaptist belief based on some 3000 passages of Scripture. It remains one of the Bruderhof's basic guidebooks. Produced in 1970 by Plough Publishers, it concludes with a brief account of Hutterite life and work during their first four centuries.

3. *Hutterite Life*, John A. Hostetler, Herald Press, Scottdale PA 15683. A 48-page overview of the approximate 400 Hutterite Bruderhofs in the United States and Canada.

4. *Hutterian Brethren*, 1528-1931, John Horsch. 1977. Macmillan Colony, Cayley, Alberta Canada. A story of martyrdom and loyalty by Hutterite Anabaptists.

5. The Hutterites, Plain People of the West, William Allard, National Geographic, July 1970. A good article with illustrations portraying life on a Bruderhof cattle ranch operated by the Hutterites.

(Mennonites)

1. *An Introduction to Mennonite History* edited by Cornelius J. Dyck, Herald Press, 1988.

2. *The Complete Writings of Menno Simons.* Translated by J. C. Wenger, 1956, Herald Press.

3. *Mennonite Society,* Calvin Redekop, 1989, John Hopkins University Press.

4. *The Mennonite Encyclopedia,* Mennonite Publishing House, 1956.

5. The Mennonite statements on peace are from Mennonite Statements on Peace and Social Concerns, 1900-1978, published by the Mennonite Central Committee, Akron, Pa.

(Amish)

1. *The Riddle of Amish Culture,* Donald Kraybill, 1989 John Hopkins University Press.

2. *A History of the Amish,* Steven Nolt, 1992, Good Books, Intercourse, PA 17534.

3. *20 Most Asked Questions about the Amish and Mennonites,* Merle and Phyllis Good, 1979, Good Books.

4. *Amish Society,* John Hostettler, 1980, John Hopkins University Press.

5. *The Puzzles of Amish Life,* Donald B. Kraybill. 1990, Good Books Publication.

6. *The 1993 Mennonite Year Book* by Herald Press, has an excellent summary of the Amish, entitled, The Amish Story 1693-1993, commemorating the 300th Anniversary of the Amish church.

7. For an answer to questions on Mennonites, Amish, and Hutterites, write: Anabaptist Center, Elizabethtown PA 17022.

Chapter 7 - Repent and Believe the Gospel

1. 20 Hot Potatoes Christians Are Afraid To Touch, Tony Campolo, 1988, Word Publishers, Dallas TX.

2. Pope John Paul's pastoral Letter is quoted from *Origens*, Catholic News Service, November 24, 1994.

3. The poem, 'I saw you on the front page', is by Edie Garrett, taken from the April, 1999, *Ministry of Money Newsletter*, 11315 Neelsville Church Road Germantown, MD 20876-4147.

4. *The Bible Story*, William Neil, 1971, Fountain Books; William Collins Son & Co. Ltd. London

5. *Brethren Society*, Carl F. Bowmann, 1995, Johns Hopkins University Press, Baltimore MD.

6. *The Jesus I Never Knew*, Philip Yancey, 1995, Zondervan Publishing House, Grand Rapids, MI.

7. *The Religions of Man*, Huston Smith, 1958, Harper and Row, New York, NY.

8. *The Gospel in Hymns*, Albert Edward Bailey, 1950, Charles Scribner's Sons. The hymn, Faith of our Fathers, was written in 1849 by Frederick W, Faber, a friend and follower of John Henry Newman quoted on the book's flyleaf. Like Newman, the author of this hymn was drawn from the Church of England to the Catholic Church in Rome. Faber joined Newman's Oratory, an association of secular priests, not monks, based on a life of prayer, hence the name "Oratory" (a place of prayer) for all their places of residence.

Faber was sent by Newman to London where he founded an Oratory on Brompton Road in the city's West End. Before he died Faber composed more than 150 hymns to help fill the

lack of hymns in England's Catholic Church.

Although "the faith of our fathers" Faber wrote about referred to the Catholic faith, the original stanza 3 referring to "Mary's prayers" winning England back to God, the hymn as here revised is one of the few hymns which echo Jesus' Sermon on the Mount in loving "both friend and foe in all our strife . . . in spite of dungeon, fire, and sword". Since Catholics, Protestants, and those in the Church of England spent considerable time butchering each other, each branch of the church can recall times of strife and persecution. What a difference the church would make if all Christians, true to Jesus, loved friend and foe alike.

10. *A History of the Christian Church*, Williston Walker and others; 1985, Fourth Edition, Charles Scribner & Sons.

11. *He is our Peace: Meditations on Christian Nonviolence.* Howard Goeringer, Eberhard Arnold, and Christoph Blumhardt 1994, Plough Publishing House, Farmington, PA.

Chapter 8 - Rethinking the Schooling of our Children

1. *The People's History of the United States*, 1492-Present, Howard Zinn, 1995, Harper Perennial

2. *Christ and Man's Dilemma.* George A. Buttrick, 1945. Abingdon-Cokesbury Press, Nashville, New Tork

3. *The Jesus Journal*, Issue #55, Tallahassee FL. 32315, Howard Goeringer, Editor;(replaced in 2000 by the journal, Rabboni, edited by Dale Recinella).

4. *Rabboni*, Issue #2, Dale Recinella, Editor, Box 37469, Jacksonville FL 32236

Appendix - About the Author

1. To arrange for a weekend Conference on the Theology of Christian Nonviolence, write: Rev. Charles McCarthy, 49 Burkeside Ave., Brockton MA 02401

2. The story of Jubilee Partners is told in a book by the community's founder, Don Mosley, *With Our Own Eyes*, 1996. Herald Press, Scottdale PA 15683-1999. To arrange for a visit to Jubilee Partners, write: Don Mosley, PO Box 68, Comer GA 30629.

3. To contact Open Door, write: Ed Weir, 910 Ponce de Leon Ave., NE, Atlanta GA 30306.

4. To arrange for a visit to the Bruderhof, write: Woodcrest Bruderhof, Rifton NY 12471.

5. Direct questions about Koinonia Farm to: Koinonia Partners, Rt. 2 Americus GA 31709.

6. The International Center of Habitat for Humanity is located at 419 W. Church Street, Americus GA 31709.